# FREEZER
# COOKBOOK

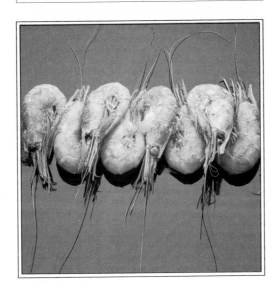

# THE NEW *St Michael*

# FREEZER COOKBOOK

## HEATHER LAMBERT

Sundial

# CONTENTS

## ACKNOWLEDGEMENTS

Photography: Robert Golden

Photographic styling:
Antonia Gaunt

Preparation of food for
photography: Heather Lambert
assisted by Rosalind Maxwell

The publishers would like to
thank the following companies
for the loan of props for photography:

Alcan Polyfoil Limited (freezer containers)
℅ Field Communications, 49
Perrymount Road, Haywards
Heath, Sussex.

Elizabeth David Ltd (kitchen equipment)
46 Bourne Street, London SW1

Divertimenti (kitchen utensils)
68/72 Marylebone Lane,
London W1

Tupperware Company (freezer containers)
43 Upper Grosvenor Street,
London W1

First published in 1981
by Octopus Books Limited
59 Grosvenor Street, London W1.
© Hennerwood Publications Limited 1981
ISBN 0 906320 24 0
Produced by Mandarin Publishers Limited
Printed in Hong Kong

## FREEZING INFORMATION    8

| | |
|---|---|
| The freezer process | 10 |
| Storage of frozen food | 11 |
| Choosing a freezer | 11 |
| Freezer care | 12 |
| Packaging | 13 |
| Stocking a freezer | 16 |
| Thawing and cooking frozen food | 19 |
| Storage times | 21 |
| Freezing fruit | 22 |
| Freezing vegetables | 30 |

## SOUPS, STARTERS & CANAPES 40

The wide range of soup recipes are all in ready-to-use quantities, but if you are short of space in the freezer, half the liquid may be omitted from the recipe, and added when the soup is thawed. Terrines and pâtés may be divided up and frozen in smaller quantities to prevent wastage.

## SAUCES & STUFFINGS 58

Sauces are an invaluable standby to have in the freezer for immediate use. Remember never to freeze stuffed poultry, always freeze the bird and the stuffing separately to avoid a health hazard.

## FISH 66

Fish soon loses its texture and delicate flavour when stored in a freezer for any length of time, so it is best to use it within 1 month. In general, it is more satisfactory to cook fish before freezing it, unless you can buy your fish virtually straight from the sea.

## MEAT & POULTRY 78

Many butchers and freezer supermarkets nowadays offer bulk buys of various meats at competitive prices. These meat and poultry recipes are specifically for the most readily available cuts, with ideas for ready frozen and fresh meat.

## VEGETABLES 104

This chapter offers a choice of recipes using fresh, raw ingredients, or if you find yourself with a glut of home grown produce, or a large quantity of vegetables from a pick-your-own farm, the recipes using ready frozen vegetables will be useful.

## ICE CREAMS & DESSERTS 116

Included here are recipes for soft fruits, which have a limited season, as well as different ways of using apples, many varieties of which do not store well in their raw form. There are also some more time-consuming desserts, which can be prepared in advance for a special occasion.

## BAKING 130

Baking lends itself as a subject for batch-baking. As home-made bread freezes extremely well, it is a good idea to set aside the best part of a day to make several loaves. Cakes, scones and biscuits are all useful additions to the freezer especially when catering for a large family or entertaining.

# NOTES

## GENERAL NOTE

1. All recipes serve 4 unless otherwise stated.
2. All eggs are sizes 3, 4, 5 (standard) unless otherwise stated.
3. All spoon measurements are level.
4. Metric and imperial measurements have been calculated separately. Use one set of measurements only as they are not exact equivalents.
5. Cooking times may vary slightly depending on the individual oven. Dishes should be placed in the centre of the oven unless otherwise specified.
6. All sugar is granulated unless otherwise stated.
7. Spoon measures can be bought in both imperial and metric sizes to give accurate measurement of small quantities.

## SERVING WITHOUT FREEZING

If you wish to prepare and serve these recipes without freezing the following instructions will give you some guidelines.

**1.** When food is required cold, omit the freezing instructions and place in the refrigerator until required.

**2.** When the food is to be served hot immediately after cooking, omit the freezing instructions and complete the recipe as given in the serving method.

**3.** In cases where the recipe method involves dealing with food taken directly from the freezer to the oven, omit the freezing instructions and cut down the cooking time by approximately one third, unless otherwise stated in the recipe. This applies particularly to recipes using pastry, and those with toppings, such as Scallop Nests.

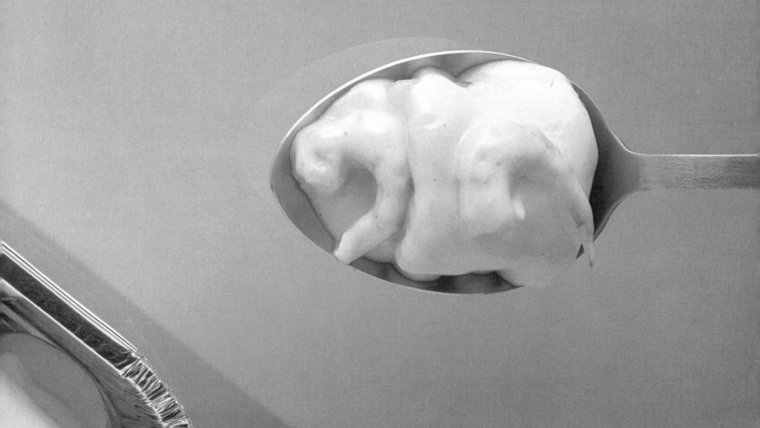

# FREEZING INFORMATION

# THE FREEZER PROCESS

From earliest recorded history mankind has searched for ways of preserving food. To do so in times of plenty was both a means of preventing famine in times of scarcity and, in later years, a means of storing food while at its cheapest.

Drying, salting, canning and bottling were all ways of preserving food but flavour, nutritive value and texture were often affected. Freezing is the easiest method so far devised and the one in which the food, when ready to be served, most nearly duplicates its original state.

Each family will use a freezer in the way which suits its own life-style. Its prime use may be for the storage of home-grown garden produce or to store bulk-buy offers. Alternatively, it may be used as a supply of special dishes or to store everyday dishes for family meals.

## WHAT CAUSES FOOD TO PERISH?

**Micro-organisms** – bacteria, moulds and yeasts that float in the air and form on most surfaces and feed on food. Many can contaminate food but freezing makes them inactive.

**Enzymes** – chemical substances naturally present in food, some of which cause undesirable changes in flavour, texture, food value, odour and colour. Freezing slows down their activity but it is because of them that food cannot be kept indefinitely in a freezer. Most of the enzymes in vegetables are destroyed by blanching.

**Drying** – the evaporation of moisture from food causes shrivelling and a general unpalatability. Unwrapped or inadequately wrapped food in a freezer would perish quickly.

**Atmospheric oxygen** – alone or in conjunction with enzymes causes food to discolour, fat to go rancid, etc. Frozen food must be adequately wrapped to keep it air-tight.

These are causes of food perishing under any conditions. When freezing food there is an additional factor which affects its quality.

**The speed of freezing** – when food is frozen slowly large ice crystals are formed in the food. These puncture the walls of the cells and moisture leaks from them during thawing and flavour is lost.

## HOW DOES FREEZING PRESERVE FOOD?

When food is frozen quickly micro-organisms are completely inactivated, the action of enzymes is slowed down and only small crystals are formed in the food. Correct packaging (see page 13) is essential to prevent drying and to keep out air.

## FAST FREEZING OF FOOD

The normal running temperature of a freezer ($-18°C$, $0°F$) is not sufficiently cold for fast freezing. By using the fast-freeze switch, or turning the setting as low as possible, the temperature will be reduced to $-28°C$, $-8°F$ or even less. This lower temperature is essential to counteract the rise in temperature caused by putting in food at room temperature, or even from the refrigerator. The instruction book supplied with the freezer will explain how long in advance this should be done but if the book is lost, allow 2-3 hours. If the machine has a fast-freeze compartment always use it – if not put the food against the base or walls because that is the coldest place.

After food is placed in the freezer, leave it at the very low setting for 4-24 hours, depending upon the amount of food put in.

*Allow about 2 hours for meat, fish and for made-up dishes. For other items allow 1-1½ hours per 450 g/1 lb.*

Never leave the deep freeze at this very low setting for more than 24 hours at a time or the motor may be damaged.

However, you should use your discretion in these matters. A small quantity of one item, e.g. left-over vegetables, will freeze quickly at the normal running temperature, especially if placed against the sides.

## AMOUNT OF FOOD WHICH CAN BE FROZEN IN A 24-HOUR PERIOD

Follow the instruction book or fast-freeze up to ⅒th of the freezing capacity in any 24 hours. The capacity of a freezer is approximately 13 kg/25 lb of food per cubic foot of freezer space. So in an 8 cubic ft freezer which will hold up to 91 kg/200 lb food, up to 9 kg/20 lb can be frozen at one time.

# STORAGE OF FROZEN FOOD

The normal running temperature in a freezer is −18°C, 0°F and if there is a choice of freezer settings it is advisable to check that the correct one is being used.

Opening the lid or door lets out some of the cold air and so increases the running cost. So it is advisable to have a storage plan so food can be located quickly.

In an upright freezer this is fairly simple. Allocate 1 or 2 types of food per shelf, moving food from the fast-freeze shelves as appropriate, also making full use of the door shelves.

Divide a chest freezer into compartments using wire baskets, large polythene or string bags, preferably in a variety of colours, or even cardboard boxes. If, for example, all vegetables are in a large green container or are marked with green, they will be easy to find in a full freezer. Different colours should be chosen for fruit, meat, etc.

It is important to appreciate that a well-filled freezer will cost less to run than a half-filled one. This is because the frozen food is colder than the air in the freezer and stays cold much longer. So just cooling down air is an expensive way of running a freezer.

## REFRIGERATORS, CONSERVATORS AND FREEZERS

All three can be used to store frozen food, but with great differences. **Refrigerators** have compartments marked with 1, 2 or 3 stars indicating frozen food can usually be stored for 1 week, 1 month or 3 months depending on the product. They are not suitable for the freezing of fresh food as their lowest temperatures are −6°C, 21°F; −12°C, 10°F and −18°C, 0°F. **Conservators,** too, are suitable only for storing already frozen food, but for the same time as in a freezer. There is no way of reducing the temperature for fast freezing. **Freezers** can be used for freezing food and for storing it.

# CHOOSING A FREEZER

### Site
A freezer can be sited almost anywhere providing the floor is strong enough to support it and air can flow freely around it. The area should be dry, or the machine may rust. If it is in a cool place the running costs will be reduced, as air entering when opened will not raise the temperature as much as warm air.

In or near the kitchen is the obvious choice but a passageway, spare bedroom or even a garage or outbuilding will do. Remember, heat is given off by the freezer to add extra warmth to its area. If in a damp area, stand it on wooden blocks and examine it frequently for rust.

If the freezer is outside the house or in a spare room, it is advisable to fit a warning light or bell in the kitchen to warn if the freezer breaks down, and a lock for safety purposes.

### Type
There are three types of freezer:
1. Chest type (4-24 cubic ft.)
2. Upright type (up to 20 cubic ft.)
3. Combined refrigerator/freezer type (4-6 cubic ft. for the freezer compartment)

**Chest freezer** (top opening)
*Advantages:*
1. Maximum storage for its capacity
2. Easy to accommodate bulky, large or awkward items in it
3. Usually cheaper to buy
4. Running costs are lower as less cold air escapes when the lid is opened. Cold air is heavier than warm and sinks below it
5. Needs less defrosting than other types – usually once a year
*Disadvantages:*
1. Needs at least twice the floor space of an upright of the same capacity
2. Difficult for a short person to reach to the bottom of the cabinet

**Upright freezer** (front opening)
*Advantages:*
1. Takes up less floor space than a chest freezer of the same capacity
2. Shelves, including those in the door, make it easier to organize the stock, to find items and to remove them
*Disadvantages:*
1. Slightly more expensive to buy
2. Slightly more expensive to run as more cold air escapes when door is opened.

However, some models have two doors or have doors or flaps fitted to each shelf to minimize this loss of cold air
3. Needs defrosting more often; usually two or three times a year

**Combined refrigerator/freezer**
*Advantages:*
As the freezer fits on top of the refrigerator or vice versa it takes up no extra floor space. It is suitable for very small kitchens.
*Disadvantages:*
The freezer usually has only a small capacity and so very little food can be frozen at one time.

## RUNNING COSTS

These cannot be given accurately. The actual cost will depend upon the number of times the lid or door is opened, how much fresh food is frozen and the siting of the freezer. An approximate guide is that a freezer will use 1 unit of electricity per week for each 15 litre capacity (or 1½-2 units per cubic ft. capacity). Most manufacturers give some guidance on this in their literature.

## USEFUL EXTRAS

It is wise to look for the following features. Not all are essential but most are desirable.
**Fast freeze switch** (see page 10).
**Interior light** which lights when the lid or

door is opened. This is essential if the freezer is sited in a dark area.
**Wire partitions and baskets or trays** to fit into cabinets. The wire partitions fit at the bottom of the freezer and the baskets or trays slide sideways across the top.
**Castors or slide rails** to enable the freezer to be moved for cleaning.
**Lock** which is almost essential if the freezer is outside the house or if there are small children.
**Alarm system** to indicate by buzzer or light if the temperature rises or if there is a fault in the electrical system.

## BUYING A SECOND-HAND FREEZER

Precautions are always essential when buying any type of second-hand appliance. Obviously make sure it is in working order. Have it connected and make sure the fast freeze switch works, if there is one. Find out from manufacturers for how long spare parts will be available giving serial number or date of manufacture. Find out if service is available.

## BUYING A NEW FREEZER

There is no doubt that by shopping around the same freezer can be found at different prices. So it is important to find out exactly what the price covers and what servicing facilities are available before making a final choice.

# FREEZER CARE

Even if you have owned a freezer before, when a new one is purchased you should read the booklet or other material provided by the manufacturer. It will tell you how to use and care for the appliance and that information may save you a lot of trouble later on.

## BEFORE IT IS FIRST USED

Wash the inside of the machine with a solution of 1 tablespoon bicarbonate of soda in about 1 litre/1¾ pints warm water. Dry well.
Wipe the outside and polish with a silicone polish. (Polishing is not essential.) Connect correctly to earthed power point, ideally one used only for the freezer.
Stick tape across both plug and switch so it cannot be switched off by accident.

Hang a notice saying 'Freezer' on main electricity switch to remind you not to turn off when going on holiday.
Set controls according to the literature and leave for at least 12 hours. You can check the temperature with a thermometer.
Put in the food, remembering restrictions on the amount to be frozen at one time, see page 10.

## CLEANING & DEFROSTING

Defrost when frost and ice on sides of freezer is ½-1 cm/¼-½ inch thick and when food stocks are at their lowest.
Set the refrigerator to its lowest setting and store as much food as possible from the freezer there, especially the smaller packs which thaw the quickest.

Pile the rest of the food close together and cover with several thicknesses of newspaper and a heavy blanket. The food should stay frozen for at least two hours.

Turn the freezer switch to Defrost or to Off and take out the plug. Follow manufacturer's instructions but if they are lost, proceed as follows:

Put towels, cloths or sponges in the base to absorb water. Put bowls of very hot water in the freezer and shut the door or lid. Leave for 20 minutes, changing the water 2 or 3 times.

Use a plastic or wooden scraper to remove ice – never a metal one. From a chest freezer remove the ice with rubber-gloved hands or a dust-pan or something similar. With an upright freezer, consider getting a handyman to make a piece of metal sloping to a hole in the centre to fit on the lowest shelf, and put a basin underneath. Wipe the inside with the bicarbonate of soda solution. If any odour remains use 1 tablespoon of vinegar in 1 litre/1¾ pints warm water. Rinse and dry.

Leave at the lowest setting for 1 hour before replacing the food. Meanwhile, wash and replace shelves, baskets, etc.

Take this opportunity to review the contents and bring the record up to date.

## HOW TO COPE WITH POWER FAILURES

It is wise to arrange for a yearly service and the information on this and on an emergency service should be kept near the freezer. This could be the manufacturer's local agent or the Electricity Board.

If the freezer stops working check the following points:
1. If the electricity supply to the house has been interrupted. If not:
2. If there is power to the socket by plugging in another appliance. If there is:

3. Check if the plug is still connected and that the fuse is in order. If they are, then you need the emergency service.

Meanwhile, take steps to keep the food in good condition:
4. Do not open the freezer.
5. Reduce the temperature round the freezer as much as possible by opening windows.

If the service man is unable to effect immediate repairs he may be able to offer storage facilities for the food. Breakdowns are rare but there is a good case for insuring the freezer contents, which is a service handled by any insurance company.

### If there are power cuts
If these occur they are likely to be at the coldest time of the year and do not last long enough to cause damage, especially if the freezer is not opened.

### How to tell if food is still usable
If the pack appears hard frozen there is no reason to worry.

If there are still ice crystals present there will be no damage.

If the food has thawed but is still very cold it can be cooked at once and then refrozen.

If the food has thawed to room temperature or it does not feel cold – *don't risk it*. Throw it away without tasting it. It is much the safest course.

### Moving house and freezer
Discuss the position with the removal firm and ensure that the freezer is the last item into the van and the first off. Reconnect it at once. Ensure the food cannot move on the journey by packing crumpled newspaper between the packs and to completely fill all available space. Fast freeze for several hours before the move; it should last at least 10 hours. Do not remove the paper for at least 12 hours after the freezer has been reconnected.

# PACKAGING

Without correct packaging freezing food cannot be successful. Packing material must have several properties. It must be:
**Strong** enough to prevent damage during storage, e.g. when someone is searching around for a particular pack and moving others around.
**Moisture proof** to keep liquids in and so prevent drying out and to stop unwanted liquids getting in.
**Vapour proof** to prevent flavours and/or aromas being transferred from one food

to another. If air is able to get into the pack it causes food to dry up and become unpalatable and the oxygen in the air could spoil colour and also break down the nutrients.
**Non-toxic** so that neither moulds nor bacteria can grow on it, especially if re-using the packaging, as vestiges of food not visible to the naked eye may still be present after washing. And it must not become dry or brittle in the cold of the freezer.

## HOW TO WRAP IN FOIL

### Butcher's wrap
1. Place food diagonally across one corner. Fold the corner over the food and then give one complete roll.
2. Fold up sides of foil close to the sides of the food and up over the top. Continue to roll to the opposite corner. Mould to the food with the hands and, if necessary, seal with freezer tape.

## CHOICE OF PACKAGING

There is a wide choice of packaging materials available to suit all purposes. Starting with the cheapest they are:

### POLYTHENE BAGS
The minimum thickness should be 120 gauge but 150-250 gauge are stronger, better for long storage and easier to re-use. If used for liquid and soft foods they tend to become awkward shapes which waste freezer space as they are difficult to stack, but this can be overcome by putting the bag in a rigid container (even an empty sugar box will do) before filling and removing when frozen.

To extract air, gather the neck close to the food, insert a straw and suck out air until the bag forms round the food. Remove the straw, tightening the neck at the same time and seal with a tie fastener. Equally effective is lowering the bag into cold water letting the weight of water force air out and then moulding the bag round the food. Take care to dry the bag thoroughly or it will stick to the freezer or to other food.

Bags with labels on them are available, on which details can be written with an ordinary ball-point pen. With others, use freezer labels, fasten ordinary labels in place with freezer tape or slip labels inside the bags.

Secure the bags with paper or plastic-covered wire ties which can be bought separately.

### PLASTIC CLING FILM & PLASTIC FREEZER FILM
These are easily moulded round any shape to exclude air. The thinner film can be used to wrap single items, e.g. chops, bread rolls, etc. These can then be packed in bags or overwrapped with more film so that single items can be taken out as required. Several thicknesses of thin film are required for overwrapping when the freezer strength is not available.

### BOIL-IN BAGS
The food is frozen in the bag in the usual way. When it is required the bag is dropped into boiling water until the food is hot. Several bags of different foods can be reheated in one pan together quite safely. Seal by using a specially designed small machine or use an electric iron on its coolest setting, protecting the polythene from direct heat by two thicknesses of tissue paper. If a wire tie is used, choose a plastic-covered one.

## ALUMINIUM FOIL & FREEZER FOIL
These can be moulded round awkward shapes to exclude all the air and to pad the sharp ends of bones which could pierce plastic film. Do not use where acid, such as fruit acid, will create small holes in the aluminium foil through which air can enter the pack.

A single thickness of aluminium foil is not suitable for long term storage. If freezer foil is not available, use a double thickness of ordinary foil.

### How to wrap in foil
There are two methods of wrapping food in foil; the butcher's wrap and the chemist's wrap which are illustrated on the left and right.
*Note:* if the food is to be reheated in foil it is important to unwrap the food and rewrap loosely first.

## RIGID CONTAINERS
These come in a variety of shapes and sizes, with lids or without, and vary in cost from expensive to free.

## ALUMINIUM FOIL CONTAINERS
These are possibly the most useful type as they can be taken straight from freezer to oven. A wide range of sizes and shapes is available from plates, pie dishes and pudding basins to round, square and oblong trays of various depths. Many styles have cardboard lids with the side to go against the food covered with foil. The plain side should be used for labelling. Some pudding basins are specially coated so that fruit puddings can be stored in them. Wash aluminium foil containers thoroughly before re-use. The lids cannot be re-used and instead use freezer cling film or freezer film, then place in a polythene bag before freezing.

## WAXED OR LINED CARDBOARD CONTAINERS
The waxed ones cannot be filled with hot food as the wax melts. Those with a foil or polythene lining are better but do not use the foil-lined type for fruit. They usually need sealing with freezer tape and cannot be re-used.

## POLYTHENE OR PLASTIC CONTAINERS
These can be re-used if very carefully washed. Some have snap-on lids making them air-tight when first used but with use these loosen and freezer tape is needed. They are excellent for fruit storage.

## HOW TO WRAP IN FOIL

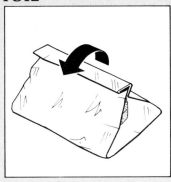

### Chemist's wrap

1. Place the food in the centre of a piece of foil large enough to fold over food with an 8-11 cm/3-4 inch overlap. Bring the longer ends together over the food, fold them over and over until the foil is folded tightly across the food.
2. Fold shorter ends over once or twice with small folds and then fold each end tight against the food. If necessary, seal with freezer tape.

## TOUGHENED GLASS & CERAMIC CONTAINERS

These are the casseroles and other dishes normally used for cooking and so it is sensible to use them in the freezer only when they contain a special recipe for a special occasion in the near future. Only use those dishes that the manufacturer recommends for freezer to oven use.

There are several ways of using them for cooking and for reheating food without having them packed away in the freezer and so out of use.

1. After the food is cooked and cooled, open freeze still in the container. Dip the dish quickly in hot water so food can be freed and overwrapped. Return the food to the freezer.
2. Before cooking, line the container with a piece of foil large enough to enclose the food completely later. After cooking, cool quickly, open freeze, and when firm remove from the container and wrap to enclose the food. Overwrap and store. This method may not be suitable for fruit dishes containing acid fruits.
3. Cook stews and similar foods in the container or a pan in the usual way. Line a dish with cling film or foil, pour in the cooled food, open freeze, etc., as in 2 above.

To reheat remove the wrapping and place the food in the container in which it was open frozen. Put at once into a cold oven, then reheat in the oven at the temperature given in the recipe, or leave to thaw thoroughly in the container first before heating.

## MICROWAVE OVEN CONTAINERS

When food is to be thawed or reheated in a microwave oven it is very important that the correct packaging is used. Metal containers, including foil, metallic glazed dishes and those with a metallic trim cannot be used, but polythene and plastic containers and toughened glass and ceramic ones, without metal trim, are all suitable. There is also a range of dishes especially designed for freezer to microwave. Polythene bags, with wire tie removed, can be used for defrosting (thawing) and 'boil-in' bags for both defrosting and cooking.

## GLASS JARS & BOTTLES

Only ones which are labelled as specially toughened to withstand low temperatures are suitable and ones with straight sides and a wide mouth are best. Leave room for the contents to expand on freezing and always pack glass in a polythene bag as an additional precaution.

## FREE CONTAINERS

Many convenience foods are packed in containers which fill all the requirements for freezer packaging. Examples are those holding yogurt, cottage cheese, salads, etc. Wash very well, rinse in hot water and drain dry.

### FREEZER TAPE

This is tape which remains adhesive at the low temperatures in freezers.

### Difficult packages

If a package has a sharp edge or is an irregular shape, it may damage others or be damaged itself, during storage. To avoid this overwrap in cotton stockinette or put into a thick polythene bag.

## WHERE TO BUY FREEZER PACKAGING

There is a wide range available in frozen food supermarkets, supermarkets, department stores and in some stationers and chemists. Some firms supply by post and will supply in larger quantities than can be bought elsewhere and therefore at a cheaper cost per unit. This is useful if large quantities of polythene bags are used as they take up little space. Electricity showrooms usually have the relevant information.

## LABELLING

It is important to label every package before it is put in the freezer and it should carry the following information:
Type of food and variety
Quantity, weight or portions
Date of freezing
Information on reheating, thawing, adding other ingredients.

Use special freezer labels, felt-tipped marking pens, or tie labels on polythene bags. It is helpful to use labels of different colours for different groups of foods for easy identification.

## FREEZER RECORD

It is advisable to keep a record of frozen food so that it is used in rotation and the recommended maximum storage time is not exceeded – a school exercise book will do. Keep a separate page for each group and list the food, quantity, weight or portions and the date – as on the label. Cross off each package removed. Check that the record is correct when defrosting.

# STOCKING A FREEZER

## FREEZER SUPERMARKETS & SPECIAL FIRMS

Freezer owners can save money by buying frozen food in bulk from freezer supermarkets. A wide variety of basic foods such as fruit, vegetables, meat, fish, etc., as well as ready prepared foods such as pies and ice cream are available in large packs. Some of the larger supermarkets and food sections in department stores often have some large packs in their range.

In many areas there are small firms or individuals who have a limited range available for immediate delivery or who will prepare food to order.

## BULK-BUYING MEAT

There is no doubt that buying half a lamb, pig or cow is cheaper than buying individual cuts, but like so many good things there are snags. So before being tempted, stop and think.

*Have you room to store all that meat at one time in addition to the food you usually freeze?*

### Just what do you get for your money?

The cheapest way is to buy the half animal, take it home and cut it up yourself – if you know how to.

It costs a little more if it is cut up for you – and sometimes the trimmings are minced as well.

With both of these you also get quantities of fat and bone which you may not want. With a further rise in the cost the butcher will trim the meat and bone the joints you specify. He might even keep the fat and bones if you wish.

One step further is when the meat is prepared, correctly wrapped and labelled by the butcher and quick frozen in his commercial freezer more quickly than in yours. All you need to do is take it home and use it. That leads to another question.

### Are you confident you can use all the various cuts?

Remember you will have meat for stewing and braising as well as grilling cuts and roasting joints. There may even be half a pig's head. To help you, the Meat Chapter starting on page 78 contains ideas for using half a lamb and also some of the cheaper cuts of meat.

## Where do you bulk-buy meat?

Make sure it is a reliable source from which you have previously bought meat of good quality, so there is no danger of being sold inferior meat. Most butchers, especially those who are part of a large chain that can itself bulk-buy, offer meat for the freezer in large quantities for a reduced price per kilogram/pound. Another good source is a frozen food supermarket from which you have previously bought meat.

## BATCH COOKING

There are occasions when it is sensible to devote a day, or half a day, to cooking for the freezer. Take one basic food or a basic recipe and produce from it a variety of dishes to last for a length of time.

**After a bulk-buy of meat:** in the chapter on meat you will find several ways of cooking stewing steak, minced beef and cooked chicken.

**Towards the end of term:** in preparation for the school holidays, a selection of tasty, inexpensive dishes.

**Before family holiday periods:** Christmas, Easter and the summer holidays cook a batch of breads, rolls and cakes.

**For a party:** plan it so that much of the food can be prepared well before the day and frozen. In that way the hostess as well as the guests can enjoy the party.

**For freezing fruit and vegetables:** take, for example, tomatoes or apples, when there is a glut and freeze them in a variety of cooked dishes as well as the ways given in the fruit and vegetable charts, see pages 22 to 37.

## COMPLETE MAIN COURSES

The meat from a large joint always tastes better than that from a small one. One way of utilizing the meat not eaten when freshly cooked is to package complete main courses. Foil plates divided into sections are available so that meat and two vegetables can be packed separately. Always cover the meat with gravy to prevent it from drying out. Boiled, roast or mashed potatoes with a wide choice of vegetables, but not green leaf ones, complete the main course. Cover with a lid or with foil, excluding as much air as possible. Reheat from frozen, at 200°C, 400°F, Gas Mark 6 for 45 minutes.

# TIME SAVING IDEAS (& SPECIAL USES)

**Grated cheese:** to give added flavour and food value to many dishes and to assist browning; sprinkle on slices of French bread, brown in the oven and serve with soup; useful for sandwiches; sprinkle on baked or grilled fish, vegetables, etc.

**Fresh breadcrumbs** – brown or white: to provide quick toppings for sweet dishes (with sugar) or savoury dishes (with cheese, chopped, cooked onion, etc.); for making charlottes; for thickening stews in an emergency, etc.

**Flavoured butters:** put small pats still frozen on grilled meat or fish; toss with cooked vegetables; allow to thaw and use instead of plain butter in sandwiches, etc.

**A variety of sauces:** to add distinction to many dishes, especially grilled ones and vegetables; to form the base of other dishes such as curries.

**Concentrated stock cubes:** freeze broken chicken carcasses and giblets until there are enough to make a rich chicken stock with vegetables to flavour, or start with fresh beef bones. Strain the stock, then boil rapidly in an open pan until it is reduced to one-third of its original volume. Store in small quantities or freeze in ice cube trays. Turn out and store (see Ice cubes).

To use, measure out two-thirds of the required liquid as water and then add concentrated stock cubes to bring it up to the level required.

**Baby foods, puréed:** great care must be taken in preparing baby foods and all the items cooked separately. They should not be fed on food cooked for the rest of the family and puréed as babies must not have as much salt as adults tend to eat. A variety to last for 2 or 3 weeks can be prepared at one session and stored in one-portion packs.

**Packed meals:** when one or more of the family takes sandwiches to work or to school it can be a rush to make them each morning – instead make several varieties at one time, pack separately, making enough to last for up to six weeks; taken out of the freezer after breakfast they will be thawed by lunchtime; they can also be useful for short-notice picnics.

**Toast toppings:** using a thick cheese sauce as a base, a great number of ingredients such as finely chopped onions, mushrooms, meat, fish, vegetables, nuts, etc., can be added; pack small quantities frozen in a thin, flat layer and when required place on a slice of toast and grill until hot and bubbly.

**Omelette fillings** based on a sauce or on fried onions, etc., a great number of fillings can be devised; pack in small quantities and reheat in a double boiler or, carefully, in a pan without thawing before putting into the omelette.

**Ice cubes:** when required for a party they can be made in advance and put into plastic bags with a squirt of soda water to prevent them from sticking together.

**Concentrated coffee and tea cubes:** brew coffee or tea that is 4 times the usual strength and freeze in ice cube trays. Pack in plastic bags (see Ice cubes) and make into cold drinks by adding water, soda water or milk.

**Croûtons:** fried croûtons are one way of using stale bread. Drain well before freezing. Serve with soups and salads.

# PREPARING FOOD FOR THE FREEZER

In general no special techniques are needed. The rules are simple.
1. Follow your usual hygiene rules.
2. Use only top quality food and vegetables and fruits as soon as they are gathered.
3. Cool food quickly and keep it covered.
4. Package correctly and label.
5. Fast freeze.
6. Keep to recommended storage times.
7. Thaw or cook from frozen as recommended on the packet or in these recipes.

**One special technique:** Soups and sauces thickened with flour and then frozen tend to separate when thawed or when reheated. To prevent this use cornflour as all or part of the thickening, as given in many recipes in this book.

**Open freezing** is used for delicate foods. It is also for those items you wish to keep separate so that you may use a small quantity at a time from one large pack. Stand the food on trays, which can be lined with foil or with plastic cling film, and fast freeze until firm. Pack in the usual way. *Do not open freeze food with a strong aroma.*

## DAIRY PRODUCTS

Dairy produce is available all the year round and, except in very isolated areas, there is little need to freeze dairy foods. However, there are occasions when, due to change of plans, there are surplus quantities, and supplies in the freezer when returning home after a holiday can be useful. It is a good idea always to have some grated cheese stored for emergency meals or for toppings.

## Milk

Homogenized milk in a wax carton is best as it does not separate during thawing.
THAW: 6-8 hours at room temperature, overnight in the refrigerator and shake well or, when time is short, heat slowly in a pan.

## Cream

Only clotted, double or whipped cream should be frozen. Cream with less than 40% butterfat content separates when thawed. Choose a pasteurised (heat treated) one and, as 12 cm/½ inch headroom must be allowed for expansion, it is usually best to transfer cream to a new container for freezing. Often cream that has been frozen has a 'grainy' texture but this can be avoided if 5 ml/1 teaspoon caster or icing sugar is added and double cream can be half-whipped before freezing. Or, fully whip cream, sweeten and pipe into rosettes or whirls. Open freeze and then package. Use, still frozen, to decorate sweets and puddings. They thaw rapidly.
THAW: Some cream can be bought already frozen and this, like home frozen, should be thawed slowly in the refrigerator overnight.

## Butter

Butter easily absorbs odours from other foods so it must be carefully over-wrapped.
THAW: At room temperature.

## Cheese

Cheese may be more crumbly after freezing but the flavour is not impaired. Hard, soft and blue cheese freeze well but freezing stops the maturing process so that, for example, Brie must be just ripe before freezing. A bag or two of grated cheese can be used for a variety of purposes and can be used without thawing. If the cheese is dry before grating it will not form a solid lump but if soft it may. In this case rub it against the side of a grater.
THAW: Pieces of cheese thawed in the refrigerator will take about 6 hours per 450 g/1 lb; at room temperature 4 hours per 450 g/1 lb.

## Eggs

Eggs cannot be frozen in their shells because expansion during freezing cracks the shells.
1. Beat white and yolk lightly together adding a pinch of salt or sugar, and mark which has been used.
2. Break eggs into individual plastic or paper containers. Open freeze, wrap and store.
3. Store egg whites together in small quantities – 30 ml/2 tablespoons equals 1 egg white when thawed.
4. Beat 6 yolks lightly with 5 ml/ 1 teaspoon salt or 15 ml/1 tablespoon sugar and mark which has been used. 15 ml/1 tablespoon equals 1 yolk when thawed.
THAW: Overnight in the refrigerator or at room temperature.

## HERBS

Wash in cold water and dry on kitchen paper.
1. Pack sprays into polythene bags.
2. Chop leaves, and pack in usable amounts in small polythene bags.
3. Make into herb butters.
USE:
1. Crumble frozen leaves between fingers instead of chopping or use sprays whole, e.g. in soups and stews.
2. Add herb cubes to sauces, soups and stews or thaw in a small strainer so water drains away and use in salads, sandwiches, etc.

**Bouquet Garni:** tie small bundles in cheesecloth, wrap individually and put together in polythene bags.

Frozen herbs are not suitable for garnishing but their flavour is better than that of dried herbs.

## CAKES AND BISCUITS

Plain cakes should be wrapped and then frozen. Thaw whilst still wrapped.

Cakes decorated with soft icing or butter cream should be open frozen and then wrapped. Remove wrapping before thawing to prevent it from sticking. Sponge sandwiches and Swiss rolls can be frozen filled with cream or butter cream but put jam fillings in after thawing.

Biscuit dough can be formed into a roll and frozen. Thaw until it can be cut into slices and baked.

## PASTRY DISHES

These are usually considered best when frozen uncooked but they can be cooked first if preferred. If fillings are put in brush the pastry with oil, melted butter or egg white to protect it and thicken fruit juices with cornflour. Bake from frozen and make steam vents in the top when the pastry is partly thawed. Uncooked pastry is best frozen in small blocks, as these thaw more quickly.

Package pastry dishes carefully and, if possible, store in rigid containers as added protection.

Always cook choux pastry before freezing.

### YEAST MIXTURES

Freeze fresh yeast for up to 1 month.

Freeze prepared yeast dough after the first rising in an oiled and floured plastic bag. Some of the yeast cells will be destroyed by the cold so the rising time will be longer or a little extra yeast can be used. Rolls and croissants are best cooked completely, then frozen and warmed through when required.

### SANDWICHES

Sandwich fillings should not contain hard-boiled eggs, which go leathery, moist salad ingredients such as lettuce and only very small amounts of mayonnaise. Otherwise, make in the usual way, spreading butter evenly and right up to the crusts to prevent the filling from making the bread soft. Wrap tightly in plastic film and then in polythene bags.
THAW: Remove from polythene bag and leave at room temperature for 2½-3 hours. For packed school and office lunches, take out of the freezer at breakfast time.

Thaw sandwiches before toasting.

### PASTA

As most types of pasta only need about 15 minutes or less cooking time, there is no point in freezing them. Left-over pasta can be added to dishes such as stews and frozen. Lasagne, cannelloni and other dishes, which require quite a bit of preparation, freeze well. Home made ravioli can be open frozen and then packed in plastic bags and frozen before cooking.
SERVE: Reheat from frozen with the dish covered to begin with, then remove the cover to allow the top to brown.

### NUTS

All nuts can be frozen, in their shells or after shelling; left whole, chopped or slivered.

### JELLIES AND GELATINES

Changes occur in frozen jellies and when thawed they have a gritty texture, they are not clear and they tend to 'weep'. Gelatine can be used quite safely to set dishes which contain whipped cream, whipped egg whites or purées (fruit, meat, fish, vegetables, etc.). Creams, mousses, soufflés, cheesecakes, etc., should be open frozen, then the surface covered closely with plastic cling film before being packaged.

### DO NOT FREEZE:

The following foods cannot be frozen because their texture or flavour is not acceptable when thawed or cooked.
**Salad vegetables** which contain a lot of water, except as purées for cold soups. They are not crisp.
**Mayonnaise** which separates into egg yolk and oil.
**Hard-boiled eggs.** The whites go leathery unless finely chopped.
**Whole eggs in their shells** which crack.
**Single or whipping cream** which separates.
**Soured cream and yogurt.** Their texture is altered.
**Food flavoured with synthetic flavouring.** The flavour alters during freezing.
**Icings (other than soft icing)** which lose their texture.
**Carbonated drinks.** They often cause a minor explosion and the spilt contents freeze on the other packages.

# THAWING AND COOKING

When food is thawed the temperature rises and the food will only keep in good condition as long as fresh food does. If food is thawed before cooking or reheating it is best done in the refrigerator, if time permits.

No exact timings can be given. Small packs thaw more quickly than large ones and some food is more 'dense' than others. Once raw food is thawed it should be cooked and eaten as quickly as possible or cooked, cooled and returned to the freezer. Cooked food, once thawed, must never be refrozen.
In the same way the time in the oven may vary a little from the times given in the

recipes, depending upon the shape of the container. For example meat stewed in a large shallow container reheats more quickly than one in a deeper container.

### SOUPS

**Hot:** turn frozen soup into a pan, adding the additional liquid if it is concentrated soup. Heat gently, stirring often.
**Cold:** thaw in the refrigerator.

### STOCK

Turn into a pan and heat. Alternatively, drop concentrated cubes into the correct amount of liquid, which can be water or the liquid in soups, stews, etc.

## SAUCES

**Hot:** delicate sauces should be wholly or partially thawed before reheating carefully. Heat others slowly from frozen, stirring often.
**Cold:** thaw in the refrigerator.

## FISH

Thin pieces may be cooked from frozen unless they are to be coated first, when they should be partially thawed so that the coating will stick. Thicker pieces should be partially thawed, however they can be cooked from frozen, if necessary, but the outer layer of flesh may become overcooked in the time it takes the heat to penetrate right through. Thaw cooked prawns and shrimps in the refrigerator and serve chilled. Frozen, shelled cooked prawns may be added to sauces direct from the freezer.

## MEAT

Meat will be more succulent if it is thawed in the refrigerator still in its original wrappings allowing about 6 hours per 450 g/1 lb.

Allow 3 hours per 450 g/1 lb at room temperature.

Small pieces, such as steaks, chops or sliced liver, may be grilled or fried from frozen if cooked a little more slowly than usual until thawed through. If they are to be coated before cooking they must be thawed.

You must decide, depending on time and flavour, whether you prefer your roasting joints thawed or not. Once thawed cook at the usual temperature and timing. If cooked from frozen a joint must be cooked slowly at 160°C, 325°F, Gas Mark 3, allowing about 45 minutes per 450 g/1 lb for beef and lamb and 1 hour for pork. If you adopt this latter method you are advised to buy a meat thermometer. By recording the temperature in the thickest part of the meat, this will enable you to get the same result time after time.

Minced meat or chopped meat for stews can be fried slowly without thawing, breaking it up carefully, or dropped into boiling stock.

## POULTRY & GAME

**Poultry and game must ALWAYS be fully thawed before they are cooked** or they will be dangerous to health, because salmonella bacteria possibly present will begin to activate before the heat has penetrated the meat enough to destroy them. Thaw in the refrigerator in their wrappings allowing about 3 hours per 450 g/1 lb. Then cook in the usual way.

## VEGETABLES

Drop frozen vegetables into a small quantity of boiling salted water. Time from when the water returns to the boil and cook with the lid on the pan. Take care not to overcook them. Vegetables may also be steamed or cooked in a covered casserole in the oven with a knob of buttered foil and bake in the oven for about 30 minutes.

See, also, the vegetable chart on pages 30-37.

## FRUIT

**Cold:** thaw in the refrigerator. Leave unopened to prevent it from discolouring. Serve slightly chilled.
**Hot:** partially thaw before stewing.

## BREAD & CAKES

**Bread** will thaw in about 2 hours at room temperature. However, frozen slices can be toasted or fried. Bread can be thawed in a moderately hot oven but will then go stale more quickly.
**Crisp rolls, French bread and croissants** taste better if reheated in the oven before serving.
**Scones:** thaw in their wrappings for about 1 hour or split when frozen, toast and butter.
**Cream cakes:** cut into wedges or slices whilst still frozen. This aids thawing and gives wedges of a better shape.
**Iced cakes:** remove wrapping or it may stick to the icing.
**Other cakes:** thaw in their wrappings. If a whole cake is not needed at one time, cut into wedges, wrap each piece in plastic cling film, reassemble and overwrap so that a small portion can be removed when required.

## DAIRY PRODUCE

**Eggs:** thaw in opened containers and use at once.
**Butter, cream and milk:** thaw overnight in the refrigerator or for about 2 hours at room temperature.

## PUDDINGS & SWEETS

**Cold:** thaw in the refrigerator.
**Hot:** steamed and baked puddings can be reheated from frozen.

## SANDWICHES

Leave in wrappings. They will thaw in 2 hours, or longer, the time varying with the size of the pack.

## COMMERCIALLY FROZEN FOOD

Follow the instructions on the pack.

# STORAGE TIMES

Once food is frozen, even if it is in the peak of condition, it can only be stored for a definite period. Assuming it is stored at −18°C/0°F or less and that it is correctly packaged a recommended storage time can be given. After that the food will still be edible for a considerable period but there will be some deterioration in texture and in flavour. The alteration in flavour is most noticeable when a lot of fat is present, either occurring naturally in the food (e.g. mackerel) or when fat has been used in its preparation. Fat may go rancid and that is why the shortest storage times are for foods such as sausages and bacon.

| | |
|---|---|
| **Giblets** | 3 months |
| **Blanched vegetables** | 12 months |
| **Herbs** | 12 months |
| **Pasta** | 4 months |
| **Fruit** (raw and cooked) | 12 months |
| **Uncooked pastry** | 3 months |
| **Cooked foods*** see below | 4 months |
| **Plain unrisen yeast dough** | 2 months |
| **Rich unrisen yeast dough** | 5 weeks |
| **Risen yeast doughs** | 3 weeks |
| **Baked bread** | 6 months |
| **Sandwiches** (depending on filling) | 1-3 months |
| **Baked cakes, Pastry and Biscuits** | 6 months |
| **Eggs** | 10 months |
| **Butter** – unsalted | 6 months |
| – salted | 3 months |
| **Milk** | 3 months |
| **Cream** (minimum 40% butterfat content) | 3-4 months |
| **Soft cheese** (must be ripe before freezing) | 8 months |
| **Hard cheese** | 6 months |
| **Blue cheese** (must be ripe before freezing) | 3 months |
| **Ice cream** | 3 months |
| **Soups, Stocks and Sauces** | 4 months |
| **Savoury breads** | 3 months |
| **White fish** | 6 months |
| **Oily fish** | 4 months |
| **Shellfish** | 3 months |
| **Cooked shellfish and other cooked fish** | 1 month |
| **Beef and Lamb** | 12 months |
| **Pork** | 9 months |
| **Veal** | 6 months |
| **Minced meat** | 2 months |
| **Offal** – hearts, liver, kidneys, tripe and tongue | 2 months |
| **Sausages, Smoked and Delicatessen meats** | 6 weeks |
| **Smoked bacon joints** | 2 months |
| **Unsmoked bacon joints** | 5 weeks |
| **Bacon rashers and chops** | 1 month |
| **Chickens, Hens, Turkeys and Capons** | 12 months |
| **Ducks and Geese** | 6 months |
| **Game** (must be fully hung and plucked) | 6 months |

*This is only a very general recommendation and you should also consult the recipe section.

# FREEZING FRUIT

Freezer owners can enjoy fruit out of season and have ready to hand the basis for interesting sweets, puddings and desserts. Home-grown fruit should be picked and frozen as quickly as possible and some farmers and market gardeners encourage customers to pick their own fruit. Bought fruit should be carefully checked.

There are 5 basic ways of preparing food for the freezer although not all fruit can be prepared in all 5 ways.

## DRY PACK
METHOD:
1. Choose fully-ripe, but not over-ripe fruit. Prepare.
2. Spread single layers of fruit on trays, which can be lined with greaseproof paper if wished, and open freeze until firm.
3. Pack into bags or boxes and return to freezer.
USE:
For pies, tarts, puddings, etc., and for making jam or jelly.

## SUGAR PACK
METHOD:
1. Choose fully-ripe, but not over-ripe, fruit. Prepare.
2. Pack alternate layers of fruit and sugar. Leave 1 cm/½ inch headroom. Freeze.
*or:*
Stir fruit and sugar carefully until fruit is coated with sugar. (Some fruits may be damaged by this method.)
*Note:* this method is not suitable for fruits which discolour rapidly.
USE:
For pies and desserts or serve in fruit salad or on its own. Because a syrup forms as the fruit thaws it may be necessary to strain this off for some recipes.

## SYRUP PACK
METHOD:
1. Prepare syrup in advance and chill.
2. Choose fully-ripe but not over-ripe fruit. Prepare.
3. Put fruit in a container and pour in enough syrup to cover the fruit and leave only 1-2 cm/½-1 inch headspace. If the fruit floats in the syrup the top layer will discolour so press crumpled greaseproof or non-stick silicone paper on top before sealing, to hold the fruit down in the syrup.
*or:*
1. Use slightly under-ripe fruit. Prepare.
2. Make syrup, add fruit and simmer carefully until just soft.
3. Cool quickly before putting into containers (see 3 above).

USE:
As Sugar Pack above.
**Syrup:** the strength of the syrup will depend upon the type of fruit, degree of ripeness and personal taste so only an average guide can be given.
To 1.2 litres/2 pints water add
– 225 g/½ lb sugar for a light syrup
– 450 g/1 lb sugar for a medium syrup
– 1 kg/2 lb sugar for a heavy syrup
Heat together until the sugar is completely dissolved. Cool and chill. Allow approximately 300 ml/½ pint syrup for each 450 g/1 lb fruit.

## PURÉES
METHOD:
1. Use fully-ripe or slightly over-ripe fruit. Remove any damaged parts.
2. **Soft fruit** – crush or blend and, if necessary, pass through a sieve to remove small seeds. Add sugar to taste, usually up to 100 g/4 oz for each 450 g/1 lb fruit.
**Other fruit** – cook until soft in just enough water or syrup to prevent it from burning. Then proceed as for soft fruit.
3. Pack and freeze, allowing 1 cm/½ inch headspace.
USE:
As a basis for fools, ice creams, sorbets, mousses, etc.

## FRUIT JUICES
Lemon, lime and orange juices are best frozen in small containers leaving a little headroom. Make sure no pips are included as they may alter the flavour of the juice during storage.

## Artificial sweeteners
It is best to add these after thawing so choose the Dry Pack method of preparing. Diabetics and those on a sugar-free diet will find this useful.

## Preventing fruit discoloration
Some fruits, such as apples, pears, apricots and peaches may discolour during preparation. This can be avoided if each piece is immediately dropped into water which has been acidified by adding the juice of 1 lemon (2 tablespoons) to

1 litre/1¾ pints cold water or by adding ¼ teaspoon ascorbic acid to 600 ml/1 pint fruit syrup.

(Ascorbic acid, also known as Vitamin C, can be bought in powder or crystal form from most chemists.)

### Fruit for jam and jelly making

If it is not convenient to make jam when the fruit is at its best or if home grown fruit does not all ripen at the same time, the fruit can be frozen and the jam or jelly made later.

1. Prepare fruit according to kind – see following chart.
2. Freeze using the dry pack method, being careful to mark weight of fruit on each container.

TO USE:
Place frozen fruit in pan adding a little water to prevent the fruit from sticking. Heat slowly until the juice runs. Then follow the usual recipe adding acid (usually lemon juice) when necessary and sugar. Note, however, that there is some loss of pectin during storage and so to aid setting increase the fruit content by 10%.

Certain fruit, such as strawberry, which is sometimes difficult to set, benefits from the addition of a little commercial liquid pectin (available from some chemists).

| Methods of freezing: | Uses: |
|---|---|

## APPLES

Choose ripe dessert or cooking apples with a good flavour. Peel, core and drop into acidified water (2 tablespoons lemon juice added to 1 litre/1¾ pints water). Dry on kitchen paper when ready to proceed. CRAB APPLES can be frozen by the sugar pack method and then used for jelly making.

| Methods of freezing: | Uses: |
|---|---|
| **Dry pack,** in slices, quartered or chopped. **Sugar pack,** in slices, quartered or chopped. | For pie and tart fillings, for puddings, etc. |
| **Syrup pack,** in slices, quartered or chopped. | As stewed fruit or part of fruit salad. |
| **Purée** | For pie and tart fillings, for charlottes, etc. |

## APRICOTS

Remove stones. If wished skin after plunging fruit into boiling water for 30 seconds. May be cut into halves.

| Methods of freezing: | Uses: |
|---|---|
| **Syrup pack** – if fully-ripe just add to syrup, if barely-ripe stew in syrup. | As stewed fruit or part of fruit salad. Drain fruit to use in pies, tarts, puddings. |
| **Purée** – when fruit is over-ripe. | As sauce, in ice cream, puddings, etc. |

## AVOCADO

Choose ripe, but not over-ripe, fruit. Peel, cut into halves and remove stone.

| Methods of freezing: | Uses: |
|---|---|
| **Dry pack** – dip slices in lemon juice first and open freeze. | In salads and snacks. |
| **Purée** – adding 1 tablespoon lemon juice to each avocado. Work quickly, to avoid discoloration. Pack in rigid containers with plastic film pressed on to surface. | For savoury dips and sauces. |

| Methods of freezing: | Uses: |
|---|---|

## BANANAS
Bananas are available all year so freezing is neither necessary nor recommended.

## BILBERRIES
Treat as Blackberries.

## BLACKBERRIES
Use only ripe blackberries; over-ripe ones often have large woody pips. Remove stalks. Wash quickly in iced water, drain and dry on kitchen paper.

| | |
|---|---|
| **Dry pack** ⎫ | For pies, tarts, puddings. |
| **Sugar pack** ⎬ | Add to fruit salad. |
| **Syrup pack** | As stewed fruit. |
| **Purée** | For making sauces, ice cream, etc. |

As blackberries are often served with apples, it is an excellent idea to freeze them together by the Dry Pack, Sugar Pack, Syrup Pack and Purée methods in any proportions, ideally in packs for specific dishes, e.g. for 1 pie.

## BLUEBERRIES
Use ripe fruit. Remove stalks. Wash quickly in iced water, drain and dry on kitchen paper.
    Methods and uses as Blackberries.

## CHERRIES
Both sweet and sour varieties may be frozen, separately. Red ones freeze better than black. Wash in iced water and remove stones and stalks.

| | |
|---|---|
| **Dry pack** | For stewing, for duck with cherries. |
| **Sugar pack** – ripe fruit only. | For pies, tarts and puddings. |
| **Syrup pack** – if under-ripe fruit, stew in syrup. | For desserts. |
| **Purée** – when fruit is very ripe. | For sweet sauces, ice creams and puddings. |

## COCONUTS
If possible choose one still containing the milk – shake to find out. Remove the outside fibres, break open. Pour off the milk and remove the inside 'meat' and grate or mince it. Then treat differently from other fruits.

| | |
|---|---|
| a) Mix with the coconut milk. | After thawing pour off the milk and use the meat in curries and sweet dishes. |
| b) Dissolve sugar to taste in the coconut milk and then mix with the meat. | Only for sweet dishes. |
| c) Toast meat carefully in a hot oven or under a grill. | Use within 2-3 months for decoration. |

**Methods of freezing:**                    **Uses:**

## CRANBERRIES
Choose ripe, bright red berries. Remove
stems, wash, drain and dry.

**Dry pack**       }
**Sugar pack**      }    Usually as a sauce or make into a jelly.

**Purée** – sweetened to taste.

## CURRANTS, BLACK, RED AND WHITE
Sort and strip from stems, with a fork. Use
fine, fully-ripe fruit. Wash, drain and dry.

**Dry pack**                                 For making into jams and jellies, for
                                             general cooking, as below.

**Sugar pack**     }          For pies, tarts, fruit salads and other
**Syrup pack**     }          sweets.

**Purée**, sweetened to taste.               As a sauce, especially with ice cream or
                                             as a base for fruit ices.

## DAMSONS
Choose ripe, unblemished fruit. Wash,
drain and dry. Remove stones (might
affect flavour if left in). Avoid Dry Pack
and Sugar Pack methods which tend to
make the skins tough. See Plums.

## DATES
Choose large, juicy, ripe dates. Slit and
remove stones. Wash and dry.

**Dry pack**                                 In cakes, puddings and sweets.
                                             Stuff as sweetmeats or eat as they are.

## FIGS
Use fully-ripe green or purple figs. Wash,
drain and dry. Remove the stems. They
are usually peeled as the skins tend to
toughen. Leave whole, halve or slice.

**Dry pack**                                 As desserts.

**Syrup pack**                               As dessert on their own or add to fruit
                                             salad.

## GOOSEBERRIES
Choose ripe cooking or dessert varieties.
Wash in iced water. Top and tail – if they
are open frozen the 'tops' and 'tails' can
be broken off after freezing.

**Dry pack**                                 For jam or jelly making and for sauce to
                                             serve with mackerel, etc.

**Sugar pack** – crush the fruit a little with   For desserts, pies, tarts, etc.
the sugar.

**Syrup pack**                               As stewed fruit.

**Purée**, sweetened to taste.               For sweet sauces, fool , and ice creams.

| Methods of freezing: | Uses: |
|---|---|

## GRAPEFRUIT

Only the flesh is frozen. Peel, and with a sharp knife cut out sections of the flesh separating it from the membranes on each side. This is easier to do if the whole fruit is thoroughly chilled but not frozen, in the freezer. An easier way is to cut the fruit into halves and prepare as for the table taking out half segments to freeze.

**Sugar pack** — For breakfast, for fruit starters, etc.

## GRAPES

Choose ripe, juicy, sweet black and white grapes. Wash and remove stems. Skin, halve and remove pips or choose the seedless varieties.

**Syrup pack** — Add to fruit salads.

If frozen in a very light syrup they can be drained and used in savoury dishes such as chicken and fish, e.g. Sole Véronique, and as a garnish for many dishes.

## KIWI FRUIT OR CHINESE GOOSEBERRIES

Peel off the brownish-green skins. Halve or slice the fruit leaving in edible seeds.

**Syrup pack** — Serve on its own or add to fruit salads.

## LEMONS AND LIMES

Choose ripe fruit. Wash and dry.

**Dry pack**
Strips of peel.
Thin slices, with or without skin. } — Add frozen to cold drinks.
Thick slices with peel. }
¼'s or ⅛'s, with peel. } — To serve with veal, fish, etc.
Whole fruit, wrapped in plastic cling film. — For marmalade or, when thawed, as fresh lemons.

Grated rind. — For flavouring cakes, buns, biscuits and sauces.

**Juice,** in small containers. — As fresh lemon juice.

## LYCHEES

Remove the rough, brown skin, cut white flesh into halves and remove the stone.

**Syrup pack** — On their own or in fruit salads.

## MANGOES

Choose ripe, firm fruit. Peel, halve and remove the stone. Cut into cubes.

**Syrup pack** — On their own or in fruit salads.

**Purée** — To make ice creams and sorbets.

| Methods of freezing: | Uses: |
|---|---|

## NECTARINES
Treat as Peaches.

## ORANGES
Treat the flesh as for Grapefruits and the flesh and skin as for Lemons and Limes. Also:

| | |
|---|---|
| **Dry pack** – whole peeled oranges. | For desserts. |
| **Syrup pack** | For breakfasts, as desserts, as part of fruit salads, etc. |

SEVILLE ORANGES for making marmalade can be frozen. Pack several into a polythene bag or wrap individual ones in plastic cling film and a bag. They can also be cut up ready for marmalade making, adding an extra 10% of fruit to aid the setting.

## PASSION FRUIT
Remove the hard, purplish skin. Leave whole or slice, collecting the juices.

| | |
|---|---|
| **Sugar pack** **Syrup pack** | Serve as a starter or mix with other fruits. Excellent in fruit salads. |
| **Purée** | To make ice cream, sorbet or mousse. |

## PAWPAW or PAPAYA
The juice is used as a meat tenderizer so the flesh can be added to meat dishes. Peel, halve, remove the seeds and slice or cube.

| | |
|---|---|
| **Dry pack** | Add to meat, poultry or vegetable casseroles, or fry slices and use as a garnish. |
| **Syrup pack** | As a dessert or to add to fruit salad. |

## PEACHES
Choose soft, ripe fruit. Over-ripe fruit will go mushy. Cover with boiling water for half a minute, dip into cold water and remove the skin. Some varieties can be skinned without boiling water. Cut into halves and remove the stone. Slice if wished. Drop immediately into cold syrup to prevent discoloration. Make sure the fruit remains submerged by using a heavy syrup and, if necessary, using greaseproof or waxed paper as well. Peaches may discolour as they thaw unless the unopened pack is thawed in the refrigerator. Use when not completely thawed.

| | |
|---|---|
| **Syrup pack** | For a wide variety of sweet dishes. |
| **Purée** | For ice cream, sorbets, fools. |

| Methods of freezing: | Uses: |
|---|---|

### PEARS
Choose only very firm varieties. It is often best to peel and core slightly under-ripe ones and simmer carefully in syrup. Chill before freezing. Use ascorbic acid to prevent discoloration – page 22.

| **Syrup pack** | As a dessert, or with other fruits. |

### PERSIMMONS or DATE PLUMS
Only really ripe fruit should be used as unripe ones are too astringent. Peel and freeze whole or cut up.

| **Syrup pack** | As a dessert alone or with other fruits. |
| **Purée** | In ice cream, sorbet or as a sauce. |

### PINEAPPLE
Peel fully ripe fruit, take out the eyes and discard the core. Cut into slices, cubes or wedges.

| **Dry pack** | To add to fruit drinks and punches. As an hors d'oeuvre. Cook and serve with meat, especially lamb, ham, veal and with chicken, fish and shellfish. |
| **Sugar pack** / **Syrup pack** | For hot and cold desserts, especially those with meringue. |

### PLUMS and GREENGAGES
Use fully-ripe fruit. Wash and dry. Remove stones or they may give an almond flavour to the fruit. Leave stones in only for short storage, e.g. for jam making.

| **Dry pack** | For jam making. |
| **Sugar pack** / **Syrup pack** | For desserts, pies, tarts, puddings, e.g. plum cobbler. |
| **Purée** | For sauces, fools, mousses, ice cream. |

### POMEGRANATES
Choose juicy fruit, cut into halves, take out juice sacs or squeeze juice into a sieve over a bowl. Rub flesh through and discard the seeds.

| **Syrup pack** – adding juice sacs. | Add to fruit salads. |
| **Juice** – if liked add a little cold syrup. | To add flavour to fruit salads and to drinks. Unsweetened juice is sometimes used in meat dishes. |

| Methods of freezing: | Uses: |
|---|---|

## RASPBERRIES and LOGANBERRIES

Choose fresh, unblemished berries, discarding any with hard seeds. Remove the stalks. Wash in iced water, drain and dry on kitchen paper. Use slightly over-ripe fruit for purée.

| | |
|---|---|
| **Dry pack** | For decoration and for jams. |
| **Sugar pack** | For pies, tarts, puddings, desserts, fruit salads. |
| **Syrup pack** | The least satisfactory method. |
| **Purée** | For sauces, ice creams and sorbets. |

## STRAWBERRIES

These are usually disappointing as they go flabby when thawed. Choose small berries but larger ones can be cut into halves or quarters. Use slightly over-ripe ones for purée.

| | |
|---|---|
| **Dry pack** | For jam and for decoration. |
| **Sugar pack** | For whole fruit jam, puddings and desserts. |
| **Syrup pack** (use small amount of syrup). | For fruit salad. |
| **Purée** | For sauces, ice creams and sorbets. |

## RHUBARB

Choose young, slender sticks of well-flavoured rhubarb. Cut off the leaves and trim the root end. Cut into short lengths. To keep the flavour blanch (see Vegetables) for 1 minute.

| | |
|---|---|
| **Dry pack** | For jam, tarts, pies, puddings and for stewing. |
| **Sugar pack** | For pies and for stewing. |
| **Syrup pack** (use small amount of syrup). | As stewed fruit. |
| **Purée** | As a sauce. |

## UGLI FRUIT

These are a cross between a grapefruit and an orange. Treat as Grapefruit.

## WHORTLEBERRIES

Treat as Blueberries.

# FREEZING VEGETABLES

All vegetables except potatoes and mushrooms should be blanched in boiling water to slow down the action of enzymes (see page 10). Some people may tell you they omit this process, but without blanching or cooking the vegetables slowly lose colour, flavour and texture as storage continues. They should be blanched as soon as possible after gathering.

Blanching reduces the cooking time later.

## To blanch

1. Bring about 4.5 litres/1 gallon water to the boil in a large pan.
2. Put up to 450 g/1 lb prepared vegetables in a wire basket or a bag made from nylon net and plunge them into the water. It should return to the boil within 1 minute, and then time the blanching.
3. Plunge immediately into a large container of iced water to stop further cooking and to cool them.
*The time the vegetable takes to cool will be the same as its blanching time.*
4. Drain well, dry and package, and freeze as appropriate. The same water can be used for 7 or 8 batches of the same vegetable but plenty of ice cubes will be needed.

In the notes on vegetables which follow some ways of serving have been included but there are, of course, many more.

## ARTICHOKES, GLOBE

Choose small to medium artichokes.
PREPARE as for immediate use, removing coarse outer leaves, trimming tips of others and rubbing cut surfaces with lemon to prevent browning. Soak up to 1 hour in acidified water (1 tablespoon lemon juice to 600 ml/1 pint water).
BLANCH AND COOL: 3 or 4 at a time with lemon added *or* cook completely in salted water if they are to be served cold. Discard the choke.

SERVE: Hot – boil in salted water for 15-25 minutes, depending upon size. Serve with melted butter or Hollandaise Sauce. Cold – thaw 4 hours or overnight and serve with vinaigrette sauce or herb mayonnaise.

## ARTICHOKE HEARTS

These are the delicious, saucer-shaped base of artichokes, which are often served separately. Rub with lemon juice before freezing.
BLANCH AND COOL: 3 or 4 at a time for 2 minutes, or cook completely if they are to be served cold.

SERVE: Hot – boil in salted water for about 15 minutes. Serve with Mornay or Hollandaise Sauce or stuff and bake. Add to chicken and delicately flavoured dishes. Cold – as a starter with prawns and vinaigrette sauce or chop and add to salads.

## ARTICHOKES, JERUSALEM

Choose fresh, straw-coloured tubers.
PREPARE: Scrub in cold water, removing any discoloured parts and rub cut surfaces with lemon. Boil in salted water for 15-20 minutes, until tender. Drain and put in cold water until they are cool enough to peel off skins. Reduce to a purée. Season.

BLANCHING is not, therefore, necessary.
SERVE: Use as a basis for soups or thaw, reheat in a little butter and mix with sieved potatoes and a little milk or cream.

## ASPARAGUS

Choose young, freshly cut stalks.
PREPARE: Cut into lengths to fit containers and grade according to thickness. Use potato peeler to remove outer skin of stalk below green buds.
BLANCH AND COOL: 2-4 minutes according to thickness or cook completely if to be served cold.

PACK: in rigid containers, head to tail to save space.
SERVE: Hot – boil in salted water about 5 minutes. Serve with melted butter or Hollandaise Sauce.
Cold – thaw for 2-3 hours and serve in salads or in hors d'oeuvres. Use as a garnish on cold dishes. Add to quiches, etc.

## AUBERGINES

Choose young small aubergines, before their seeds become woody.
PREPARE: Wash well and trim ends. Cut into 1 cm/½ inch slices and blanch immediately to prevent discoloration.
BLANCH AND COOL: 4 minutes, then open freeze.
SERVE: Use in a variety of cooked dishes such as moussaka. Alternatively, coat with batter and fry, or brush with oil, grill and serve as a vegetable.

Aubergines can also be stuffed and cooked before freezing. They are also an essential ingredient of Ratatouille which can be frozen to serve hot or cold.

## BEANS, BROAD

Choose small, young beans.
PREPARE: Shell and grade.
BLANCH AND COOL: 3 minutes, and open freeze before packing.

SERVE: Hot – boil in salted water for 5-10 minutes. Serve with Italian Tomato Sauce or parsley sauce.
Cold – cool and add to mixed salads.

## BEANS, FRENCH or RUNNER

Choose young, tender beans, if possible before the string develops. They should snap easily.
PREPARE: Cut off both ends and, if necessary, remove the strings. Leave small French beans whole. Cut runner beans into slices or chunks.

BLANCH AND COOL: Whole beans or chunks for 2 minutes, slices for 1 minute.
SERVE: Boil in salted water for 8-10 minutes. Toss in butter.

## BEETROOT

Choose small, young beetroot up to 7.5 cm/3 inch diameter.
PREPARE: Cook completely, cool and skin. Leave whole or cut into slices or dice.
BLANCHING is, therefore, not necessary.
SERVE: Hot – reheat in butter and coat with a béchamel sauce.

Cold – reheat with butter and orange slices without peel, and cool for a salad.
Slices can be covered with sweetened, spiced vinegar for a while before serving with salads.

## BROCCOLI and CALABRESE

Choose compact heads.
PREPARE: Cut off woody stalks and any large leaves. Divide into sprigs and trim to equal lengths. Wash thoroughly in salted water.

BLANCH: 3-4 minutes, according to thickness.
SERVE: Boil in salted water for 5-8 minutes and toss in butter or coat with Hollandaise Sauce or cheese sauce.

## BRUSSELS SPROUTS

Choose small, tight sprouts.
PREPARE: Trim off any coarse or discoloured outer leaves.
BLANCH AND COOL: 3 minutes.

SERVE: Boil in salted water for 5-8 minutes. They also make an excellent soup.

## CABBAGE, WHITE and RED

Choose small firm heads with a good colour.
PREPARE: Shred or cut into wedges. Wash very well.
BLANCH AND COOL: 1½-2 minutes.
SERVE: Add to a little boiling, salted water and cook 3-5 minutes. Once cabbage has been frozen it cannot be used in salads.

Cabbage, especially red, can be braised with onion, apple, etc., in continental-style before freezing.
  Cabbage leaves can be stuffed, rolled and cooked in the oven with tomato sauce before freezing.

## CARROTS, YOUNG

Choose young, finger thick, whole carrots.
PREPARE: Trim off tops and wash.
BLANCH AND COOL: for 5 minutes and rub off their skins whilst they are cooling in iced water.

SERVE: Boil in salted water for about 8 minutes, toss in butter melted with parsley or mint. They can be cut into rings or strips and used as garnish.

## CARROTS, OLDER

Choose freshly dug, medium-sized carrots.
PREPARE: Scrape and cut into slices, strips or dice.
BLANCH AND COOL: 3 minutes.
SERVE: Boil in salted water for about 8 minutes, toss in butter as above. Older carrots can be used to make carrot soup.
  Carrots can also be cooked with turnips or with parsnips until soft. Mash with

butter and pepper and freeze. Reheat in a double boiler or thaw and reheat, stirring constantly. They are often mixed with celery, peas, sweetcorn or other vegetables and are sometimes frozen in a sauce made with the cooking liquid, adding cornflour mixed to a paste as a final thickener. They are an essential part of a Vegetable Stew Pack, see page 37.

## CAULIFLOWER

Choose white, compact heads with fresh green leaves.
PREPARE: Separate into florets of fairly even size, splitting large ones as necessary.
BLANCH AND COOL: 3 minutes.

SERVE: Boil in salted water for 5-8 minutes. Serve with a sauce (see below). See also Mixed Vegetables (page 37).
  Cauliflower can also be frozen in a cheese, cream or tomato sauce.
  Fry in batter for fritters, open freeze and reheat in the oven until crisp.

## CELERIAC

Choose small to medium firm and unblemished ones.
PREPARE: Slice, peel and drop into water with lemon juice added. If liked, cut into large dice.
BLANCH AND COOL: 6 minutes or cook completely for 40-60 minutes and purée.

SERVE: Cook in boiling salted water for 12-15 minutes. Serve with a cheese or white sauce. The purée can be heated with butter and freshly ground pepper or may be mixed with a potato purée.

## CELERY

Choose crisp young celery before it becomes stringy.

PREPARE: Discard root end and outer stalks. Trim heart to about 10 cm/4 inches. If large cut into halves or quarters. Wash very well to remove grit and dirt. Cut removed tops of stalks, or cut all stalks into 2.5 cm/1 inch lengths.

BLANCH AND COOL: 3 minutes for stalks, 6 minutes for hearts.

SERVE: Boil in salted water for 3-5 minutes for stalks or about 10 minutes for hearts.

Serve hearts braised in chicken stock or in Italian Tomato Sauce. The stalks can also be used to make soup or for flavouring a variety of cooked dishes. Pack in small quantities. See also Vegetable Stew Pack (page 37).

Celery cannot be frozen to serve raw in salad.

## CHICORY

Choose small compact white heads.

PREPARE: Trim root end and remove any marked outside leaves.

BLANCH AND COOL: 2 minutes in water with lemon juice added to keep the vegetable white. Drain well and squeeze out excess moisture.

SERVE: Chicory is rarely served as a plain vegetable. Use for dishes such as braised chicory or wrap in cooked ham, coat with a cheese sauce and bake. These dishes can be prepared and frozen rather than just blanching the chicory.

## CHILLIS

Choose glossy, unwrinkled red and/or green pods.

PREPARE: Very carefully as the volatile oil in the flesh will make the skin tingle and the eyes burn. It is best to wear rubber gloves and never touch the face with them. Work under running cold water. Cut off the stalk, and split open the pod. Brush out the seeds.

BLANCH AND COOL: 2 minutes. Open freeze for a short period and then wrap in plastic film or foil in very small quantities and then overwrap these in a thick polythene bag.

SERVE: Thaw and use to flavour a wide variety of savoury dishes including chilli con carne, curries, barbecue sauce, etc.

## CORN

Choose young tender corn with fresh looking husk and silk.

PREPARE: Remove husk and silk and cut off any immature top.

BLANCH AND COOL: 4-6 minutes, according to size. For kernels, blanch 4 minutes then strip off kernels.

SERVE: Thaw corn on the cob for about 4 hours. Boil in salted water for 4 minutes, kernels for 3 minutes. Corn on the cob can also be baked in foil after thawing. Kernels can be used in salads, especially rice salads and as a colourful decoration.

Small cubes of red and green pepper can be blanched separately and mixed with the kernels before freezing.

## COURGETTES

Choose small tender courgettes of good colour.

PREPARE: Cut off each end. Wash and cut into 2.5 cm/1 inch lengths. Larger courgettes should be cut into halves for stuffing.

BLANCH AND COOL: 3 minutes.

SERVE: Boil in salted water for 3 minutes, then toss in melted butter and herbs.

If to be stuffed, do not blanch, but bake before freezing. Courgettes may also be frozen as part of a ratatouille.

## CUCUMBER

Cucumbers are usually served raw in salads and it is impossible to freeze them for this purpose. They can be made into soups, to be served hot or cold, or added to casseroles. These are all prepared before freezing.

## FENNEL, FLORENCE

This is a relative of the herb fennel, with a delicate anise flavour.

Choose a compact fresh looking bulb.
PREPARE: Cut into slices lengthways or crossways.

BLANCH AND COOL: 3 minutes.
SERVE: Boil in salted water for 7-10 minutes. Drain and braise, or serve with a cheese or tomato sauce.

## KOHLRABI

Choose small, tender roots. Trim off tops and root ends, Leave whole if small, slice or dice if larger.
BLANCH AND COOL: 3 minutes if whole, 2 minutes if sliced or diced.

SERVE: Boil in salted water 8-10 minutes. Toss in melted butter. It can be layered with a savoury mixture based on minced cooked meat, tomatoes, garlic, etc. and served with a Milanese or mushroom sauce.

## LEEKS

Choose young, thin, tender leeks with bright green tops. Pick clean, not dirty leeks.
PREPARE: Trim off root end and remove outer leaves. Wash very well and cut into lengths which will fit into the container.
BLANCH AND COOL: 1 minute.

SERVE: Boil in salted water for 3-5 minutes. Drain very well and toss in melted butter. Or put, still frozen, into a sieve or colander to drain as they thaw. Cook gently in butter for 5 minutes. Leeks are often served with a variety of sauces.

Leeks may also be frozen as a purée to be made later into Leek and Potato Soup or vichyssoise, or the soup can be made and frozen.

## MANGE TOUT (Sugar peas) and ASPARAGUS PEAS

Choose flat young pods with a good green colour before strings form.
PREPARE: Trim off ends.
BLANCH AND COOL: 2 minutes.

SERVE: Boil in salted water 3-5 minutes and toss in melted butter. They can be thawed and fried as part of Chinese Vegetables.

## MARROW

Choose young, tender marrows.
PREPARE: If very young they need not be peeled. Cut into slices and remove seeds. Dice, if wished.
BLANCH AND COOL: 3 minutes.
SERVE: Boil in salted water for 3 minutes or thaw and drain slices, dip into batter and fry.

Blanched halves of marrow can be stuffed with a well flavoured stuffing and baked before freezing. Even young marrows have very little flavour. They can be stewed with onions, tomatoes and herbs until almost all the moisture is evaporated and then frozen.

The flesh of older marrows can be steamed and puréed. Reheat carefully with butter, pepper and herbs.

## MUSHROOMS

Choose cultivated mushrooms. They must be very fresh with white, unwrinkled upper skin.
PREPARE: Trim off ends of stalks. Wipe with a damp cloth or rinse quickly in cold water. *Never* leave in water even for a minute or two as they quickly absorb water. If large, slice them.

BLANCH AND COOL: Do not blanch.
FREEZE: Open freeze. They may, instead be fried lightly in butter and drained very well before freezing.

## OKRA (Ladies' fingers)

Choose young, tender pods with a good green colour.
PREPARE: Cut off the stems and wash well.
BLANCH AND COOL: 3-4 minutes, according to size.

SERVE: Boil in salted water for 5-8 minutes and toss in melted butter.
　Okra is rather gelatinous and so is often added to stews, both for flavouring and thickening. These can, of course, be frozen.

## ONIONS

Onions are available all the year so there is little point in freezing them as a general rule, but a few small packs can be useful.
　Choose firm onions. Ordinary, Spanish, small pickling onions or shallots can all be frozen by the method below. The last two are often unobtainable and can also be frozen in a variety of sauces or can be added to Mixed Vegetables and Vegetable Stew Packs (see page 37).
PREPARE: Peel. Slice large onions into rings or chop.

BLANCH AND COOL: 1 minute or fry in oil or butter and drain well. Pack into small packages and overwrap because of the strong aroma.
SERVE: Use to flavour stews, casseroles, etc. and to add to sauces, omelette fillings and stuffings.
　Onion rings, coated in batter and deep fried freeze well and can be reheated in a hot oven.

## PARSNIPS

Choose small young tender parsnips.
PREPARE: Trim and peel. Cut into quarters, strips or dice.
BLANCH AND COOL: 3 minutes or cook completely and purée. The purée can be mixed with other purées either before or after freezing.

SERVE: Boil in salted water for 5-8 minutes or allow quarters to thaw and roast them round the joint. Reheat purée carefully over a low heat.

## PEAS and PETITS POIS

Choose freshly picked young peas. Older ones are tough with little flavour.
PREPARE: Shell and look over for any discoloured ones.

BLANCH AND COOL: 1-2 minutes.
SERVE: Boil in salted water for 4-7 minutes. They are usually included in Mixed Vegetables (see page 37).

## PEPPERS, SWEET, RED and GREEN

Although used as a vegetable, peppers are really fruits so do not need to be blanched.

Choose firm, glossy ones with a good colour.

PREPARE: Wash. Remove stems and take out seeds and white pith if they are to be frozen whole for stuffing later. Or cut into halves, remove stem, seeds and pith and cut into strips.

SERVE: Use to flavour a wide variety of savoury dishes. Whole peppers can be stuffed and baked after thawing. They can be frozen in cooked dishes such as Ratatouille. Peppers can be stuffed before freezing but they then take up more freezer space.

## POTATOES, NEW

Choose small even-sized potatoes.

PREPARE: Remove skins by scrubbing or scraping.

COOK: In the usual way until almost tender.

SERVE: Boil in salted water for 3-5 minutes. Drain, toss in melted butter and chopped fresh parsley.

## POTATOES, OLD

There are a variety of ways in which potatoes can be frozen. Follow your favourite recipes for:

STUFFED POTATOES: Open freeze. Reheat in the oven.

DUCHESS POTATOES: Pipe rosettes on to a baking tray, brush with beaten egg and brown lightly in the oven. Open freeze. Reheat in the oven until browned. These can be flavoured with tomato purée, cheese, etc.

MASHED POTATO OR POTATO PURÉE: Freeze in a container. Reheat in a double boiler or carefully over a low heat with butter. Other purées can be mixed in before or after freezing.

POTATO CROQUETTES: Fry until lightly browned in deep fat. Drain very well. Open freeze. Reheat on a baking tray in a hot oven.

CHIPS: Fry in deep fat at 180°C/350°F until cooked but not browned. Drain very well. Open freeze. Complete frying in deep or shallow fat without thawing. Watch carefully as there may be some splattering.

ROAST POTATOES: Roast in the usual way. Drain well and freeze. Reheat from frozen in a hot oven without adding more fat.

## PUMPKIN

Prepare, blanch, cool and freeze as Marrow. Use the purée for sweet pie fillings adding the spices after thawing as their flavour may change a little during freezing.

## SALSIFY (Oyster Plant) and SCORZONERA

These are long thin roots – the salsify has a brown skin and scorzonera a black one. They are dealt with in the same way. Choose unwrinkled, unblemished roots.

PREPARE: Scrub.

BLANCH AND COOL: 2 minutes. Remove skins whilst still warm and cut into 5 cm/2 inch lengths.

SERVE: Boil in salted water for about 5 minutes. Drain. Toss in butter or mix with béchamel or cheese sauce. Or thaw, dry well, dip in butter and fry in deep fat until brown and crisp.

## SPINACH

Choose fresh, young leaves before the centre stalks have thickened.
PREPARE: Wash each leaf carefully.
BLANCH AND COOL: Small quantities at a time for 2 minutes or put into a pan with the water sticking to the leaves and cook in the usual way. Drain very well. If wished, chop.

SERVE: Boil in salted water for 2-3 minutes. Or put frozen, chopped spinach into a sieve, thaw and drain. Reheat with a little butter, seasonings and nutmeg.
   Serve topped with poached egg and cheese sauce. Use in quiches, etc.

## SWEDES

See Turnips.

## SWEET POTATOES

See Potatoes, Old. They can be baked, fried, roasted, made into croquettes, duchess potatoes, or mashed.

## TOMATOES

Although used as a vegetable, tomatoes are really fruits so do not need to be blanched. Because they contain so much moisture they are too soft when thawed to be served raw.
1. Freeze whole, cut into halves straight from freezer and grill or fry.

2. Skin, freeze whole or in quarters and add to stews towards end of cooking time so they retain their form.
3. Purée. Cut up and simmer with very little water until tender. Sieve and freeze. Use in soups, sauces, stews, etc.
4. They can be frozen as tomato juice.

## TURNIPS

Choose small, firm unblemished turnips.
PREPARE: Peel, cut into slices, dice or strips.
BLANCH AND COOL: 3 minutes or cook fully in the usual way and purée.
SERVE: Boil in salted water for 8-10 minutes. Reheat purée carefully with butter and pepper.

   The purée may be mixed with potato or carrot purée before or after freezing.
   Turnips are usually included in Vegetable Stew Packs (see below) or in a simple mixed vegetable pack of carrots and turnips.

## YAM

These are dealt with in the same way as Potatoes, Old.

## MIXED VEGETABLES and VEGETABLE STEW PACKS

Making up these mixed packs at home gives us the chance to mix vegetables as we want and in the quantities we prefer. When preparing them, each vegetable should be prepared according to kind and mixed together after open freezing. Try to choose vegetables which are boiled for the same time after freezing; otherwise vary the sizes of the cut vegetables. Small pieces cook more quickly than larger ones.

# SOUPS, STARTERS & CANAPES

## HONEYDEW SOUP

*Preparation time: 10 minutes*
*Cooking time: 10 minutes*
*Recommended freezer life: 4 months*

1 medium honeydew melon,
    halved
4 spring onions, chopped
1 tablespoon ground almonds
150 ml/¼ pint plain
    unsweetened yogurt
2 teaspoons lime or lemon juice
salt
freshly ground black pepper
1 tablespoon cornflour
2 tablespoons water
**TO SERVE:**
120 ml/4 fl oz double cream
melon balls

1. Remove and discard the melon seeds
and chop the flesh.
2. Place the flesh in a blender with the
onions, ground almonds, yogurt, lime or
lemon juice, and salt and pepper.
Liquidize the mixture to a purée.
3. Pour the soup into a saucepan, and
bring gently to the boil, stirring well.
Blend the cornflour with the water and
stir it into the soup. Simmer, stirring, for
2-3 minutes. Allow to go cold and chill in
the refrigerator.

**TO FREEZE:** Pour into a rigid container,
cover and freeze.

**TO SERVE:** Allow to thaw in the
refrigerator for 6-8 hours, then pour into
a bowl, and whisk well. Stir in the cream,
and serve cold with a few melon balls to
garnish the soup.

## ICED CURRIED SOUP

*Preparation time: 10 minutes*
*Cooking time: 35 minutes*
*Recommended freezer life: 3 months*

50 g/2 oz onion, peeled and
    chopped
50 g/2 oz carrot, chopped
1 tablespoon oil
1 tablespoon curry powder
450 g/1 lb tomatoes, skinned
    and chopped
300 ml/½ pint chicken stock
1 bay leaf
1 teaspoon dried basil
1 teaspoon sugar
2 tablespoons tomato purée
lemon juice, to taste
**TO SERVE:**
150 ml/¼ pint single cream
sprigs of parsley

1. In a saucepan, fry the onion and carrot
in the oil for 2-3 minutes, then stir in the
curry powder. Cook for a further 2
minutes, stirring well.
2. Add the tomatoes, stock, herbs, sugar
and tomato purée. Bring to the boil, cover
and simmer for 20 minutes.
3. Remove the bay leaf and liquidize the
soup in an electric blender, or rub it
through a sieve.
4. Strain the soup into a bowl if you have
used the liquidizer. Taste and adjust the
seasoning and add lemon juice to taste.
Chill the soup in the refrigerator.

**TO FREEZE:** Pour into a rigid container,
cover and freeze.

**TO SERVE:** Allow to thaw for 8 hours in
the refrigerator. Stir in the cream, and
serve garnished with parsley sprigs.

# SMOKED HADDOCK SOUP

*Preparation time: 10 minutes*
*Cooking time: 40 minutes*
*Recommended freezer life: 4 months*

600 ml/1 pint milk
1 kg/2 lb Finnan haddock
225 g/8 oz potatoes, peeled and diced
2 onions, peeled and chopped
sprig of parsley
salt
freshly ground black pepper
lemon juice, to taste
**TO SERVE:**
40 g/1½ oz butter
150 ml/¼ pint single cream
cayenne

1. Put the milk and haddock in a saucepan and bring gently to boiling point. Cover and simmer for 5 minutes.
2. Strain the haddock, reserving the liquor. Flake the flesh, removing all bones.
3. Bring the reserved liquor to the boil, and add the potatoes, onions and sprig of parsley. Add salt and pepper, cover and simmer for 20 minutes.
4. Add the fish to the liquid and cook for a further 10 minutes. Remove the parsley sprig and add lemon juice to taste.

**TO FREEZE:** Allow to go cold, pour into a rigid container, cover and freeze.

**TO SERVE:** Allow to thaw over a gentle heat in a pan, then gradually stir in the butter, a little at a time. Stir in the cream and serve sprinkled with cayenne.

# TOMATO & ORANGE SOUP

*Preparation time: 15 minutes*
*Cooking time: 45 minutes*
*Recommended freezer life: 4 months*

40 g/1½ oz butter
1 large Spanish onion, peeled and chopped
175 g/6 oz carrot, diced
750 g/1½ lb tomatoes, skinned and roughly chopped
1 tablespoon tomato purée
450 ml/¾ pint chicken stock
2 bay leaves
3 parsley stalks
1 teaspoon dried basil
salt
freshly ground black pepper
1 teaspoon sugar
**TO SERVE:**
rind and juice of 1 orange
1 tablespoon cornflour
3 tablespoons water
150 ml/¼ pint single cream
chopped fresh chives

1. Melt the butter in a saucepan and add the chopped onion and carrot. Fry gently until the onion is soft and transparent.
2. Add the tomatoes to the pan and stir in the tomato purée, stock, herbs, salt, pepper and sugar. Cover and simmer for 30 minutes.
3. Remove the bay leaves and parsley stalks and liquidize the soup in an electric blender, or rub it through a sieve.

**TO FREEZE:** Allow to go cold, pour into a rigid container, cover and freeze.

**TO SERVE:** Bring to boiling point over a gentle heat, then add the rind and juice of the orange. Stir in the cornflour blended with the water and simmer for 2-3 minutes. Stir in the cream and serve garnished with chopped chives.

Top: Leek and potato soup; Smoked haddock soup
Right: Tomato and orange soup; Artichoke soup

# LEEK & POTATO SOUP

*Preparation time: 10 minutes*
*Cooking time: 50 minutes*
*Recommended freezer life: 4 months*

25 g/1oz butter
3 large leeks, trimmed and
   thinly sliced
450 g/1 lb potatoes, peeled and
   sliced
900 ml/1½ pints chicken stock
salt
freshly ground black pepper
1 tablespoon cornflour
3 tablespoons water
TO SERVE:
150 ml/¼ pint single cream
chopped fresh chives

1. Melt the butter in a saucepan, add the leeks, cover and fry for about 3 minutes.
2. Add the potatoes, stock, salt and pepper, cover and simmer for 30 minutes.
3. Liquidize the soup in an electric blender, or rub through a sieve, and return it to the pan.
4. Mix the cornflour with the water and stir it into the soup. Simmer, stirring, for 2-3 minutes.

TO FREEZE: Allow to go cold, pour into a rigid container, cover, and freeze.

TO SERVE: Allow to thaw over a gentle heat in a pan, then bring to boiling point. Remove from the heat and stir in the cream. Serve garnished with chives.

# ARTICHOKE SOUP

*Preparation time: 15 minutes*
*Cooking time: 40 minutes*
*Recommended freezer life: 4 months*

50 g/2 oz butter
1 large onion, peeled and sliced
750 g/1½ lb Jerusalem
   artichokes, peeled and sliced
600 ml/1 pint water
600 ml/1 pint milk
salt
freshly ground black pepper
1 tablespoon cornflour
3 tablespoons water
TO SERVE:
75 ml/3 fl oz single cream
chopped fresh parsley
croûtons

1. Melt the butter in a saucepan, add the onion and fry gently until transparent.
2. Add the artichokes to the pan and continue cooking for 2-3 minutes.
3. Add the water, milk, salt and pepper and bring to the boil. Cover and simmer for 20 minutes.
4. Liquidize the soup in an electric blender, or rub through a sieve, and return it to the pan.
5. Mix the cornflour with the water, and stir it into the soup. Simmer, stirring, for 2-3 minutes.

TO FREEZE: Allow to go cold, pour into a rigid container, cover and freeze.

TO SERVE: Allow to thaw over a gentle heat in a pan, then bring to boiling point. Remove from the heat and stir in the cream. Serve garnished with chopped parsley and croûtons.

# CAMEMBERT CRESCENTS

*Makes: 12 crescents*
*Preparation time: 25 minutes*
*Recommended freezer life: 4 months*

225 g/8 oz Camembert cheese
1 tablespoon chopped fresh
  chives
pinch of ground nutmeg
freshly ground black pepper
1 tablespoon double cream
1×375 g/13 oz packet frozen
  puff pastry, thawed
**TO SERVE:**
1 egg, beaten

1. Peel off and discard the skin of the Camembert cheese.
2. Put the cheese in a bowl. Beat well and stir in the chopped chives, nutmeg, pepper and cream.
3. Roll out the pastry and cut into 12 squares, each measuring 15 cm/6 inches. Cut each square diagonally in half.
4. Place 1 teaspoonful of the mixture along the longest side of each of the triangles, then roll them up to enclose the filling.
5. Twist the two ends and curve them round to form a crescent shape.

**TO FREEZE:** Open freeze for 1 hour, then pack together in a rigid container, cover and return to the freezer.

**TO SERVE:** Place the crescents on a baking sheet, and brush lightly with beaten egg. Bake in a preheated oven at 200°C, 400°F, Gas Mark 7 for 20 minutes until risen and lightly browned.

# AVOCADO ICE CREAM

*Preparation time: 20 minutes*
*Freezing time: 1½-2 hours*
*Recommended freezer life: 3 months*

2 large ripe avocado pears
75 g/3 oz full fat soft cheese
1 shallot, peeled and crushed
1 tablespoon lemon juice
2 tablespoons plain
    unsweetened yogurt
1 teaspoon sugar
dash of Worcestershire sauce
pinch of ground nutmeg
pinch of paprika
salt
freshly ground black pepper
**TO SERVE:**
4 tablespoons mayonnaise
100 g/4 oz peeled prawns
sprigs of parsley

1. Skin the avocado pears, and remove the stones.
2. Chop the avocado flesh, and liquidize it in an electric blender together with the remaining ingredients. Alternatively, mash together thoroughly in a mixing bowl.
3. Pour into a container and freeze for at least 1½-2 hours. Stir 2 or 3 times during the freezing process to prevent any crystals from forming. When the ice cream is fully frozen, cover with a lid and return it to the freezer.

**TO SERVE:** Allow the ice cream to soften in the refrigerator for 1 hour before serving. Spoon it into 4 individual glasses, top each glass with a spoonful of mayonnaise and the prawns. Garnish each serving with parsley sprigs.

# SMOKED SALMON AND CREAM CHEESE PÂTÉ

*Serves 6*
*Preparation time: 30 minutes*
*Recommended freezer life: 2 months*

225 g/8 oz full fat soft cheese
1 large avocado pear, skinned
    and chopped
3 tablespoons lemon juice
175 g/6 oz smoked salmon
salt
freshly ground black pepper
pinch of cayenne
pinch of ground nutmeg
2 tablespoons double cream
2 tablespoons finely chopped
    watercress
**TO SERVE:**
sprigs of watercress

1. Blend the cheese, avocado pear, lemon juice and 100 g/4 oz of the smoked salmon to a smooth purée in a liquidizer or mixing bowl.
2. Add the salt, pepper, cayenne and nutmeg.
3. Dice the remaining smoked salmon, and stir it into the mixture with the cream and chopped watercress. Taste and adjust the seasoning. Spoon into a pot or foil container.

**TO FREEZE:** Cover and freeze.

**TO SERVE:** Allow to thaw in a refrigerator overnight. Garnish with sprigs of watercress, and serve with lemon wedges and fingers of hot toast.

# CHICKEN & LIVER TERRINE

*Serves 6*
*Preparation time: 35 minutes*
*Cooking time: 1 hour 40 minutes*
*Recommended freezer life: 4 months*

2 large chicken breasts, boned
2 tablespoons sherry
350 g/12 oz sausage meat
350 g/12 oz lamb's liver, minced
3 onions, peeled and finely
  chopped
1 teaspoon dried thyme
2 tablespoons double cream
1 egg
salt
freshly ground black pepper
10 rashers streaky bacon, rind
  removed
4 bay leaves
3 juniper berries

1. Put the chicken breasts in a bowl, pour in the sherry and leave to marinate.
2. Beat together the sausage meat, liver, onion, thyme, cream, egg and salt and pepper.
3. Spread the bacon rashers on a board, and stretch them using a blunt knife.
4. Decorate the base of a 1 kg/2 lb loaf tin with the bay leaves and juniper berries. Place the rashers of flattened bacon over the base and sides, draping them over the rims of the tin to enable you to fold them over the pâté later.
5. Drain the chicken breasts, retaining the liquid. Beat the sausage meat mixture and liquid together.
6. Spoon half the mixture into the prepared tin and cover with the chicken breasts. Spoon the remaining mixture over the chicken and wrap the bacon rashers over the top.

7. Cover the pâté with a piece of greased foil, and place in a roasting tin half filled with water.
8. Cook in a preheated oven at 140°C, 275°F, Gas Mark 1 for 1 hour 40 minutes.
9. The pâté is cooked when it has shrunk from the sides of the tin and the juices run clear when it is pierced with a knife.
10. Cover the pâté with a clean piece of foil, and place a 2 kg/4½ lb weight on top. Leave overnight in a refrigerator.

**TO FREEZE:** Remove the weight, turn out the pâté and open freeze it. When firm, place in a polythene bag, seal and return to the freezer.

**TO SERVE:** Allow to thaw overnight in a refrigerator. Serve sliced.

# POTTED CHEESE WITH PORT

*Serves 6*
*Preparation time: 20 minutes*
*Recommended freezer life: 3 months*

225 g/8 oz mixed blue cheeses
  (Stilton, Danish Blue,
  Dolcelatte, Gorgonzola)
50 g/2 oz butter
100 g/4 oz full fat soft cheese
1 teaspoon chopped fresh
  chives
3 tablespoons port
salt
freshly ground black pepper
50 g/2 oz butter
**TO SERVE:**
herb bread or toast

1. Rub the blue cheese through a sieve and set aside.
2. Cream the butter until light, then beat in the full fat soft cheese.
3. Stir in the blue cheese, chopped chives, port, and salt and pepper.
4. Spoon the mixture into small cocotte pots and chill in the refrigerator until fairly firm.
5. Melt the butter in a pan, then leave it to stand until the sediment settles to the bottom of the pan. Carefully pour off the pure butter and use to coat the top of the potted cheese. Allow the butter to set.

**TO FREEZE:** Wrap each pot in cling wrap, pack together in a plastic box and freeze.

**TO SERVE:** Allow to thaw in a cool place for 6 hours. Serve with herb bread or toast.

# FRENCH CHICKEN LIVER PÂTÉ

*Serves 4-6*
*Preparation time: 10 minutes*
*Cooking time: 30 minutes*
*Recommended freezer life: 4 months*

50 g/2 oz butter
50 g/2 oz shallots, peeled and
  chopped
75 g/3 oz streaky bacon, rind
  removed and chopped
450 g/1 lb chicken livers
salt
freshly ground black pepper
pinch of ground nutmeg
1 tablespoon dry sherry
40 g/1½ oz butter, softened
squeeze of lemon juice
  (optional)
1 bay leaf
65 g/2½ oz butter

1. Melt the butter in a pan, add the shallots and bacon, and fry gently for 5 minutes.
2. Add the chicken livers and fry them quickly over a high heat, stirring continuously.
3. Cool the mixture, then blend to a purée in a liquidizer.
4. Beat in the salt, pepper, nutmeg, sherry, softened butter and lemon juice.
5. Spoon the mixture into a foil container or individual cocotte dishes, smoothing the top, and allow to set in the refrigerator. Decorate with a bay leaf.
6. Melt the 65 g/2½ oz butter in a pan, then leave it to stand until the sediment settles to the bottom of the pan. Carefully pour off the pure butter and use to coat the top of the pâté. Allow the butter to set.

**TO FREEZE:** Cover and freeze.

**TO SERVE:** Allow to thaw in a cool place for 6 hours. Serve with melba toast.

**Above: Potted cheese with port**
**Left: Chicken and liver terrine**

# SARDINE & PIMENTO PÂTÉ

*Serves 6*
*Preparation time: 15 minutes*
*Recommended freezer life: 2 months*

100 g/4 oz full fat soft cheese
2×100 g/4 oz cans sardines
1 tablespoon lemon juice
salt
paprika
2 tablespoons double cream
1 teaspoon chopped fresh
   chives
½ red pepper, cored, seeded
   and finely chopped

1. Cream the cheese with a wooden spoon until light and fluffy.
2. Drain the sardines and mash them with a fork, then beat them into the cheese.
3. Add the lemon juice and salt and paprika to taste.
4. Stir in the cream, chopped chives and chopped red pepper.

TO FREEZE: Turn into a rigid container, cover and freeze.

TO SERVE: Allow to thaw in the refrigerator for 6-8 hours. Serve with toast or French bread.

# SOFT HERRING ROE PÂTÉ

*Serves 6*
*Preparation time: 5 minutes*
*Cooking time: 5 minutes*
*Recommended freezer life: 2 months*

65 g/2½ oz butter, softened
225 g/8 oz herring roe
25 g/1 oz fresh breadcrumbs
1 tablespoon lemon juice
3 tablespoons double cream
salt
freshly ground white pepper
cayenne
TO SERVE:
herb bread

1. Melt 15 g/½ oz of the butter in a pan, add the herring roe and fry gently for 4 minutes. Remove from the heat.
2. Liquidize the roe with the remaining butter, the breadcrumbs, lemon juice, cream, salt, pepper and cayenne in an electric blender or rub through a sieve.

TO FREEZE: Spoon into a rigid container, cover and freeze.

TO SERVE: Allow to thaw in a cool place for 6 hours. Serve with herb bread.

# TARAMASALATA

*Serves 6*
*Preparation time: 15 minutes*
*Recommended freezer life: 2 months*

350 g/12 oz smoked cod's roe,
   skin removed
1 × 150 g/5 oz packet cream
   cheese with garlic and herbs
150 ml/¼ pint olive oil
freshly ground black pepper
paprika
1 tablespoon lemon juice
120 ml/4 fl oz double cream
TO SERVE:
sprig of parsley

1. Liquidize the cod's roe with the cheese in an electric blender.
2. Add the oil in a steady stream with the motor turned to a high setting.
3. When all the oil has been incorporated, add the pepper, paprika and lemon juice. Stir in the cream.

TO FREEZE: Spoon the mixture into a rigid container, cover and freeze.

TO SERVE: Allow to thaw in the refrigerator for at least 6 hours. Garnish with parsley and serve with warm pitta bread.

**Above, left to right: Sardine and pimento pâté; Soft herring roe pâté; Taramasalata**
**Right: Ricotta cannelloni with tomato sauce**

# RICOTTA CANNELLONI WITH TOMATO SAUCE

*Preparation time: 20 minutes*
*Cooking time: 30 minutes*
*Recommended freezer life: 4 months*

1 tablespoon oil
2 litres/3½ pints water
8 cannelloni
**FILLING:**
175 g/6 oz ricotta cheese
100 g/4 oz full fat soft cheese
25 g/1 oz Parmesan cheese,
  grated
1 egg, lightly beaten
salt
freshly ground black pepper
pinch of ground nutmeg
**SAUCE:**
1 onion, peeled and diced
1 tablespoon oil
1 × 400 g/14 oz can tomatoes
1 tablespoon tomato purée
1 teaspoon Worcestershire sauce
salt
freshly ground black pepper
1 bay leaf
1 teaspoon dried thyme
**TOPPING:**
1 tablespoon grated Parmesan
  cheese

1. Bring the oil and water to the boil in a large saucepan. Add the pasta, and simmer for 8-10 minutes, stirring occasionally to prevent the pieces sticking together. Drain and cool the pasta.
2. To prepare the filling, blend the 3 cheeses together in a mixing bowl, and stir in the beaten egg, salt, pepper and nutmeg. Mix well, then carefully spoon the filling into the cannelloni, and arrange them in a well buttered foil container.
3. To prepare the sauce, gently fry the onion in the oil over a low heat until soft and transparent.
4. Add the remaining sauce ingredients, cover and simmer for 10-15 minutes.
5. Remove from the heat and allow to go cold. Remove the bay leaf.
6. Pour the sauce over the cannelloni, and sprinkle with the Parmesan cheese.

**TO FREEZE:** Cover and freeze.

**TO SERVE:** Allow to thaw for 3-4 hours, loosen the lid, then place in a preheated oven at 180°C, 350°F, Gas Mark 4 for 45 minutes, or until heated through.

# SCALLOP NESTS

*Serves 6*
*Preparation time: 30 minutes*
*Cooking time: 50 minutes*
*Recommended freezer life: 1 month*

225 g/8 oz shortcrust pastry
**POACHING LIQUID:**
250 ml/8 fl oz water
120 ml/4 fl oz dry white wine
1 small carrot, peeled and sliced
1 shallot, peeled and sliced
1 teaspoon lemon juice
parsley stalks
1 bay leaf
salt
4 black peppercorns
6 large scallops
**SAUCE:**
25 g/1 oz butter
1 shallot, peeled and chopped
100 g/4 oz button mushrooms,
  sliced
15 g/½ oz plain flour
300 ml/½ pint fish liquor
1 tablespoon cornflour
2 tablespoons water
salt
freshly ground black pepper
2 tablespoons double cream
**TOPPING:**
25 g/1 oz toasted white
  breadcrumbs
6 slivers chilled butter
**TO SERVE:**
sprigs of parsley

1. Roll out the pastry and use it to line 6 individual foil containers, each 6 cm /2½ inches in diameter and 2.5 cm/1 inch deep.
2. Line the pastry cases with greaseproof paper, and fill them with dried peas or lentils.
3. Bake blind in a preheated oven at 190°C, 375°F, Gas Mark 5 for 10 minutes.
4. Remove the paper with the peas or lentils and return the pastry cases to the oven for 6-10 minutes, until light golden in colour. Allow to cool.
5. Place all the poaching liquid ingredients in a pan, bring to the boil and simmer for 5 minutes.
6. Wash the scallops carefully, add them to the pan, and poach very gently for 5-7 minutes.
7. Lift out the scallops, and cut each one into 6 pieces. Strain the poaching liquid into a measuring jug, and reserve 300 ml/ ½ pint for the sauce.
8. Melt the butter in a saucepan, and add the shallots. Fry gently over a low heat until transparent.

9. Add the mushrooms and cook for a further 2-3 minutes.
10. Stir in the flour, gradually add the fish liquor, then bring to the boil.
11. Blend the cornflour with the water, stir into the sauce and simmer for 2-3 minutes. Add salt and pepper, then stir in the cream.
12. Allow the sauce to go cold, then stir in the scallops.
13. Divide the mixture between the pastry cases, and sprinkle with the breadcrumbs. Top each one with a sliver of butter.

**TO FREEZE:** Wrap the scallop nests individually in cling film. Pack in a polythene bag, seal and freeze.

**TO SERVE:** Remove the polythene and cling wrap, then place the frozen nests on a baking sheet in a preheated oven at 190°C, 375°F, Gas Mark 5 for 20-25 minutes. If not frozen, reheat for 10 minutes only. Remove the nests from the foil cases, garnish with parsley sprigs and serve with lemon wedges.

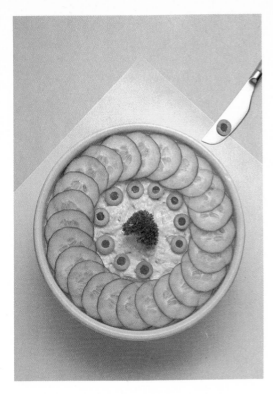

# TUNA FISH MOUSSE

*Serves 6*
*Preparation time: 10 minutes*
*Cooking time: 10 minutes*
*Recommended freezer life: 2 months*

50 g/2 oz butter
50 g/2 oz plain flour
300 ml/½ pint milk
salt
freshly ground black pepper
1 tablespoon powdered gelatine
1 tablespoon water
2×200 g/7 oz cans tuna fish,
    drained
50 g/2 oz pimento stuffed
    olives, chopped
150 ml/¼ pint mayonnaise
squeeze of lemon juice
250 ml/8 fl oz double cream
**TO SERVE:**
cucumber slices
4 pimento stuffed olives
sprigs of parsley

1.  Melt the butter in a pan, stir in the flour and cook for 2-3 minutes.
2.  Gradually stir in the milk and bring the sauce slowly to the boil. Simmer for 2-3 minutes, and add salt and pepper.
3.  Mix the gelatine with the water, and stir it into the hot sauce. Allow the sauce to cool.
4.  Flake the tuna fish and add to the cooled sauce with the olives, mayonnaise and lemon juice.
5.  Whip the cream and fold it into the mixture.

**TO FREEZE:** Pour the mixture into a 900 ml/1½ pint soufflé dish or foil container, and allow to set. Cover and freeze.

**TO SERVE:** Allow to thaw for 6-8 hours in the refrigerator. Garnish with cucumber slices, stuffed olives and parsley sprigs. Serve with hot toast and lemon wedges.

# SMOKED TROUT MOUSSE

*Serves 6*
*Preparation time: 20 minutes*
*Cooking time: 15 minutes*
*Recommended freezer life: 2 months*

40 g/1½ oz butter
40 g/1½ oz plain flour
300 ml/½ pint milk
salt
freshly ground black pepper
pinch of paprika
1 teaspoon lemon juice
2 eggs, separated
20 g/¾ oz powdered gelatine
2 tablespoons water
2 × 225 g/8 oz smoked trout,
    skinned and boned
50 g/2 oz nibbed almonds,
    toasted
175 ml/6 fl oz double cream
**TO SERVE:**
25 g/1 oz flaked almonds,
    toasted

1.  Melt the butter in a saucepan, stir in the flour and cook for 2-3 minutes.
2.  Gradually stir in the milk over a low heat, then bring to the boil and simmer for 2-3 minutes.
3.  Add the salt, pepper, paprika and lemon juice. Remove the sauce from the heat and beat in the egg yolks.
4.  Sprinkle the gelatine over the water, leave for 30 seconds, then add to the sauce, stirring until it has melted, but do not allow to boil. Allow the sauce to cool.
5.  Flake the fish flesh, and stir it into the sauce with the almonds.
6.  Whisk the egg whites and whip the cream lightly, then fold them into the fish mixture.

**TO FREEZE:** Pour into a 1.2 litre/2 pint soufflé dish or foil container, and allow to set. Cover and freeze.

**TO SERVE:** Allow to thaw in the refrigerator for 6-8 hours. Sprinkle the toasted almonds over the top, and serve with fingers of toast and lemon wedges.

**Above: Tuna fish mousse**
**Far left: Scallop nests**
**Left: Smoked trout mousse**

# ANCHOVY & MOZZARELLA PIZZA

*Preparation time: 20 minutes*
*Cooking time: 30 minutes*
*Recommended freezer life: 4 months*

225 g/8 oz Milk Bread dough
  (page 134)
1×100 g/4 oz can sardines in
  olive oil, drained and crushed
1 garlic clove, crushed
1×200 g/7 oz can tomatoes,
  drained and crushed
100 g/4 oz Mozzarella cheese,
  sliced
1×25 g/1 oz can anchovy fillets,
  halved lengthways
20 black olives
1 tablespoon grated Parmesan
  cheese

1. Roll out the dough into a 23 cm/9 inch diameter circle and place it on a greased baking sheet.
2. Spread the crushed sardines over the dough.
3. Stir the garlic into the tomatoes and spread the mixture over the sardines.
4. Arrange the Mozzarella slices over the top, then make a criss-cross pattern with the anchovy fillets. Place the black olives in the lattice squares and sprinkle with the Parmesan.
5. Bake in a preheated oven at 200°C, 400°F, Gas Mark 6 for 10 minutes. Lower the heat to 180°C, 350°F, Gas Mark 4 and continue cooking for 20 minutes.

**TO FREEZE:** Allow to go cold, pack in a polythene bag, seal and freeze.

**TO SERVE:** From frozen, place in a preheated oven at 180°C, 350°F, Gas Mark 5 for 30-40 minutes. Serve as a snack with a green salad. Alternatively, slice and pack to serve cold for a picnic.

# FRENCH ONION TART

*Serves 6*
*Preparation time: 10 minutes*
*Cooking time: 45 minutes*
*Recommended freezer life: 4 months*

250 g/12 oz Spanish onions,
  peeled and sliced
1×20 cm/8 inch shortcrust
  pastry flan case, baked blind
3 eggs
250 ml/8 fl oz double cream
salt
freshly ground black pepper
pinch of paprika
50 g/2 oz Gruyère cheese,
  grated

1. Put the onions in a pan of boiling salted water and simmer for 5 minutes. Drain and arrange the onions in the flan case.
2. Beat together the eggs, cream, salt, pepper and paprika, and pour the mixture over the onions. Sprinkle the Gruyère cheese all over the top.
3. Bake in a preheated oven at 190°C, 375°F, Gas Mark 5 for 25-30 minutes, until the filling is set and golden brown.

**TO FREEZE:** Allow to go cold, then open freeze for 3-4 hours. Remove the flan from the tin, place in a polythene bag, seal and return to the freezer.

**TO SERVE:** Remove from the polythene bag and place in a preheated oven at 180°C, 350°F, Gas Mark 4 for 50 minutes.

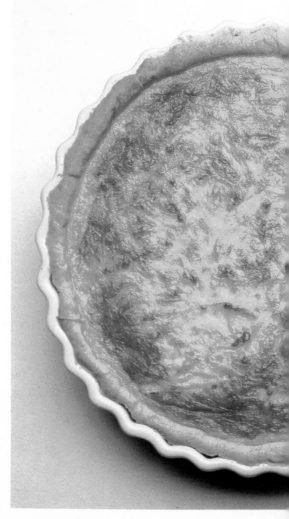

**French onion tart**

# SMOKED HADDOCK & TOMATO SHELLS

*Preparation time: 15 minutes*
*Cooking time: 45 minutes*
*Recommended freezer life: 2 months*

225 g/8 oz smoked haddock
    fillets
300 ml/½ pint milk
25 g/1 oz butter
1 small onion, peeled and
    chopped
25 g/1 oz plain flour
freshly ground black pepper
salt
175 g/6 oz tomatoes, peeled,
    quartered and seeded
2 tablespoons double cream
DUCHESSE POTATOES:
1½ potatoes, peeled
25 g/1 oz butter
1 egg yolk
salt
freshly ground black pepper
1 tablespoon grated cheese
1 tablespoon breadcrumbs
TO SERVE:
sprigs of parsley

1. Simmer the haddock fillets in the milk for 6-8 minutes. Strain, and reserve the liquor. Flake the fish and set aside.
2. Melt the butter in a pan, add the onion and fry over a low heat until soft and transparent.
3. Stir in the flour, cook for 2-3 minutes, then gradually stir in the reserved fish liquor.
4. Bring the mixture to the boil and simmer for 3 minutes. Add pepper and a little salt.
5. Cut the tomato flesh into thin strips, and fold them into the sauce with the flaked haddock and cream.
6. Divide the mixture between 4 greased scallop shells.
7. To make the Duchesse Potatoes, boil the potatoes until tender, then drain and mash them with a fork.
8. Beat in the butter, egg yolk and salt and pepper.
9. Place the potato mixture in a piping bag fitted with a star nozzle and pipe shell shapes round the edge of the scallops.

10. Combine the grated cheese and breadcrumbs and sprinkle them over the haddock filling.

**TO FREEZE:** Open freeze for 1 hour, then place each shell in a small polythene bag, seal and return to the freezer.

**TO SERVE:** Remove from the polythene bags and place the shells in a preheated oven at 190°C, 375°F, Gas Mark 5, for 25 minutes. If not frozen, reheat for 10 minutes only. Serve garnished with parsley sprigs.

**Smoked haddock and tomato shells**

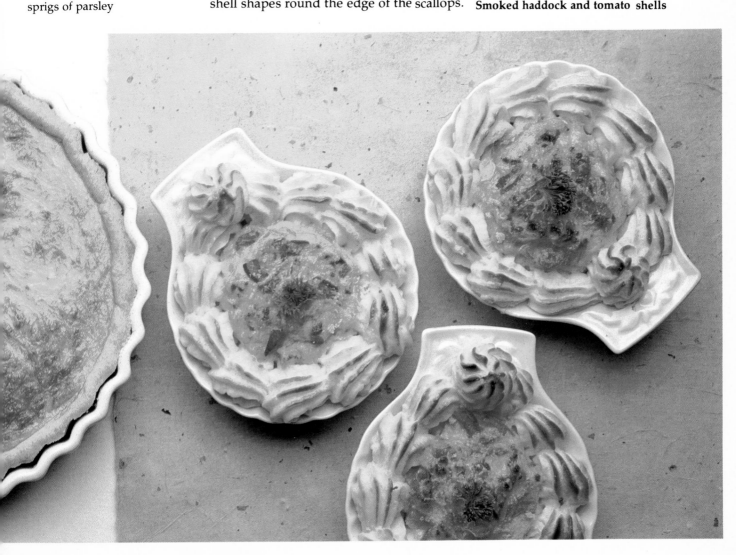

# NUTTY CHEESE TRIANGLES

*Makes 12*
*Preparation time: 20 minutes*
*Cooking time: 12 minutes*
*Recommended freezer life: 3 months*

225 g/8 oz puff pastry
   trimmings
25 g/1 oz full fat soft cheese
25 g/1 oz Cheddar cheese,
   grated
25 g/1 oz salted peanuts, finely
   chopped
1 egg, beaten, to seal and glaze
1 teaspoon grated Parmesan
   cheese

As puff pastry cannot be re-rolled, this is a good way to use trimmings while making other puff pastry items.

1. Roll out the pastry trimmings thinly and cut into 7.5 cm/3 inch squares. Cut each square in half diagonally to form triangles.
2. Mix the cream and grated cheese with the peanuts and place a teaspoonful of the mixture on half the number of triangles. Brush the edges with beaten egg and stick the remaining triangles on top to form parcels.

3. Brush each triangle with beaten egg and sprinkle with Parmesan cheese. Bake in a preheated oven at 200°C, 400°F, Gas Mark 6 for 12 minutes, until crisp and golden brown.

**TO FREEZE:** Allow to go cold and pack into a rigid container. Cover and freeze.

**TO SERVE:** From frozen, place on a baking sheet and warm through in a preheated oven at 200°C, 400°F, Gas Mark 6 for 10 minutes. Serve hot.

# COCKTAIL BEIGNETS

*Makes 30*
*Preparation time: 20 minutes*
*Cooking time: 30 minutes*
*Recommended freezer life: 3 months*

**CHOUX PASTRY:**
50 g/2 oz butter
150 ml/¼ pint water
65 g/2½ oz plain flour
1 egg
1 egg yolk
**CHEESE FLAVOURING:**
50 g/2 oz Cheddar cheese, grated
40 g/1½ oz ham, finely diced
25 g/1 oz shelled almonds,
   chopped
pinch of paprika
salt
freshly ground black pepper
oil for deep frying
**TO SERVE:**
chutney

1. Melt the butter in the water over a low heat.
2. When the butter has melted completely, bring the mixture to the boil, and quickly add the flour.
3. Beat vigorously, until the mixture thickens, and forms a smooth paste.
4. Cook the mixture beating continually for 2-3 minutes, until it leaves the sides of the pan.
5. Allow the pastry to cool for 3-4 minutes, then beat in the eggs one at a time. Beat in the cheese, ham, almonds, paprika, salt and pepper.
6. Heat the oil and drop in about 6 heaped teaspoonfuls of the mixture, to allow space for the beignets to swell. Deep fry for 4-5 minutes until puffed and golden brown. Remove from the oil and drain on kitchen paper.

**TO FREEZE:** Allow to go cold, pack into a rigid container, cover and freeze.

**TO SERVE:** From frozen, place on a baking sheet, and heat in a preheated oven at 200°C, 400°F, Gas Mark 6 for 8-10 minutes. Spear each beignet with a cocktail stick, and serve with peach chutney as a dip.

# TWISTY CHEESE STRAWS

Makes 24
Preparation time: 25 minutes
Recommended freezer life: 3 months

100 g/4 oz plain flour
50 g/2 oz butter
50 g/2 oz strong Cheddar
  cheese, grated
salt
pinch of cayenne
1 egg yolk
a little water, to bind

1. Sift the flour into a bowl and rub in the butter until the mixture resembles fine breadcrumbs. Stir in the cheese, salt and cayenne. Using a round ended knife lightly mix in the egg yolk and enough water to form a firm dough. Knead lightly and chill in the refrigerator for about 45 minutes.
2. Roll out the pastry on a floured board to 3 mm/⅛ inch thick and cut into strips 5 mm/¼ inch wide and 13 cm/5 inches long. Twist each strip to form a corkscrew shape and place on a baking sheet.

TO FREEZE: Open freeze, then pack in a rigid container, cover and return to the freezer.

TO SERVE: Place on a lightly greased baking sheet, and cook in a preheated oven at 200°C, 400°F, Gas Mark 6 for 15-20 minutes. If not freezing allow 10-12 minutes.

# SARDINE CRESCENTS

Makes 20
Preparation time: 1½ hours
Cooking time: 10 minutes
Recommended freezer life: 3 months

100 g/4 oz butter
100 g/4 oz full fat soft cheese
100 g/4 oz plain flour
FILLING:
2×120 g/4½ oz cans sardines,
  drained
1 teaspoon lemon juice
1 teaspoon curry powder
2 hard-boiled eggs, finely
  chopped
1 tablespoon chopped fresh
  parsley
dash of Worcestershire sauce
salt
freshly ground black pepper
beaten egg, to seal

1. Cream the butter and cheese together. Stir in the flour and knead gently to form a soft ball. Chill in the refrigerator for 1 hour.
2. Meanwhile prepare the filling. Mash the sardines in a bowl, then stir in all the remaining ingredients.
3. Roll out the pastry thinly and cut into 10 cm/4 inch squares. Cut each square in half diagonally to form triangles.
4. To make each crescent, place a teaspoonful of the filling on each triangle and roll up from the long side towards the point. Seal with beaten egg to stop the shape unrolling. Twist the ends and curl round to form a crescent. Place all the crescents on a baking sheet and allow to harden in the refrigerator for about 45 minutes.

TO FREEZE: Pack into a rigid plastic container, placing greaseproof paper between the layers. Cover and freeze.

TO SERVE: Place on a baking sheet and allow to thaw at room temperature for 1 hour. Bake in a preheated oven at 230°C, 450°F, Gas Mark 8 for 10 minutes and serve hot. If baking from chilled cook for 5-6 minutes only.

# CREAM CHEESE & TOMATO DIP

*Preparation time: 20 minutes*
*Cooking time: 10 minutes*
*Recommended freezer life: 3 months*

225 g/8 oz full fat soft cheese
1 tablespoon tomato purée
3 tablespoons mayonnaise
1 teaspoon caster sugar
1 tablespoon double cream
dash of Tabasco sauce
1 tablespoon fresh orange juice
salt
freshly ground black pepper
½ medium red pepper, cored,
  seeded and diced
½ medium green pepper, cored,
  seeded and diced
50 g/2 oz ham, finely diced
50 g/2 oz frozen sweetcorn,
  cooked

Blend the cheese, tomato purée, mayonnaise and caster sugar together to form a smooth mixture. Add the remaining ingredients and mix well.

**TO FREEZE:**  Spoon into a rigid container, cover and freeze.

**TO SERVE:**  Allow to thaw at room temperature for 6 hours. Serve with crudités to dip into the mixture.

# BLUE CHEESE DIP

*Preparation time: 15 minutes*
*Recommended freezer life: 3 months*

50 g/2 oz butter
50 g/2 oz full fat soft cheese
100 g/4 oz Roquefort or
  Dolcelatte or mild Stilton,
  sieved
50 g/2 oz walnuts, chopped

Cream the butter and full fat soft cheese to a smooth paste. Beat in the blue cheese and mix thoroughly. Stir in the chopped walnuts. The dip should be a smooth but firm consistency.

**TO FREEZE:**  Spoon into a rigid container, cover and freeze.

**TO SERVE:**  Allow the dip to thaw in the container at room temperature, for 4-6 hours. Serve with crudités (celery, carrot, apple, cauliflower florets), large fried croûtons and potato crisps.

# BOMBAY DIP

*Serves 10*
*Preparation time: 10 minutes*
*Cooking time: 35 minutes*
*Recommended freezer life: 3 months*

25 g/1 oz butter
1 shallot, peeled and diced
1 tablespoon curry paste
1 tablespoon plain flour
300 ml/½ pint milk
1 tablespoon cornflour
3 tablespoons water
1 tablespoon chutney
25 g/1 oz peanuts
1 small cooking apple, peeled,
  cored and diced
1 tablespoon lemon juice
1 bay leaf
150 ml/¼ pint single cream
pinch of ground coriander
salt
freshly ground black pepper

1. Melt the butter in a saucepan and gently fry the shallot for 5 minutes. Stir in the curry paste and cook for 1 minute. Stir in the flour. Gradually add the milk, stirring continually and bringing the sauce back to the boil after each addition. Simmer for 3 minutes.
2. Mix the cornflour and water together, and add to the sauce. Bring back to the boil and add the chutney, peanuts, apple, lemon juice and bay leaf. Cover and simmer for 10 minutes.
3. Cool the sauce slightly, remove the bay leaf and blend in a liquidizer, or sieve. Stir in the cream, ground coriander, salt and pepper.

**TO FREEZE:** Pour into a rigid container and allow to go cold. Cover and freeze.

**TO SERVE:** Turn the frozen sauce into a pan and gradually bring to the boil. Simmer for 2 minutes, adjusting the seasoning if necessary. Serve hot with cocktail sausages, chicken drumsticks or poppadoms.

# CHILLI SAUCE

*Serves 10*
*Preparation time: 10 minutes*
*Cooking time: 30 minutes*
*Recommended freezer life: 3 months*

25 g/1 oz butter
2 shallots, peeled and finely
  diced
40 g/1½ oz green pepper, cored,
  seeded and diced
1 tablespoon chilli powder
1 tablespoon plain flour
300 ml/½ pint milk
1 tablespoon cornflour
3 tablespoons water
1 teaspoon tomato purée
1 tablespoon Worcestershire
  sauce
1 teaspoon Tabasco sauce
salt
freshly ground black pepper
75 g/3 oz Gruyère cheese, diced
120 ml/4 fl oz single cream

Chilli powders vary in strength depending on the manufacturer, so it is best to use it cautiously until you find the right strength to suit your taste.

1. Melt the butter and gently fry the shallots and green pepper for 4 minutes. Stir in the chilli powder and cook for 1-2 minutes. Stir in the flour and gradually stir in the milk, bringing the sauce to the boil between each addition.
2. Mix the cornflour with the water, stir into the sauce and bring back to the boil. Add the tomato purée, Worcestershire sauce, Tabasco sauce, salt and pepper. Simmer the sauce for 6 minutes, remove from the heat and stir in the Gruyère cheese. Continue stirring until all the cheese has melted.
3. Stir in the cream and adjust the seasoning if necessary.

**TO FREEZE:** Pour into a rigid container and allow to go cold. Cover and freeze.

**TO SERVE:** Turn into a pan and gradually bring to the boil. Simmer for 2 minutes and serve hot with scampi, pieces of deep fried, breadcrumbed plaice or meat balls.

# SAUCES & STUFFINGS

## FRESH TOMATO SAUCE

*Makes 1½ pints*
*Preparation time: 10 minutes*
*Cooking time: 2 hours*
*Recommended freezer life: 4 months*

3 tablespoons oil
2 Spanish onions, peeled and
  finely diced
2 cloves garlic, crushed
5 tablespoons tomato purée
450 g/1 lb tomatoes, skinned
  and roughly chopped
pinch of sugar
1 teaspoon Worcestershire
  sauce
2 bay leaves
1 sprig of fresh rosemary
salt
freshly ground black pepper
250 ml/8 fl oz dry white wine
1 tablespoon cornflour
2 tablespoons water

1.  Heat the oil in a saucepan and gently fry the onions and garlic for 8-10 minutes. Stir in the tomato purée, tomatoes, sugar, Worcestershire sauce, bay leaves, the sprig of rosemary and add salt and pepper.
2.  Pour in the wine, and bring the sauce to the boil. Cover and simmer for about 40 minutes. Blend the cornflour with the water and add to the sauce. Simmer for a further 5 minutes.

**TO FREEZE:**  Allow to go cold, remove the bay leaves and rosemary then pour into a rigid container, cover and freeze.

**TO SERVE:**  Allow to gently thaw in a pan over a low heat, then bring to the boil. Serve with fish, veal, chicken, scampi or pasta.

## MUSHROOM SAUCE

*Makes ½ pint*
*Preparation time: 10 minutes*
*Cooking time: 15 minutes*
*Recommended freezer life: 4 months*

25 g/1 oz butter
100 g/4 oz button mushrooms,
  sliced
squeeze of lemon juice
3 teaspoons cornflour
150 ml/¼ pint milk
salt
freshly ground black pepper
150 ml/¼ pint soured cream

1.  Melt the butter in a saucepan, add the mushrooms and lemon juice and fry gently for 4-5 minutes. Mix the cornflour to a smooth paste with the milk, add to the mushrooms with the salt and pepper, and bring slowly to the boil.
2.  Remove the sauce from the heat, and stir in the soured cream.

**TO FREEZE:**  Allow to go cold, pour into a rigid container, cover and freeze.

**TO SERVE:**  Allow to thaw at room temperature for 5-6 hours. Heat very gently but do not allow the sauce to boil.

# CREAMY ONION SAUCE

*Makes: 1 pint*
*Preparation time: 10 minutes*
*Cooking time: 45 minutes*
*Recommended freezer life: 4 months*

450 g/1 lb Spanish onions,
  peeled and sliced
450 ml/¾ pint milk
25 g/1 oz butter
25 g/1 oz plain flour
1 tablespoon cornflour
2 tablespoons water
pinch of ground mace
salt
freshly ground black pepper
**TO SERVE:**
3 tablespoons double cream

1. Gently bring the onions and milk to the boil in a saucepan. Simmer until the onions are tender, then cool, sieve or blend in a liquidizer.
2. Melt the butter in a clean saucepan, stir in the flour and cook for 2-3 minutes. Gradually stir in the onion and milk mixture over a low heat.
3. Mix the cornflour with the cold water, and add to the sauce. Bring back to the boil and simmer for 5-6 minutes. Add the mace, salt and pepper.

**TO FREEZE:** Allow to go cold, pour into a rigid container, cover and freeze.

**TO SERVE:** Allow to thaw at room temperature for 6-8 hours. Heat gently over a low heat to boiling point, then stir in the cream.

# SPECIAL MORNAY SAUCE

*Makes 1 pint*
*Preparation time: 20 minutes*
*Cooking time: 1 hour*
*Recommended freezer life: 4 months*

15 g/½ oz butter
2 rashers streaky bacon, rind
  removed and chopped
1 onion, peeled and diced
1 stick of celery, diced
450 ml/¾ pint milk
1 bay leaf
sprigs of parsley
3 fresh sage leaves or a pinch of
  dried sage
6 black peppercorns
2 cloves
**CHEESE SAUCE:**
50 g/2 oz butter
25 g/1 oz plain flour
1 tablespoon cornflour
6 tablespoons water
50 g/2 oz Cheddar cheese,
  grated
50 g/2 oz Emmenthal cheese,
  grated
25 g/1 oz Parmesan cheese,
  grated
1 teaspoon made French
  mustard
pinch of ground nutmeg
salt
freshly ground black pepper

1. Melt the 15 g/½ oz butter in a saucepan and gently fry the bacon, onion and celery for 5 minutes, but do not allow to brown. Pour in the milk and add the bay leaf, parsley, sage, peppercorns and cloves. Cover and simmer for 20 minutes.
2. Remove from the heat and allow to stand for a further 10 minutes. Strain and reserve the liquor.
3. To make the cheese sauce, melt the 50 g/2 oz butter in a saucepan, and stir in the flour. Cook for 2-3 minutes, then gradually stir in the reserved liquor over a low heat. Bring to the boil.
4. Mix the cornflour with the cold water and pour into the sauce. Simmer for 2-3 minutes, then beat in the cheeses, mustard, nutmeg, salt and pepper.

**TO FREEZE:** Allow to go cold, then pour into a rigid container, cover and freeze.

**TO SERVE:** Allow to thaw at room temperature for 5-6 hours. Turn into a pan and bring gently to simmering point.

**Special mornay sauce**

# DEMI-GLACE SAUCE

*Makes 1½ pints*
*Preparation time: 15 minutes*
*Cooking time: 1½ hours*
*Recommended freezer life: 4 months*

25 g/1 oz butter
100 g/4 oz streaky bacon, diced
50 g/2 oz carrot, scraped and diced
50 g/2 oz onion, peeled and diced
50 g/2 oz celery, diced
25 g/1 oz plain flour
900 ml/1½ pints beef stock
1 bay leaf
2 tablespoons tomato purée
150 ml/¼ pint sherry
1 tablespoon cornflour
3 tablespoons water
salt
freshly ground black pepper

1. Melt the butter and gently fry the bacon until golden brown. Stir in the carrot, onion and celery and gently fry for 10 minutes, until the vegetables begin to brown slightly.
2. Stir in the flour and cook for a further 3 minutes.
3. Gradually stir in the stock, bringing the sauce to the boil after each addition. Add the bay leaf, cover and simmer for 30 minutes.
4. Stir in the tomato purée and sherry. Increase the heat slightly and cook for a further 15 minutes. Skim off any fat that may appear on the surface.
5. Mix the cornflour with the cold water and stir into the sauce. Bring back to the boil, and simmer for 2 minutes. Strain the sauce through a fine sieve, and add salt and pepper.

**TO FREEZE:** Allow to go cold, pour into a rigid container, cover and freeze.

**TO SERVE:** Allow to thaw slowly over a gentle heat. Bring to the boil, stirring rapidly, until the sauce is smooth.

**Demi-glace sauce**

# SWEET & SOUR SAUCE

*Makes ½ pint*
*Preparation time: 10 minutes*
*Cooking time: 45 minutes*
*Recommended freezer life: 4 months*

1 tablespoon oil
1 onion, peeled and diced
150 ml/¼ pint dry white wine
1 tablespoon wine vinegar
1 tablespoon peach chutney
1 tablespoon tomato ketchup
1 teaspoon soy sauce
1 teaspoon made mustard
salt
freshly ground black pepper
pinch of mixed spice
pinch of chilli powder
1 tablespoon cornflour
6 tablespoons water

1. Heat the oil in a pan and gently fry the onion until soft and transparent. Pour in the wine, increase the heat, and boil for 2 minutes.
2. Add the vinegar, chutney, tomato ketchup, soy sauce, mustard, salt, pepper, mixed spice and chilli powder. Cover and simmer for 20 minutes.
3. Cool slightly, then sieve or blend in a liquidizer, and return to the pan. Blend the cornflour with the water and stir into the sauce. Bring back to the boil and simmer for 2-3 minutes.

**TO FREEZE:** Allow to go cold, pour into a rigid container, cover and freeze.

**TO SERVE:** Allow to thaw slowly over a gentle heat. Bring to the boil, stirring rapidly, until smooth.

# APPLE SAUCE

*Preparation time: 10 minutes*
*Cooking time: 20 minutes*
*Recommended freezer life: 4 months*

50 g/2 oz butter
1 large Spanish onion, peeled and finely diced
12 fresh sage leaves or 2 teaspoons dried sage
salt
freshly ground black pepper
2 tablespoons demerara sugar
450 g/1 lb dessert apples, peeled, cored and sliced

To serve with duck, pork or goose.

1. Melt the butter and gently fry the onion. Add the sage, salt and pepper, and cook until the onion is soft and transparent, stirring occasionally.
2. Sprinkle over the demerara sugar, increase the heat and stir in the apples. Cook for 7-10 minutes, turning the mixture over occasionally with a wooden spoon, but taking care not to break the apple slices.
3. As soon as the apples are soft, but not mushy, remove from the heat.

**TO FREEZE:** Allow to go cold, spoon into a rigid container, cover and freeze.

**TO SERVE:** Allow to thaw in a cool place for 4-6 hours, then heat gently.

# BLACKCURRANT SAUCE

*Makes 450 ml /¾ pint*
*Preparation time: 20 minutes*
*Cooking time: 25 minutes*
*Recommended freezer life: 4 months*

350 g/12 oz fresh blackcurrants,
　topped and tailed, with
　150 ml/¼ pint water,
or 350 g/12 oz frozen
　blackcurrants
　with 50 ml/2 fl oz water
3 tablespoons caster sugar
2 tablespoons orange juice
2 teaspoons cornflour
2 tablespoons water
1 tablespoon Grand Marnier

To accompany ice cream or pancakes.

1. Put the blackcurrants, the water and caster sugar into a pan, cover and stew gently for 15 minutes.
2. Cool then pass the mixture through a sieve. Return to the heat and stir in the orange juice.
3. Blend the cornflour with the 2 tablespoons water, stir into the sauce and bring to the boil, stirring continuously. Remove from the heat and cool. When the sauce is cool, stir in the Grand Marnier.

TO FREEZE:  Pour into a rigid container, cover and freeze.

TO SERVE:  Allow to thaw at room temperature for 4 hours.

# MELBA SAUCE

*Makes ½ pint*
*Preparation time: 10 minutes*
*Cooking time: 15 minutes*
*Recommended freezer life: 4 months*

350 g/12 oz fresh raspberries
　with 150 ml/¼pint water,
or 350 g/12 oz frozen
　raspberries
　with 50 ml/2 fl oz water
1 tablespoon caster sugar
1 tablespoon arrowroot
1 tablespoon redcurrant jelly
1 tablespoon orange juice
1 tablespoon gin

1. Bring the raspberries, the water and sugar to the boil in a saucepan. Sieve or purée the mixture in a liquidizer for 2 minutes, then return to the pan.
2. Stir in the arrowroot, redcurrant jelly and orange juice, and bring back to the boil. Cook for 3 minutes. If liquidized strain the sauce into a bowl. Stir in the gin.

TO FREEZE:  Allow to go cold, pour into a rigid container, cover and freeze.

TO SERVE:  Allow to thaw at room temperature for 6 hours.

## CORNFLOUR STABILIZER FOR LIAISON BUTTER SAUCES:

Liaison butter sauces, such as Hollandaise and Bearnaise sauce, are made with warmed egg yolks with which butter is gradually incorporated to make a rich creamy sauce. Most cooks dread making them as the egg yolk can curdle. It is extremely easy and almost foolproof to make these sauces in a liquidizer or food processor. The action of the machine ensures a really good blending of the ingredients, which is essential if you are going to freeze the sauce. With the aid of the cornflour stabilizer, one also minimizes the chances of the sauces curdling when warming them through after freezing. The sauces should be served at blood heat.

*Makes 1 quantity*

1 tablespoon cornflour
3 tablespoons water

Blend the cornflour with the cold water in a small pan. Bring to the boil while beating well, until the mixture forms a thick paste and becomes transparent. Set aside to cool.

**TO FREEZE:** Pour into a rigid circular freezer container, cover and freeze.

**TO SERVE:** Allow to thaw at room temperature for 5-6 hours. Stand the container in a bowl of tepid water and stir continually while the sauce warms through.

# HOLLANDAISE SAUCE

*Preparation time: 20 minutes*
*Recommended freezer life: 4 months*

3 egg yolks
2 tablespoons lemon juice
225 g/8 oz butter, melted and cooled
freshly ground black pepper
1 quantity cornflour stabilizer, if freezing the sauce

1. Over a low heat whisk the yolks and lemon juice in a heavy cast iron saucepan until the mixture is frothy and begins to thicken. Alternatively, whisk the yolks and lemon juice in a bowl placed over a pan of simmering water. (The water should not touch the bottom of the bowl.)
2. Pour into a liquidizer or food processor and turn on the motor immediately. Add the cooled butter in a thin stream, keeping the motor running all the time. When all the butter is incorporated the sauce should be the consistency of thick double cream. Add the pepper and, if proposing to freeze the sauce, the cornflour stabilizer.

# BEARNAISE SAUCE

*Preparation time: 20 minutes*
*Recommended freezer life: 4 months*

4 tablespoons wine vinegar
1 shallot, peeled and sliced
1 bay leaf
pinch of ground mace
6 peppercorns
3 egg yolks
175 g/6 oz butter, melted and cooled
1 teaspoon chopped fresh or dried tarragon
1 teaspoon chopped fresh or dried parsley
salt
freshly ground black pepper
1 quantity cornflour stabilizer, if freezing the sauce

1. Place the vinegar, shallot, bay leaf, mace and peppercorns in a small pan and boil until the liquid is reduced to 1 tablespoon. Allow to cool slightly.
2. Beat the yolks in a heavy cast iron saucepan, or in a bowl placed over a pan of simmering water, and add the warm vinegar mixture, strained. Whisk well over a very low heat until the sauce is light and fluffy and beginning to thicken.
3. Transfer to a liquidizer or food processor and turn on the motor immediately. Add the cooled butter in a thin stream, keeping the motor running. Add the tarragon, parsley, salt, pepper and cornflour stabilizer, if proposing to freeze the sauce.

**TO FREEZE:** Pour into a rigid circular freezer container, cover and freeze.

**TO SERVE:** Allow to thaw at room temperature for 5-6 hours. Stand the container in a bowl of tepid water and stir continually while the sauce warms through.

# APRICOT & ALMOND STUFFING

*Preparation time: 15 minutes,*
*plus soaking time*
*Recommended freezer life: 4 months*

100 g/4 oz dried apricots,
   soaked in water overnight
   and finely chopped
50 g/2 oz fresh white
   breadcrumbs
25 g/1 oz flaked almonds
1 tablespoon chopped fresh
   parsley
1 teaspoon dried marjoram
rind and juice of 1 small orange
salt
freshly ground black pepper
1 egg, beaten

Enough to stuff about 4½ lb shoulder of lamb, boned or 4 lb boned veal.

Mix all the ingredients together.

**TO FREEZE:** Pack into a rigid container, cover and freeze.

**TO USE:** Allow to thaw at room temperature for 4 hours.

# MUSHROOM & BACON STUFFING

*Preparation time: 15 minutes*
*Cooking time: 15 minutes*
*Recommended freezer life: 4 months*

25 g/1 oz butter
100 g/4 oz streaky bacon, rind
   removed, diced
175 g/6 oz mushrooms, finely
   chopped
100 g/4 oz fresh brown
   breadcrumbs
1 tablespoon finely chopped
   fresh parsley
2 tablespoons soured cream
pinch of dried basil
4 juniper berries, crushed
   (optional)
salt
freshly ground black pepper

To be used for fish, chicken, turkey or game.

1. Melt the butter in a pan and gently fry the bacon for 4 minutes. Stir in the mushrooms and cook for a further 4 minutes. Remove from the heat and stir in the breadcrumbs, parsley, soured cream, basil, juniper berries, salt and pepper.

**TO FREEZE:** Allow to go cold, pack into a rigid container, cover and freeze.

**TO USE:** Allow to thaw at room temperature for 4 hours.

# APPLE & RAISIN STUFFING

*Preparation time: 10 minutes*
*Cooking time: 20 minutes*
*Recommended freezer life: 4 months*

50 g/2 oz butter
1 onion, peeled and finely
   chopped
8 fresh sage leaves or 2
   teaspoons dried sage
225 g/8 oz dessert apples,
   peeled, cored and diced
40 g/1½ oz raw long-grain rice,
   cooked and drained
50 g/2 oz raisins
salt
freshly ground black pepper
1 egg yolk, lightly beaten

To be used for duck, goose or pork.

1. Melt the butter in a pan and gently fry the onion for 4 minutes, until soft and transparent. Increase the heat, add the sage leaves and apples, and toss over the heat for 6-7 minutes, until the apples soften but do not entirely lose their shape.
2. Add the rice, raisins, salt and pepper, stirring well. Remove from the heat and cool slightly. Beat in the egg yolk to bind all the ingredients together.

**TO FREEZE:** Allow to go cold, pack into a rigid container, cover and freeze.

**TO USE:** Allow to thaw at room temperature for 4 hours.

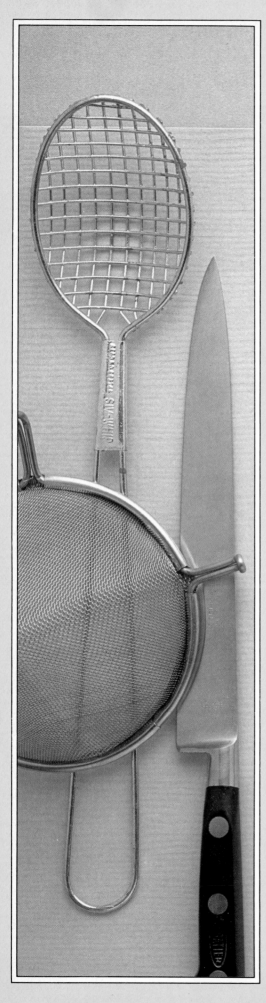

# FISH

## SALMON SURPRISE

*Serves 6*
*Preparation time: 30 minutes*
*Cooking time: 40 minutes*
*Recommended freezer life: 1 month*

450 g/1 lb salmon, skinned
2 onions, peeled and sliced
6 black peppercorns
slice of lemon
salt
50 g/2 oz long-grain rice
25 g/1 oz butter
175 g/6 oz button mushrooms,
  sliced
50 g/2 oz Gruyère cheese,
  grated
1 tablespoon lemon juice
175 ml/6 fl oz single cream
pinch of ground nutmeg
salt
freshly ground black pepper
1 tablespoon cornflour
2 tablespoons water
2 tablespoons chopped fresh
  parsley
1×375 g/13 oz packet frozen
  puff pastry, thawed
2 eggs, beaten

1. Place the salmon in a pan with the onions, peppercorns, slice of lemon and salt and cover with water. Cover and bring slowly to the boil.
2. Remove from the heat and set aside for 10 minutes. Strain and reserve the fish liquor. Bone and flake the salmon.
3. Cook the rice in the fish liquor, then strain and allow to cool.
4. Melt the butter in a saucepan and gently fry the mushrooms for 2-3 minutes. Stir in the Gruyère cheese, lemon juice, cream, nutmeg and salt and pepper. Cook until the cheese has melted and all the ingredients are thoroughly blended.
5. Mix the cornflour with the water and stir into the sauce. Simmer for 2-3 minutes, then stir in the chopped parsley and allow to cool.
6. Roll out the pastry to a 36 cm/14 inch square. Spread half the rice over the pastry to form a 18 cm/7 inch square in the centre.
7. Cover the rice with half the mushroom mixture, then all of the flaked salmon. Spread the rest of the mushroom mixture over the fish, top with the remaining rice.
8. Draw up 2 sides of the pastry to overlap by 25 cm/1 inch, and seal with beaten egg. Trim away the pastry from each end to within 25 cm/1 inch of the filling. Seal with beaten egg, and crimp the edges.
9. Cut a 5 cm/2 inch wide strip of pastry from the trimmings, and place over the join, sealing with beaten egg. Make pastry leaves from the remaining trimmings, and use to make a pattern diagonally down the sealing pastry strip.

TO FREEZE: Open freeze for 3 hours, then wrap in a freezer bag and return to the freezer.

TO SERVE: Brush with beaten egg, and, from frozen, bake in a preheated oven at 190°C, 375°F, Gas Mark 6 for 40 minutes. Lower the heat to 160°C, 325°F, Gas Mark 3, and continue to cook for a further 20 minutes. If not frozen, cook at 190°C, 375°F, Gas Mark 5 for 25 minutes, then lower the heat and continue cooking for 25 minutes.

# LEMON SOLE VERONIQUE

*Preparation time: 15 minutes*
*Cooking time: 50 minutes*
*Recommended freezer life: 1 month*

750 g/1½ lb lemon sole fillets
1 onion, peeled and sliced into
 rings
2 tablespoons wine vinegar
salt
freshly ground white pepper
**SAUCE:**
25 g/1 oz butter
2 tablespoons plain flour
250 ml/8 fl oz reserved fish
 liquor
1 tablespoon cornflour
2 tablespoons water
125 ml/4 fl oz single cream
75 g/3 oz seedless white grapes

1. Roll up the fish fillets and arrange them in a buttered ovenproof dish.
2. Scatter the onion rings over the fillets and pour over the vinegar. Pour over enough water to cover the fillets, and add salt and pepper.
3. Cover the dish with foil and cook in a preheated oven at 160°C, 325°F, Gas Mark 3 for 25-30 minutes.
4. Lift out the fillets and place them in the bottom of a lightly buttered foil dish.
5. Strain the fish liquor into a saucepan, and reduce it by boiling until approximately 250 ml/8 fl oz remain. Set the liquor aside.
6. To make the sauce, melt the butter and stir in the flour. Cook for 2-3 minutes. Gradually stir in the fish liquor over a low heat. Bring the mixture to the boil.

7. Mix the cornflour with the water, and stir into the sauce.
8. Cook for 2-3 minutes, then remove from the heat and stir in the cream and grapes. Pour the sauce over the fish fillets.

**TO FREEZE:** Allow to go cold, cover and freeze.

**TO SERVE:** Loosen the lid and, from frozen, place in a preheated oven at 160°C, 325°F, Gas Mark 3 for 45-50 minutes.

# STUFFED FILLETS OF PLAICE IN PRAWN SAUCE

*Preparation time: 20 minutes*
*Cooking time: 40 minutes*
*Recommended freezer life: 1 month*

4×175 g/6 oz plaice fillets,
 skinned
**STUFFING:**
50 g/2 oz fresh white
 breadcrumbs
2 tablespoons chopped fresh
 parsley
75 g/3 oz Gouda cheese, grated
1 tablespoon lemon juice
2 tablespoons single cream
1 egg yolk
salt
freshly ground black pepper
**SAUCE:**
150 ml/¼ pint milk
25 g/1 oz butter
2 tablespoons plain flour
1 tablespoon cornflour
2 tablespoons water
75 g/3 oz peeled prawns
salt
freshly ground black pepper
150 ml/¼ pint single cream
**TO SERVE:**
6 prawns in shells
lemon twists
sprigs of parsley

1. Lay the fillets flat on a board. Mix all the stuffing ingredients together, and divide the mixture between the fillets. Roll up each fillet to enclose the stuffing.
2. Place the rolls in a buttered ovenproof dish and pour in the milk. Cover the dish with foil and bake in a preheated oven at 160°C, 325°F, Gas Mark 3 for 20 minutes.
3. Remove the fillets to a clean buttered dish or foil container, and strain the liquor into a bowl.
4. Melt the butter in a saucepan and stir in the flour. Cook for 2-3 minutes, then gradually stir in the fish liquor over a low heat and bring to the boil.
5. Blend the cornflour with the water, and stir into the sauce. Continue simmering for 3-4 minutes.
6. Stir in the prawns, salt and pepper and then the cream. Pour the sauce over the fish fillets.

**TO FREEZE:** Allow to go cold, then cover and freeze.

**TO SERVE:** Allow to thaw at room temperature for 5-6 hours. Loosen the lid and heat gently in a preheated oven at 160°C, 325°F, Gas Mark 3 for 35 minutes. Serve garnished with prawns in their shells, lemon twists and parsley sprigs.

**Top left: Lemon sole veronique**
**Top right: Dover sole in orange sauce**
**Below: Stuffed fillets of plaice in prawn sauce**

# DOVER SOLE IN ORANGE SAUCE

*Preparation time: 15 minutes*
*Cooking time: 45 minutes*
*Recommended freezer life: 1 month*

4 fillets Dover sole, skinned
120 ml/4 fl oz water
1 large orange
pinch of salt
SAUCE:
25 g/1 oz butter
15 g/½ oz plain flour
250 ml/8 fl oz reserved fish
   liquor
1 tablespoon cornflour
2 tablespoons water
salt
freshly ground black pepper
150 ml/¼ pint single cream
TO SERVE:
1 large orange

1. Roll up the fish fillets and place them in an ovenproof dish. Pour over the water, and add the rind and juice of half of the orange. Sprinkle with the salt.
2. Cover the dish with foil, and cook in a preheated moderate oven at 180°C, 350°F, Gas Mark 4 for 20-25 minutes.
3. Transfer the fish rolls to a foil container, and reserve 250 ml/8 fl oz of the fish liquor.
4. To make the sauce, melt the butter in a saucepan and stir in the flour. Cook for 2-3 minutes, then gradually stir in the reserved fish liquor over a low heat.
5. Bring the sauce to the boil and add the rind and juice of the remaining half orange.
6. Mix the cornflour in the water together, add to the sauce and simmer for 2-3 minutes, stirring all the time.

7. Add salt and pepper, and stir in the cream. Pour the sauce over the fish rolls.

TO FREEZE: Allow to go cold, cover and freeze.

TO SERVE: Allow to thaw in the refrigerator for 6-8 hours. Place in a preheated moderate oven at 180°C, 350°F, Gas Mark 4 for 35 minutes. Grate the rind of the orange over the fish. Remove the pith from the orange, and slice the flesh. Garnish the fish with orange slices.

# CREAMY PRAWN CURRY

*Preparation time: 15 minutes*
*Cooking time: 25 minutes*
*Recommended freezer life: 1 month*

50 g/2 oz butter
bunch of spring onions,
  trimmed and sliced
1 tablespoon curry powder
25 g/1 oz plain flour
250 ml/8 fl oz milk
350 g/12 oz peeled prawns
1 green pepper, cored, seeded,
  diced and blanched
50 g/2 oz flaked almonds
juice of ½ lime or lemon
pinch of ground mace
salt
freshly ground black pepper
1 tablespoon cornflour
2 tablespoons water
150 ml/¼ pint double cream
**TO SERVE:**
long-grain rice, cooked
slices of lime or lemon

1. Melt the butter in a saucepan and fry the spring onions until lightly browned. Stir in the curry powder, and fry for 2-3 minutes to bring out the flavour.
3. Stir in the flour and cook for 2-3 minutes. Gradually stir in the milk.
4. Bring the sauce to the boil, and add the prawns, green pepper, almonds, lime or lemon juice, mace and salt and pepper. Cover and simmer gently for 10 minutes.
4. Mix the cornflour and water together and stir into the curry. Simmer for a further 2-3 minutes, then stir in the cream.

**TO FREEZE:** Pour into a freezer container and allow to go cold. Cover and freeze.

**TO SERVE:** Allow to thaw at room temperature for 5-6 hours. Pour into a heavy pan, and reheat gently. Serve on a bed of rice, with lime or lemon slices to garnish.

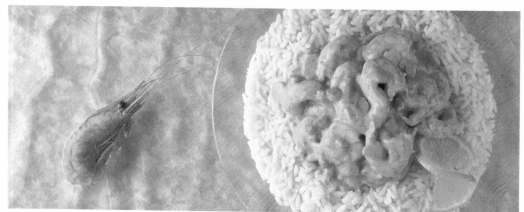

# FILLETS OF PLAICE DUGLERE

*Preparation time: 15 minutes*
*Cooking time: 50 minutes*
*Recommended freezer life: 1 month*

750 g/1½ lb plaice fillets,
  skinned
salt
freshly ground black pepper
1 teaspoon lemon juice
**SAUCE:**
25 g/1 oz butter
1 small onion, peeled and
  chopped
15 g/½ oz plain flour
150 ml/¼ pint dry white wine
65 ml/2½ fl oz water
150 ml/¼ pint single cream
1 tablespoon cornflour
2 tablespoons water
225 g/8 oz tomatoes, skinned,
  seeded and shredded
1 teaspoon sugar
1 teaspoon dried basil
1 tablespoon chopped fresh
  parsley
salt
freshly ground black pepper
40 g/1½ oz fresh brown
  breadcrumbs
**TO SERVE:**
sprigs of parsley

1. Roll up the fish fillets and place them in a buttered ovenproof dish or foil container. Sprinkle with salt, pepper and lemon juice. Set aside.
2. To make the sauce, melt the butter in a saucepan and gently fry the onion until it becomes transparent. Stir in the flour, and cook for 2-3 minutes. Stir in the wine and the 65 ml/2½ fl oz of water.
3. Bring the sauce to the boil and slowly add the cream.
4. Mix the cornflour with the 2 tablespoons water and add to the sauce. Simmer for 2-3 minutes.
5. Stir in the tomatoes, sugar, dried basil, chopped parsley, and salt and pepper. Pour the sauce over the fish.
6. Sprinkle the breadcrumbs over the fish. Cook in a preheated oven at 180°C, 350°F, Gas Mark 4 for 25 minutes.

**TO FREEZE:** Allow to go cold, then cover and freeze.

**TO SERVE:** Allow to thaw at room temperature for 5-6 hours. Uncover and place in a preheated oven at 160°C, 325°F, Gas Mark 3 for 30 minutes. Serve garnished with parsley sprigs.

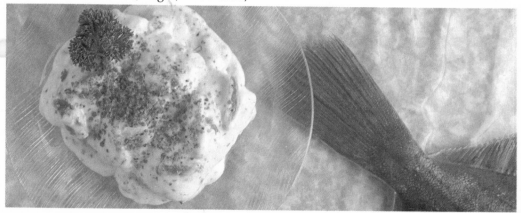

# CHINESE SEAFOOD ROLLS

*Preparation time: 20 minutes*
*Cooking time: 20 minutes*
*Recommended freezer life: 1 month*

**BATTER:**
2 eggs
150 ml/5 fl oz water
½ teaspoon salt
50 g/2 oz plain flour

**FILLING:**
1 tablespoon grated carrot
1 tablespoon finely chopped
   celery
1 tablespoon finely chopped
   spring onion
50 g/2 oz drained canned or
   fresh beansprouts
100 g/4 oz cooked flaked
   haddock
100 g/4 oz peeled prawns
2 teaspoons oil
1 teaspoon caster sugar
salt
freshly ground black pepper

**TO SERVE:**
Sweet and Sour Sauce (page 62)

1. Beat the eggs together, and reserve 2 tablespoons of beaten egg to use later.
2. Beat the water, salt and flour into the remaining beaten egg until smooth. This can be done in a liquidizer or food processor.
3. Use the batter to make 12 thin pancakes – approximately 15 cm/6 inches in diameter.
4. Blanch the carrot and celery together in boiling water for 2 minutes, then drain, and mix with all the remaining filling ingredients.

5. Divide the mixture between the pancakes and roll them up, folding in the sides and using the reserved beaten egg to seal the edges together.

**TO FREEZE:** Pack the rolls in a rigid container, cover and freeze.

**TO SERVE:** While still frozen, deep fry the rolls in hot oil for 5-7 minutes, until crisp and golden brown. Serve with Sweet and Sour Sauce.

# SALMON FISHCAKES

*Serves 6*
*Preparation time: 20 minutes*
*Cooking time: 1 hour 30 minutes*
*Recommended freezer life: 1 month*

750 g/1½ lb fresh salmon
1 bay leaf
1 carrot, peeled and sliced
1 onion, peeled and sliced
salt
6 black peppercorns
strip of lemon rind
sprig of parsley
450 g/1 lb potatoes, peeled and
   cut into even-sized chunks
3 egg yolks
25 g/1 oz butter
1 tablespoon chopped fresh
   parsley
freshly ground black pepper
COATING:
seasoned flour
2 eggs, beaten
100 g/4 oz fresh white
   breadcrumbs
TO SERVE:
oil for frying
150 ml/½ pint Hollandaise
   Sauce (page 64)

If fresh salmon is not available, use canned salmon which will not need any initial cooking.

1. Place the salmon in a large saucepan with the bay leaf, carrot, onion, salt, peppercorns and lemon rind. Cover with water and bring to the boil.
2. Remove from the heat and allow to stand for 45 minutes.
3. Meanwhile, boil the potatoes gently in salted water until just cooked. Drain, and leave in a colander for 2-3 minutes to dry.
4. Transfer to a bowl and mash well. Beat in the egg yolks, butter, chopped parsley and add salt and pepper.
5. Drain the fish and flake finely, then blend it into the potato mixture.

6. Divide the salmon mixture into 12, and form each piece into a round cake. Chill in the refrigerator for 30 minutes.
7. Dip the fishcakes into seasoned flour, then beaten egg, and coat with breadcrumbs.

**TO FREEZE:** Place the fishcakes in 2 large shallow foil containers, cover and freeze.

**TO SERVE:** Allow to thaw in the refrigerator for 3-4 hours. Fry in deep fat for 8-10 minutes and serve with Hollandaise Sauce.

**VARIATION:**
Replace the fresh salmon with fresh cod or haddock.

Top: Scallops à la bretonne
Below: Salmon fishcakes

# SCALLOPS A LA BRETONNE

*Preparation time: 20 minutes*
*Cooking time: 20 minutes*
*Recommended freezer life: 1 month*

4 large fresh scallops
40 g/1½ oz butter
2 shallots, peeled and finely
    chopped
150 ml/5 fl oz dry white wine
1 tablespoon brandy
1 tablespoon chopped fresh
    parsley
40 g/1½ oz fresh white
    breadcrumbs
salt
freshly ground black pepper
1 quantity Duchesse Potato
    (see recipe for Smoked
    Haddock and Tomato Shells,
    page 53)
4 small slivers of chilled butter
TO SERVE:
sprigs of parsley
1 lemon, quartered

1.  Wash the scallops thoroughly, and divide each one into 4 pieces.
2.  Melt the butter in a saucepan, and add the shallots. Cook gently until transparent.
3.  Add the scallops, wine and brandy, bring to simmering point, then stir in the parsley and breadcrumbs.
4.  Add salt and pepper, then cover and cook very gently for 7 minutes.
5.  Remove from the heat and divide the mixture evenly between 4 buttered scallop shells.
6.  Pipe the Duchesse Potato round the filling in a shell pattern and place a small sliver of chilled butter on the top of each filling.

**TO FREEZE:** Open freeze for 2-3 hours, then pack individually in freezer bags and return to the freezer.

**TO SERVE:** Allow the shells to thaw at room temperature for 3 hours, then place in a preheated oven at 160°C, 325°F, Gas Mark 3 for 25 minutes. Before serving, place under a hot grill to brown the potato. Serve garnished with parsley sprigs and lemon wedges.

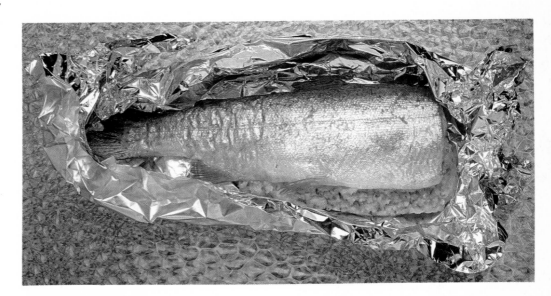

# STUFFED TROUT PARCELS

*Preparation time: 15 minutes*
*Cooking time: 7 minutes*
*Recommended freezer life: 1 month*

STUFFING:
50 g/2 oz butter
175 g/6 oz soft herring roes
1 tablespoon lemon juice
1 teaspoon creamed horseradish
1 tablespoon chopped fresh
    parsley
salt
freshly ground black pepper
pinch of cayenne pepper
2 tablespoons fresh white
    breadcrumbs
4×350 g/12 oz trout, gutted
TO SERVE:
tomato wedges
lemon wedges
sprigs of parsley
Hollandaise Sauce (page 64)

1.  Melt the butter in a saucepan, add the roes, and fry gently for 5 minutes.
2.  Mash the roes gently with a fork. Add the lemon juice, creamed horseradish, parsley, salt, pepper and cayenne pepper. Cook, stirring, for 2 minutes.
3.  Remove from the heat and stir in the breadcrumbs. Allow the stuffing to go cold.
4.  Meanwhile, remove the heads from the trout and take out the backbones. Divide the stuffing between the fish, re-shape the trout, and place each one on a strip of well buttered foil. Wrap each trout with the foil to form a parcel.

**TO FREEZE:** Place in a polythene bag, seal and freeze.

**TO SERVE:** Allow to thaw at room temperature for 3-4 hours. Bake in a preheated oven at 190°C, 375°F, Gas Mark 5 for 35 minutes. Remove the fish from the foil, and place on a serving dish. Garnish with tomato and lemon wedges and parsley sprigs. Serve with Hollandaise Sauce.

**VARIATION:**
The trout may also be stuffed with a Mushroom and Bacon Stuffing (page 65).

# SPECIAL COD PIE

*Preparation time: 30 minutes*
*Cooking time: 1 hour*
*Recommended freezer life: 1 month*

450 g/1 lb cod fillet, skinned
100 g/4 oz peeled prawns
100 g/4 oz button mushrooms
175 ml/6 fl oz dry white wine
120 ml/4 fl oz water
few sprigs of parsley
1 bay leaf
4 black peppercorns
salt
2 egg yolks
1 tablespoon chopped fresh
    parsley
1 teaspoon grated lemon rind
pinch of ground mace
120 ml/4 fl oz double cream,
    lightly beaten
2 egg whites, stiffly whisked
100 g/4 oz frozen shortcrust
    pastry, thawed
1×225 g/7 oz packet frozen puff
    pastry, thawed
**TO SERVE:**
beaten egg

1. Place the cod, prawns and mushrooms in a pan and pour in the wine and water. Add the parsley sprigs, bay leaf, peppercorns and salt. Cover and bring slowly to the boil.
2. Remove the pan from the heat and set aside for 10 minutes.
3. Strain the fish liquor into a small pan, then boil it over a high heat until it is reduced to about 120 ml/4 fl oz.
4. Pound the mushrooms, prawns and about a quarter of the cod together to form a smooth paste. Beat in the egg yolks, chopped parsley, lemon rind and reduced fish liquor. Add the mace and taste and adjust the seasoning.
5. Fold in the cream with the whisked egg whites.
6. Line the base of a 20 cm/8 inch pie plate with the shortcrust pastry and bake it blind in a preheated oven at 200°C, 400°F, Gas Mark 6 for 10 minutes. Allow the pastry to cool slightly.
7. Cover the pastry base with half of the fish mixture, leaving a 2.5 cm/1 inch rim around the edge. Gently break up the remaining cod, spread it over the fish mixture, then finish with the remaining fish mixture.
8. Roll out the puff pastry thinly and use it to top the pie. Seal and scallop the edges, and use any pastry trimmings to make leaves to garnish the pie.

**TO FREEZE:** Open freeze, then place in a polythene bag, seal and return to freezer.

**TO SERVE:** Remove from the polythene bag. Brush the pie with beaten egg and cook in a preheated oven at 190°C, 375°F, Gas Mark 5 for 1 hour.

# SPINACH PARCELS WITH MUSHROOM SAUCE

*Preparation time: 20 minutes*
*Cooking time: 40 minutes*
*Recommended freezer life: 1 month*

8 large spinach leaves, stalks
    removed
450 g/1 lb whiting, skinned and
    filleted
250 ml/8 fl oz milk
1 bouquet garni
1 shallot, peeled
1 small carrot, sliced
rind and juice of ½ lemon
salt
freshly ground black pepper
25 g/1 oz butter
2 tablespoons plain flour
1 tablespoon tomato purée
pinch of ground nutmeg
1 tablespoon cornflour
2 tablespoons water
3 tablespoons double cream
600 ml/1 pint Mushroom Sauce
    (page 58)

1. Blanch the spinach leaves in boiling water for 2 minutes. Drain, and spread the leaves out to dry.
2. To make the filling, put the whiting in a pan with the milk, bouquet garni, shallot, carrot slices, lemon rind and juice and salt and pepper.
3. Poach the fish gently for 10-15 minutes. Strain and reserve the poaching liquor.
4. Flake the fish, and discard the vegetables and herbs.
5. Melt the butter in a saucepan, stir in the flour and cook for 2-3 minutes. Gradually add the reserved fish liquor over a low heat.
6. Stir in the tomato purée and a pinch of nutmeg. Bring to the boil, cover and simmer for 4-5 minutes.
7. Mix the cornflour with the water and add to the sauce. Simmer for 2-3 minutes, then remove from the heat and fold in the fish and cream. Allow the mixture to cool.
8. Divide the fish mixture between the spinach leaves, and fold them up

carefully to form individual parcels.
9. Place the parcels in a buttered foil container or dish, and pour over the Mushroom Sauce.

**TO FREEZE:** Cover and freeze.

**TO SERVE:** Loosen the lid of the container, and, from frozen, place in a preheated oven at 180°C, 350°F, Gas Mark 4 for 45 minutes.

# HADDOCK MAISON

*Preparation time: 30 minutes*
*Cooking time: 1 hour*
*Recommended freezer life: 1 month*

750 g/1½ lb fresh haddock
    fillets, skinned
1 bay leaf
1 garlic clove, crushed
150 ml/¼ pint red wine
65 ml/2½ fl oz water
POTATO BASE:
450 g/1 lb potatoes, peeled
25 g/1 oz butter
1 egg yolk
1 teaspoon French mustard
salt
freshly ground black pepper
SAUCE:
1 green pepper, cored, seeded
    and cut into thin strips
1 red pepper, cored, seeded and
    cut into thin strips
50 g/2 oz butter
2 shallots, peeled and finely
    chopped
25 g/1 oz plain flour
4 tomatoes, skinned, seeded
    and shredded
1 tablespoon cornflour
2 tablespoons water
25 g/1 oz Cheddar cheese, grated
2 tablespoons single cream
salt
freshly ground black pepper
TO SERVE:
2 tablespoons chopped fresh
    parsley

1. Fold the fish fillets in half and place them in a buttered ovenproof dish. Add the bay leaf and garlic, and pour over the red wine and water.
2. Cover the dish with buttered foil and bake in a preheated oven at 160°C, 325°F, Gas Mark 3 for 20-25 minutes.
3. Meanwhile, cut the potatoes into even sized pieces, and boil them until tender.
4. Drain the potatoes well, then mash them and beat in the butter, egg yolk, mustard and salt and pepper. Set aside.
5. Blanch the strips of green and red pepper in boiling salted water for 3 minutes, then drain.
6. Melt the butter in a saucepan and add the shallots. Fry them over a gentle heat until transparent.
7. Stir in the flour and cook for 2-3 minutes.
8. Remove the sauce from the heat, and strain in the liquor from the cooked fish. Stir until the sauce is smooth, then add the peppers and tomatoes. Bring to the boil, stirring well.
9. Mix the cornflour with the water, and stir into the sauce. Continue simmering for 2-3 minutes.
10. Remove the sauce from the heat and stir in the cheese, cream and salt and pepper.
11. Spread the potato mixture over the base of a shallow serving dish or foil container. Arrange the haddock fillets on top and pour over the sauce.

**TO FREEZE:** Allow to go cold, then cover and freeze.

**TO SERVE:** Allow to thaw at room temperature for 5-6 hours. Loosen the lid of the container, and place in a preheated oven at 160°C, 325°F, Gas Mark 3 for 35-40 minutes. Serve garnished with a sprinkling of chopped fresh parsley.

# COD STEAKS WITH PARSLEY & LEMON SAUCE

*Preparation time: 20 minutes*
*Cooking time: 40 minutes*
*Recommended freezer life: 1 month*

4×175 g/6 oz cod steaks
175 ml/6 fl oz milk
175 ml/6 fl oz water
2 parsley sprigs
slice of lemon
salt
freshly ground black pepper
**SAUCE:**
40 g/1½ oz butter
25 g/1 oz plain flour
1 tablespoon cornflour
2 tablespoons water
2 tablespoons finely chopped
    fresh parsley
1 teaspoon grated lemon rind
2 tablespoons lemon juice
pinch of ground mace
120 ml/4 fl oz single cream
**TO SERVE:**
sprigs of parsley
1 lemon, quartered
Duchesse Potatoes (page 53)

1. Place the cod steaks in a buttered shallow ovenproof dish, and pour in the milk and water. Add the parsley sprigs, lemon slice and salt and pepper.
2. Cover the dish with buttered foil, and bake in a preheated oven at 160°C, 325°F, Gas Mark 3 for 25 minutes.
3. Lift out the steaks, and arrange them in a clean ovenproof dish or foil container.
4. Strain the fish liquor, and reserve 350 ml/12 fl oz for the sauce.
5. To make the sauce, melt the butter in a saucepan, and stir in the flour. Cook for 2-3 minutes, then gradually stir in the reserved fish liquor over a low heat.
6. Bring the sauce to the boil.
7. Mix the cornflour with the water, and stir into the sauce. Simmer for 2-3 minutes, then remove from the heat.
8. Add the parsley, lemon rind, lemon juice and mace, then taste and adjust the seasoning. Stir in the cream and pour the sauce over the fish.

**TO FREEZE:** Allow to go cold, then cover and freeze.

**TO SERVE:** Allow to thaw at room temperature for 3-4 hours, then loosen the lid of the freezer container, and place in a preheated oven at 160°C, 325°F, Gas Mark 3 for 25-30 minutes, until heated through. Garnish with parsley sprigs and lemon wedges. Serve with Duchesse Potatoes and buttered peas.

# BAKED POTATOES PROVENCALE

*Preparation time: 20 minutes*
*Cooking time: 1 hour 20 minutes*
*Recommended freezer life: 1 month*

4 large potatoes
25 g/1 oz butter
2 egg yolks
2 tablespoons milk
salt
freshly ground black pepper
**STUFFING:**
25 g/1 oz butter
1 Spanish onion, peeled and
    chopped
175 g/6 oz prawns
1 tablespoon plain flour
225 g/8 oz tomatoes
1 teaspoon chopped fresh
    parsley
salt
freshly ground black pepper
25 g/1 oz cheese, grated

1. Scrub the potatoes then bake them in a preheated oven at 200°C, 400°F, Gas Mark 6 for 45-60 minutes.
2. Slice off the top of each potato and scoop the flesh into a bowl.
3. Mash the flesh well, and beat in the butter, egg yolks, milk and salt and pepper, and set aside.
4. To prepare the stuffing, melt the butter in a pan and gently fry the onion until soft and transparent.
5. Add the prawns, then sprinkle in the flour and cook for 2-3 minutes. Skin, seed and shred the tomatoes, and add the shreds to the pan.
6. Rub the tomato seeds and juices through a sieve, and add to the pan with the chopped parsley. Bring to the boil and cook for 2-3 minutes. Add salt and pepper to taste.
7. Spoon the prawn mixture into the

potato shells and sprinkle the grated cheese over the top.
8. Put the reserved potato mixture into a piping bag with a star nozzle and pipe generous whirls of potato over the stuffing.

**TO FREEZE:** Open freeze for 2-3 hours, then wrap in a freezer bag and return to the freezer.

**TO SERVE:** From frozen, place on a greased baking sheet and cook in a preheated oven at 200°C, 400°F, Gas Mark 6 for 40 minutes. If not frozen, cook the potatoes for only 7-10 minutes. Serve with buttered peas.

# SEAFOOD CRUMBLE

*Serves 6*
*Preparation time: 30 minutes*
*Cooking time: 50 minutes*
*Recommended freezer life: 1 month*

450 g/1 lb smoked haddock
    fillets
450 g/1 lb fresh haddock fillets
40 g/1½ oz butter
1 shallot, peeled and finely
    chopped
25 g/1 oz plain flour
300 ml/½ pint milk
350 g/12 oz prawns, shelled
1 tablespoon lemon juice
salt
freshly ground black pepper
4 tablespoons cornflour
8 tablespoons water
CRUMBLE TOPPING:
175 g/6 oz plain flour
75 g/3 oz butter
75 g/3 oz cheese, grated
pinch of paprika

1. Place the haddock fillets in a buttered ovenproof dish and cover with water. Cover the dish with buttered foil.
2. Place in a preheated oven at 190°C, 375°F, Gas Mark 5 and cook for 30 minutes.
3. Drain, skin, and flake the fish, reserving 300 ml/½ pint of the fish liquor.
4. Melt the butter and gently fry the shallot for 4 minutes. Stir in the flour, and gradually add the milk, bringing back to the boil after each addition. Stir continually.
5. Pour in the reserved fish liquor, bring back to the boil and simmer for 3 minutes.
6. Add the shelled prawns, lemon juice, and salt and pepper. Cover and simmer for 5 minutes.
7. Mix the cornflour and water together, and stir into the mixture.
8. Bring the mixture back to the boil, then remove from the heat and set aside to cool. Stir in the reserved flaked fish.
9. To make the topping, sift the flour into a bowl and rub in the butter and then the grated cheese, until the mixture resembles fine breadcrumbs. Stir in the paprika.
10. Spoon the fish mixture into a large rectangular foil container and sprinkle the crumble topping over the fish.

**TO FREEZE:** Cover and freeze.

**TO SERVE:** Allow to thaw for 4 hours. Place in a preheated oven at 190°C, 375°F, Gas Mark 5 for 45 minutes. Serve with buttered new potatoes and a green salad.

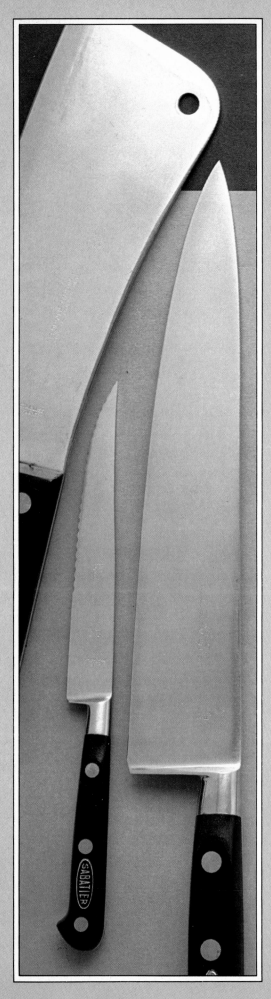

# MEAT & POULTRY

## SPINACH STUFFED BREAST OF LAMB

*Preparation time: 30 minutes*
*Cooking Time: 1 hour 10 minutes*

1×750 g/1½ lb breast or loin of
  lamb, boned

**STUFFING:**
25 g/1 oz ham, finely diced
2 lamb's kidneys, peeled, cored
  and finely chopped
75 g/3 oz fresh spinach, finely
  chopped
25 g/1 oz fresh white
  breadcrumbs
1 small onion, peeled and finely
  chopped
3 tablespoons double cream
salt
freshly ground black pepper
pinch of ground nutmeg

25 g/1 oz butter
1 teaspoon French mustard
1 tablespoon orange juice
2 tablespoons redcurrant jelly
**TO SERVE:**
Demi-Glace Sauce (page 61)

1. Arrange the breast or loin of lamb flat on a board and trim off the excess fat.
2. Combine all the stuffing ingredients together, and spread the stuffing over the lamb.
3. Roll up the joint, and secure it with string.
4. Place the joint in a roasting tin, and spread the butter over it. Sprinkle over a little salt and pepper, then loosely cover with buttered greaseproof paper or some foil.
5. Cook in a preheated oven at 160°C, 325°F, Gas Mark 3 for 45 minutes.
6. Put the mustard, orange juice and redcurrant jelly in a small pan, and warm them over a low heat until the jelly has melted.
7. Remove the covering from the joint, and pour over the redcurrant glaze.
8. Increase the oven heat to 200°C, 400°F, Gas Mark 6 and cook the joint for a further 10-15 minutes, basting it with the glaze 2 or 3 times during the cooking period.

**TO FREEZE:** Allow to go cold, then pack in a polythene bag and freeze.

**TO SERVE:** Allow to thaw at room temperature for 5-6 hours. Serve cold for a picnic or buffet meal, or wrap in buttered foil and heat the joint gently through in a preheated oven at 160°C, 325°F, Gas Mark 3 for 35 minutes. Serve with Demi-Glace Sauce.

**VARIATION:**
Replace the stuffing with Apricot and Almond Stuffing (page 65), or Apple and Raisin Stuffing (page 65).

# GLAZED LEG OF LAMB WITH PORT & HONEY

*Serves 8-10*
*Preparation time: 20 minutes, plus marinating*
*Cooking time: 2¼ hours*
*Recommended freezer life: 4 months*

1×1¾ kg/4 lb leg of lamb
2 garlic cloves, peeled and cut into strips
1 large onion, peeled and chopped
2 large carrots, peeled and chopped
6 black peppercorns
sprigs of fresh rosemary
120 ml/4 fl oz port
175 ml/6 fl oz water
1 tablespoon tomato purée
1 teaspoon anchovy essence
2 tablespoons clear honey
salt
freshly ground black pepper

This dish is very useful for a buffet lunch or special picnic.

1. Make slits in the skin of the lamb, and push the garlic strips into the slits.
2. Put the onion, carrot, peppercorns and rosemary sprigs in a large casserole and place the joint on top.
3. Blend together the port, water, tomato purée and anchovy essence and pour it over the meat.
4. Cover and leave in a cool place for 3-4 hours, turning the meat occasionally.
5. Cook the casserole in a preheated oven at 180°C, 350°F, Gas Mark 4 for 1½-2 hours.
6. Remove the joint and place it in a roasting pan. Strain the liquid from the casserole into a saucepan, discarding the vegetables, and add the honey.
7. Reduce the liquid by boiling over a high heat until approximately 120 ml/ 4 fl oz remain. Pour over the joint.
8. Increase the oven temperature to 200°C, 400°F, Gas Mark 6, and cook the joint for 20-30 minutes, basting frequently. Serve immediately or follow freezing instructions.

**TO FREEZE:** Allow to go cold. Open freeze for 6 hours, then wrap in a polythene bag, seal and return to the freezer.

**TO SERVE:** Allow to thaw at room temperature for at least 12 hours. Carve and serve cold.

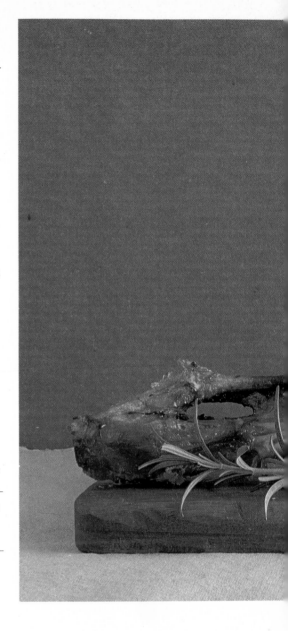

TWO RECIPES FOR COOKING PREVIOUSLY FROZEN LEGS OF LAMB

# FRENCH ROAST LAMB

*Preparation time: 20 minutes*
*Cooking time: 1¾ hours*

1×1¾ kg/4 lb leg of lamb, thawed
3 garlic cloves, peeled and cut into 4 lengthwise
75 g/3 oz butter, softened
salt
freshly ground black pepper

1. Make 12 small incisions in the skin of the lamb, and push a piece of garlic into each.
2. Spread the butter over the joint, and sprinkle with salt and pepper. Place the joint in a roasting tin, and cover it with foil.
3. Cook in a preheated oven at 180°C, 350°F, Gas Mark 4 for 1¼ hours.
4. Remove the foil and baste the meat with the pan juices.
5. Continue cooking for a further 30 minutes to brown the skin.
6. Serve the lamb, accompanied by the buttery pan juices.

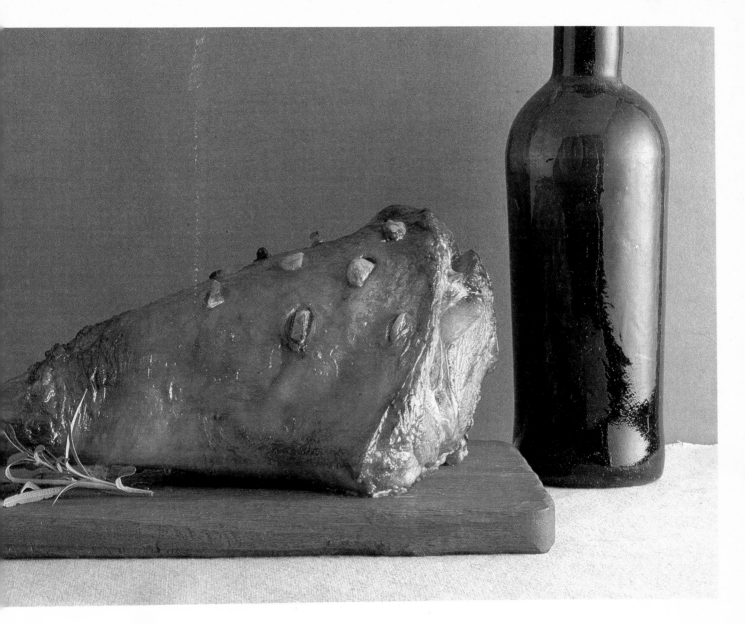

# WINTER BRAISED LAMB

*Preparation time: 20 minutes*
*Cooking time: 2½ hours*

225 g/8 oz carrots, peeled and
  diced
1 onion, peeled and diced
3 celery sticks, diced
225 g/8 oz turnips, peeled and
  diced
1×1¾ kg/4 lb leg of lamb,
  thawed
1×400 g/14 oz can consommé
salt
freshly ground black pepper

1. Put the carrot, onion, celery and turnip in the bottom of a roasting tin, and place the leg of lamb on top.
2. Pour the consommé over the lamb, and sprinkle with salt and pepper. Cover the joint with foil.
3. Cook in a preheated oven at 180°C, 350°F, Gas Mark 4 for 2 hours. Remove the foil from the joint and continue cooking for a further 30 minutes to brown the skin.
4. Place the joint on a carving dish, and liquidize the vegetables and pan juices in an electric blender.
5. Reheat the sauce, adding a little water if it is too thick. Serve the sauce hot with the lamb.

# STUFFED SHOULDER OF LAMB EN CROUTE

*Serves 6*
*Preparation time: 50 minutes, plus*
*  making stuffing*
*Cooking time: 1½ hours*
*Recommended freezer life: 4 months*

1 × 1¾ kg/4 lb shoulder of lamb,
  boned
1 quantity Apricot and Almond
  Stuffing (page 65)
2 tablespoons oil
1 × 375 g/13 oz packet frozen
  puff pastry, thawed
**TO SERVE:**
1 egg, beaten

1. Put the boned shoulder on a board. If the butcher has not already done so, slit a pocket in the meat to hold the stuffing, taking care not to pierce the outer skin.
2. Fill the pocket with the apricot and almond stuffing, and roll up the joint.
3. Sew up the edges using a trussing needle and kitchen string. Push the flap through the hole left by the removed bone, and secure with more string, taking care to keep a good rectangular shape.
4. Transfer the joint to a roasting tin, and brush it with oil.
5. Cook in a preheated oven at 160°C, 325°F, Gas Mark 3 for 1½ hours. Allow to go cold.
6. Roll out the pastry, then wrap it around the joint, sealing the edges well. Make criss-cross indentations over the

surface of the pastry, and use any trimmings to make pastry leaves to garnish.

**TO FREEZE:** Open freeze for 4-5 hours, then wrap in a polythene bag, seal and return to the freezer.

**TO SERVE:** Allow to thaw for at least 8 hours, or overnight. Place on a baking sheet and brush with beaten egg. Cook in a preheated oven at 200°C, 400°F, Gas Mark 6 for 15 minutes, then lower the heat to 160°C, 325°F, Gas Mark 3, and continue cooking for a further 45 minutes.

# LAMB WITH YOGURT & DILL

*Preparation time: 20 minutes*
*Cooking time: 2 hours*

50 g/2 oz butter
1½ kg/3 lb boned shoulder of
   lamb, cubed
3 tablespoons plain flour
450 g/1 lb courgettes, sliced
bunch of spring onions, sliced
2 tablespoons chopped fresh dill
1 tablespoon chopped fresh
   mint
salt
freshly ground black pepper
300 ml/½ pint chicken stock
2 tablespoons cornflour
6 tablespoons water
**TO SERVE:**
150 ml/¼ pint plain unsweetened
   yogurt

1. Melt the butter in a large saucepan.
2. Toss the meat in the flour, then add to the pan and fry for 10 minutes, stirring occasionally.
3. Add the courgettes and spring onions and fry for a further 15 minutes.
4. Stir in the dill, mint, salt, pepper and stock. Cover and simmer for 1½ hours.
5. Taste and adjust the seasoning. Mix the cornflour with the water and stir into the lamb. Bring to the boil and simmer for 2-3 minutes.

**TO FREEZE:** Pour into a foil container and allow to go cold. Cover and freeze.

**TO SERVE:** Bring slowly to the boil and stir in the yogurt.

# IRISH STEW

*Preparation time: 20 minutes*
*Cooking time: 2 hours 40 minutes*
*Recommended freezer life: 4 months*

50 g/2 oz dripping
1 kg/2 lb stewing lamb
2 onions, peeled and sliced
600 ml/1 pint chicken stock
1 bouquet garni
salt
freshly ground black pepper
2 tablespoons pearl barley
450 g/1 lb potatoes, peeled and
   cut into chunks
1 tablespoon chopped fresh
   parsley

1. Heat the dripping in a large frying pan, and quickly fry the meat until it is lightly browned on all sides. Remove the meat to a deep ovenproof dish.
2. Fry the onions in the remaining pan juices until lightly browned, then add them to the meat.
3. Pour in the stock and add the bouquet garni, salt and pepper. Sprinkle the barley over the meat.
4. Cover and cook in a preheated oven at 160°C, 325°F, Gas Mark 3 for 1½ hours, stirring the stew occasionally.
5. Add the potatoes to the stew, and continue cooking for a further 30-40 minutes, or until the meat is tender and the potatoes are cooked. Stir in the parsley.

**TO FREEZE:** Allow to go cold, then remove any excess fat from the surface, and discard the bouquet garni. Spoon the stew into a rigid container, cover and freeze.

**TO SERVE:** Allow to thaw at room temperature for 5-6 hours, then reheat gently in a large saucepan, stirring occasionally, taking care not to break up the potato chunks.

# LAMB CUTLETS WELLINGTON

*Preparation time: 30 minutes*
*Cooking time: 40 minutes*
*Recommended freezer life: 4 months*

4 best end of neck lamb cutlets
25 g/1 oz butter
1 medium onion, peeled and
    finely chopped
175 g/6 oz button mushrooms,
    finely chopped
pinch of ground nutmeg
1 tablespoon chopped fresh
    parsley
salt
freshly ground black pepper
100 g/4 oz liver pâté
1 tablespoon single cream
1×200 g/7 oz packet frozen puff
    pastry, thawed
1 egg, beaten
TO SERVE:
1 egg, beaten
sprigs of watercress

1. Trim the excess fat from the cutlets, and scrape the last 7.5 cm/3 inches of the bones clean with a sharp knife.
2. Melt the butter in a frying pan, and quickly brown the cutlets on both sides to seal in the juices.
3. Remove the cutlets from the pan, and set them aside to cool.
4. Stir the onion and mushrooms into the pan juices, and gently fry for 20-25 minutes until they are cooked through, and most of the liquid has evaporated.
5. Remove the pan from the heat, and stir in the nutmeg, parsley, and salt and pepper. Set aside to cool.
6. Beat the pâté with the cream, and spread this mixture over one side of the 'eyes' of meat on the cutlets.
7. Roll out the pastry thinly, and cut it into four triangles. Divide the mushroom mixture equally and place in the centre of each of the triangles.
8. Lay the lamb cutlets pâté side down on top of the mushroom mixture. Fold the sides of the pastry triangles over the cutlets, trimming off any excess pastry, and seal the parcels with beaten egg.
9. Turn the cutlets over, and garnish the top of each one with leaves, made from the pastry trimmings.

**TO FREEZE:** Open freeze for 2 hours, then pack in a polythene bag, seal and return to the freezer.

**TO SERVE:** Allow to thaw at room temperature for 1½-2 hours. Place on a baking sheet, and brush with beaten egg. Cook in a preheated oven at 200°C, 400°F, Gas Mark 6 for 15-20 minutes, until they are risen and golden brown. Place the cutlets on a serving dish, and garnish with watercress sprigs.

# SPICY LAMB CHOPS

*Preparation time: 30 minutes*
*Cooking time: 1 hour 10 minutes*
*Recommended freezer life: 4 months*

2 tablespoons oil
4 lamb chump chops
1 Spanish onion, peeled and
  sliced
1 green pepper, cored, seeded
  and sliced
1 teaspoon ground cumin
1 teaspoon chilli powder
1 tablespoon apricot jam
1 teaspoon tomato purée
1 teaspoon Worcestershire
  sauce
1 tablespoon wine vinegar
300 ml/½ pint chicken stock
4 tomatoes, peeled, seeded and
  chopped
50 g/2 oz salted peanuts
salt
freshly ground black pepper
1 tablespoon cornflour
2 tablespoons water

Chilli powder should be used cautiously since it is very hot, and the strength of it varies according to the manufacturer.

1. Heat the oil in a large frying pan, and quickly fry the chops on both sides, then remove them to a large casserole.
2. Fry the onion and pepper in the pan juices until lightly browned.
3. Add the cumin and chilli powder to the onions, and cook over a high heat for 2-3 minutes, stirring constantly.
4. Lower the heat, and add the apricot jam, tomato purée, Worcestershire sauce, vinegar, stock, tomatoes and peanuts to the pan, and bring to the boil. Add salt and pepper, then pour over the chops.
5. Cover and cook in a preheated oven at 160°C, 325°F, Gas Mark 3 for 40 minutes.
6. Remove the chops from the casserole and arrange them in a deep serving dish or foil container.
7. Mix the cornflour and water together, and stir into the sauce. Cook, stirring, until it is thickened, then pour over the chops.

**TO FREEZE:** Allow to go cold, then cover and freeze.

**TO SERVE:** Loosen the lid and put the chops and sauce, from frozen, in a preheated oven at 160°C, 325°F, Gas Mark 3 for 50-60 minutes, stirring occasionally. Serve with boiled rice.

**VARIATION:**
Use neck or loin of lamb, or pork chops.

# LAMB CHOPS WITH ORANGE

*Preparation time: 20 minutes*
*Cooking time: 50 minutes*
*Recommended freezer life: 4 months*

4 lamb loin chops
25 g/1 oz butter
50 g/2 oz shallots, peeled and
  chopped
rind and juice of 1 large orange
250 ml/8 fl oz chicken stock
2 tablespoons redcurrant jelly
1 tablespoon chopped fresh
  parsley
25 g/1 oz red lentils
½ teaspoon ground nutmeg
salt
freshly ground black pepper
2 teaspoons cornflour
2 tablespoons water
**TO SERVE:**
bunch of watercress

1. Trim the excess fat from the chops and form them into rounds.
2. Melt the butter in a heavy pan, add the chops and fry until golden brown on both sides. Remove the chops from the pan.
3. Add the chopped shallot to the pan and fry briskly for a few minutes, then stir in the orange rind and juice, stock, redcurrant jelly, parsley, lentils, nutmeg, salt and pepper.
4. Return the chops to the pan, coating them well with the sauce. Cover and simmer gently for 20-25 minutes.
5. Remove the chops from the pan and place them in a freezer container.
6. Mix the cornflour with the water, stir into the sauce and simmer for 2-3 minutes, stirring occasionally. Pour the sauce over the chops.

**TO FREEZE:** Allow to go cold, cover and freeze.

**TO SERVE:** Loosen the lid, and place in a preheated oven at 180°C, 350°F, Gas Mark 4 for 50-60 minutes. Arrange the chops on a serving dish and pour the sauce over. Serve garnished with watercress.

**VARIATION:**
Neck or loin of lamb, or pork chops can be used to make this dish.

# SUMMER BEEF CASSEROLE

*Serves 6*
*Preparation time: 30 minutes*
*Cooking time: 2 hours 20 minutes*
*Recommended freezer life: 4 months*

25 g/1 oz butter
2 tablespoons oil
1 kg/2 lb stewing steak, cut into
  2.5 cm/1 inch cubes
175 g/6 oz small onions, peeled
225 g/8 oz young carrots, peeled
1 tablespoon plain flour
1 tablespoon tomato purée
450 ml/¾ pint beef stock
1 bay leaf
sprig of parsley
sprig of marjoram
salt
freshly ground black pepper
175 g/6 oz French beans, cut
  into 2.5 cm/1 inch lengths
175 g/6 oz courgettes, thickly
  sliced
75 g/3 oz small button
  mushrooms
**TO SERVE:**
4 tablespoons double cream
½ teaspoon paprika

1. Melt the butter and oil in a frying pan, add the meat and fry quickly until browned on all sides. Remove the meat from the pan to a large casserole.
2. Add the onions and carrots to the pan, and cook until lightly browned, stirring constantly.
3. Stir in the flour and tomato purée, then gradually add the stock, stirring well. Add the herbs, and salt and pepper.
4. Pour the mixture over the meat.
5. Cover and cook in a preheated oven at 160°C, 325°F, Gas Mark 3 for 1¼-1½ hours.
6. Add the beans, courgettes and mushrooms to the casserole. Continue cooking for 30 minutes, or until the meat is tender.

**TO FREEZE:** Allow to go cold, pour into a rigid container, cover and freeze.

**TO SERVE:** Loosen the lid and place in a preheated oven at 180°C, 350°C, Gas Mark 4 for 50-60 minutes, stirring occasionally. Transfer to a serving dish and trickle over the cream. Sprinkle with paprika and serve at once.

**VARIATION:**
For a winter casserole, replace the courgettes and beans with peeled and diced turnips and swedes.

# HUNGARIAN GOULASH

*Serves 6*
*Preparation time: 30 minutes*
*Cooking time: 2½ hours*
*Recommended freezer life: 4 months*

3 tablespoons oil
1 kg/2 lb stewing steak, cut into
  2.5 cm/1 inch cubes
2 Spanish onions, peeled and
  sliced
1 green pepper, cored, seeded
  and thinly sliced
1 red pepper, cored, seeded and
  thinly sliced
2 tablespoons paprika
1×400 g/14 oz can tomatoes
300 ml/½ pint beef stock
1 teaspoon dried thyme
1 teaspoon dried marjoram
salt
freshly ground black pepper
3 tablespoons cornflour
150 ml/¼ pint plain
  unsweetened yogurt
**TO SERVE:**
2 tablespoons plain
  unsweetened yogurt

1. Heat the oil in a frying pan, and quickly fry the meat until lightly browned on all sides. Remove the meat to a large casserole.
2. Add the onions and peppers to the pan and gently fry them until soft and lightly browned.
3. Stir in the paprika and cook for a further 2-3 minutes.
4. Stir in the tomatoes, stock, herbs and salt and pepper. Pour the mixture over the meat.
5. Cover and cook the goulash in a preheated oven at 180°C, 350°F, Gas Mark 4 for about 2 hours, or until the meat is tender.
6. Blend the cornflour with the yogurt, and stir into the casserole. Return the dish to the oven for 5 minutes to thicken the goulash.

**TO FREEZE:** Pour into a rigid container. Allow to go cold, cover and freeze.

**TO SERVE:** Allow to thaw at room temperature for 3-4 hours. Turn the

goulash into a casserole, and place in a preheated oven at 180°C, 350°F, Gas Mark 4 for 45 minutes, stirring occasionally. Trickle over the yogurt before serving.

**VARIATION:**
Use lean lamb or veal.

# MILD BEEF CURRY

*Serves 6*
*Preparation time: 20 minutes*
*Cooking time: 2 hours 20 minutes*
*Recommended freezer life: 3 months*

25 g/1 oz butter
2 tablespoons oil
1 kg/2 lb stewing steak, cut into
  2½ cm/1 inch cubes
1 large onion, peeled and diced
100 g/4 oz carrots, peeled and
  diced
1 teaspoon curry paste
1 teaspoon ground turmeric
1 teaspoon ground coriander
1 teaspoon ground cumin
1 teaspoon chilli seasoning
1 large cooking apple, peeled,
  cored and diced
1 teaspoon lemon juice
1 tablespoon chutney
75 g/3 oz sultanas
50 g/2 oz cashew nuts
300 ml/½ pint beef stock
1 bay leaf
salt
freshly ground black pepper
2 tablespoons cornflour
2 tablespoons water
TO SERVE:
cooked rice
poppadums
sliced bananas
chutney

If you prefer a hotter curry more curry
paste may be added. The chilli seasoning
should be used cautiously as it is
extremely hot, and varies in strength
according to the manufacturer.

1.  Melt the butter and oil in a frying pan,
add the meat and fry quickly until
browned on all sides. Remove the meat
from the pan.
2.  Add the onion and carrot to the
remaining fat and fry until golden brown.
3.  Add the curry paste with all the spices
and cook for 2-3 minutes, stirring
constantly.
4.  Add the apple, lemon juice, chutney,
sultanas and cashew nuts.
5.  Return the meat to the pan, pour over
the stock, and add the bay leaf, salt and
pepper.
6.  Cover and simmer gently, stirring
occasionally, for 2 hours, or until the meat
is tender.
7.  Mix together the cornflour and water,
stir into the curry and simmer for 2-3
minutes.

**TO FREEZE:**  Allow to go cold, spoon into a
rigid container, cover and freeze.

**TO SERVE:**  Loosen the lid and place in a
preheated oven at 180°C, 350°F, Gas Mark
4 for 50-60 minutes. Serve on a bed of
rice, accompanied by poppadums, sliced
bananas and chutney.

# SPANISH BEEF

*Serves 6-8*
*Preparation time: 20 minutes*
*Cooking time: 2 hours 20 minutes*
*Recommended freezer life: 4 months*

2 tablespoons oil
1 kg/2 lb stewing steak, cut into
  2.5 cm/1 inch cubes
1 large onion, peeled and sliced
1 garlic clove, crushed
2 red peppers, cored, seeded
  and sliced
1×150 g/5 oz can tomato purée
1 teaspoon sugar
450 ml/¾ pint beef stock
½ teaspoon mustard seeds
1 teaspoon dried oregano
salt
freshly ground black pepper
450 g/1 lb tomatoes, skinned
  and chopped
1-2 tablespoons cornflour
4 tablespoons water
TO SERVE:
croûtons
chopped fresh parsley

1.  Heat the oil in a frying pan and quickly
fry the meat until lightly browned on all
sides. Remove the meat to a large
flameproof casserole.
2.  Add the onion and garlic to the pan
and fry gently for 3-4 minutes.
3.  Add the peppers and continue frying
for 2 minutes, stirring constantly.
4.  Stir in the tomato purée, sugar and
stock. Add the mustard seeds, oregano,
salt and pepper.
5.  Bring the sauce to the boil, then pour it
over the meat in the casserole. Cover and
simmer gently for 1½ hours, or until the
meat is tender.
6.  Add the tomatoes to the casserole and
bring back to the boil. Mix the cornflour
with the water, stir into the casserole and
simmer for 2-3 minutes, stirring
occasionally.

**TO FREEZE:**  Allow to go cold. Pour into a
rigid foil container, cover and freeze.

**TO SERVE:**  Loosen the lid and place in a
preheated oven at 180°C, 350°F, Gas Mark
4 for 50-60 minutes, stirring occasionally.
Pour into a serving dish and garnish
with croûtons.

**VARIATION:**
Use lamb chops instead of stewing steak.

# STEAK, KIDNEY & MUSHROOM PIE

*Serves 6*
*Preparation time: 20 minutes*
*Cooking time: 1 hour 50 minutes*
*Recommended freezer life: 4 months*

50 g/2 oz butter
2 tablespoons oil
500 g/1¼ lb stewing steak, cut into 2.5 cm/1 inch cubes
350 g/12 oz kidneys, skinned, cored and thinly sliced
1 onion, peeled and thinly sliced
1 tablespoon sherry
2 teaspoons Worcestershire sauce
175 ml/6 fl oz beef stock
½ teaspoon dried marjoram
½ teaspoon dried thyme
pinch of ground cloves
salt
freshly ground black pepper
175 g/6 oz button mushrooms, sliced
1 tablespoon cornflour
3 tablespoons water
1×335 g/13 oz packet frozen puff or shortcrust pastry, thawed
1 egg, beaten
**TO SERVE:**
1 egg, beaten

1. Heat the butter and oil in a frying pan and quickly fry the meat until lightly browned on all sides. Remove the meat to a large casserole.
2. Add the onion to the pan, and fry gently until soft.
3. Stir in the sherry, Worcestershire sauce, stock, marjoram, thyme, ground cloves, and salt and pepper.
4. Pour the mixture over the meat in the casserole.
5. Cover and cook in a preheated oven at 160°C, 325°F, Gas Mark 3 for 1½ hours.
6. Stir in the mushrooms. Blend the cornflour with the water and stir into the casserole. Return it to the oven for 5 minutes, to thicken the mixture.
7. Allow to go cold, then transfer the mixture to a large enamel or foil pie dish. Roll out the pastry, and use it to cover the pie, sealing the edges well with beaten egg. Use any pastry trimmings to make leaves for the pie top.

**TO FREEZE:** Open freeze until the pastry is hard, then wrap in a polythene bag, seal and return to the freezer.

**TO SERVE:** Allow to thaw for 4-6 hours in the refrigerator, then brush with beaten egg, and cook in a preheated oven at 200°C, 400°F, Gas Mark 6 for 20-25 minutes, or until the pastry is well risen and golden brown. Lower the heat to 180°C, 350°F, Gas Mark 4 and cook for a further 30 minutes.

# COTTAGE PIE

*Preparation time: 20 minutes*
*Cooking time: 1 hour*
*Recommended freezer life: 4 months*

1 tablespoon oil
1 onion, peeled and chopped
450 g/1 lb minced beef
1×225 g/8 oz can tomatoes
1 tablespoon tomato purée
1 teaspoon dried thyme
½ teaspoon mustard powder
salt
freshly ground black pepper
1 tablespoon cornflour
2 tablespoons water
25 g/1 oz butter
225 g/8 oz button mushrooms, sliced
1 tablespoon chopped fresh parsley
350 g/12 oz cooked potato, mashed and seasoned
15 g/½ oz Cheddar cheese, grated

1. Heat the oil in a large pan, add the onion and fry gently until light golden.
2. Stir in the minced beef, and continue cooking until the meat is lightly browned.
3. Stir in the tomatoes and their juice, tomato purée, thyme, mustard powder, salt and pepper, then bring to the boil. Cover and simmer for 25 minutes, stirring occasionally.
4. Mix the cornflour with the water and stir into the mixture. Simmer for a further 3-4 minutes, then remove from the heat and set aside.
5. Melt the butter in a small pan, add the mushrooms and fry gently for 2-3 minutes. Stir in the parsley, then allow them to cool.
6. Spoon half the meat mixture into a 1.2 litre/2 pint pie dish or foil container, then cover with the mushroom mixture.
7. Spoon over the remaining meat mixture, then top the pie with the mashed potato.

8. Smooth the surface of the potato, then make a pattern on the top with a fork. Sprinkle the pie with grated cheese.

**TO FREEZE:** Open freeze for 3-4 hours, then cover and return to the freezer.

**TO SERVE:** Uncover and, from frozen, bake in a preheated oven at 160°C, 325°F, Gas Mark 3 for 1 hour. If not frozen, bake for only 35-40 minutes. Put under a preheated hot grill to brown the top of the pie, and serve immediately.

# PICNIC PASTIES

*Makes 6*
*Preparation time: 40 minutes*
*Cooking time: 40 minutes*
*Recommended freezer life: 4 months*

350 g/12 oz plain flour
175 g/6 oz butter, cut into pieces
1 egg yolk
5 tablespoons cold water
FILLING:
450 g/1 lb minced beef
1 onion, peeled and finely
   chopped
1 large carrot, peeled and grated
1 beef stock cube, dissolved in 3
   tablespoons hot water
1 tablespoon chopped fresh
   parsley
salt
freshly ground black pepper
1 medium potato, peeled,
   halved and thinly sliced
1 egg, beaten, to seal and glaze

1. To make the pastry, sift the flour into a bowl, and rub in the butter until the mixture resembles fine breadcrumbs.
2. Add the egg yolk and water, mixing together with a round bladed knife.
3. Lightly knead the mixture into a ball, then place it in the refrigerator.
4. To make the filling, mix together all the filling ingredients, except the potato slices.
5. Divide the pastry into 6 equal pieces and roll out each piece.
6. Place a 15 cm/6 inch diameter saucepan lid on each piece, and cut around it to form a neat circle of pastry. Remove the trimmings and set them aside.
7. Divide the meat mixture into 6, and place one portion on each circle of pastry.
8. Use the potato slices to form an overlapping wall around the meat.
9. Brush the pastry edges with beaten egg, draw up the pastry over the meat and crimp the edges together.
10. Roll out the pastry trimmings and use them to form the initials of the family or friends and stick the initials on the sides of the pasties with beaten egg.
11. Place the pasties on a baking sheet, and brush with beaten egg.
12. Cook in a preheated oven at 200°C, 400°F, Gas Mark 6 for 20 minutes. Lower the heat to 160°C, 325°F, Gas Mark 3 and continue cooking for 20 minutes.

**TO FREEZE:** Allow to go cold, then pack into a polythene bag, seal and freeze.

**TO SERVE:** From frozen, place the pasties in a preheated oven at 180°C, 350°F, Gas Mark 4 for 35-40 minutes. Serve hot with vegetables or cold for a picnic.

# LASAGNE

*Preparation time: 30 minutes*
*Cooking time: 1 hour 10 minutes*
*Recommended freezer life: 4 months*

1 tablespoon oil
50 g/2 oz carrots, diced
50 g/2 oz onions, peeled and
    diced
100 g/4 oz bacon, rind removed
    and diced
450 g/1 lb minced beef
1×225 g/8 oz can tomatoes
1 tablespoon tomato purée
1 teaspoon French mustard
2 teaspoons Worcestershire
    sauce
1 teaspoon caster sugar
salt
freshly ground black pepper
1 tablespoon cornflour
3 tablespoons water
salt
2 tablespoons oil
100 g/4 oz lasagne
75 g/3 oz ricotta or cottage
    cheese
175 g/6 oz fresh spinach,
    cooked and well drained
**TOPPING:**
300 ml/½ pint Special Mornay
    Sauce (page 60)
1 tablespoon grated Cheddar
    cheese
1 tablespoon grated Parmesan
    cheese

1. Heat the oil in a pan, add the carrots, onions and bacon and fry gently for 5 minutes.
2. Add the minced beef and continue cooking, stirring occasionally, until the meat is browned.
3. Stir in the tomatoes, tomato purée, mustard, Worcestershire sauce, sugar, salt and pepper. Simmer for 30 minutes.
4. Mix the cornflour with the water, and stir into the sauce. Cook, stirring, for 3-4 minutes, then remove from the heat and allow to go cold.
5. Fill a large saucepan with water, add salt and the oil.
6. Bring the water to the boil, and cook the pieces of lasagne for 12 minutes, making sure they do not stick together while cooking.
7. Drain the lasagne and pat dry with kitchen paper.

8. Grease a 1.75 litre/3 pint ovenproof dish or foil container, and place a layer of lasagne in the bottom of the dish. Cover the lasagne with a layer of meat sauce, then a thin layer of ricotta or cottage cheese, followed by a layer of spinach.
9. Continue layering until the 3 items are used up, finishing with a layer of lasagne.
10. Pour the Mornay Sauce over the top and sprinkle over the grated Cheddar and Parmesan cheese.

**TO FREEZE:** Allow to go cold, then cover and freeze.

**TO SERVE:** Uncover and, from frozen, place in a preheated oven at 160°C, 325°F, Gas Mark 3 for 1 hour. If not frozen, cook the lasagne for only 30-35 minutes. Brown the top of the lasagne under a preheated hot grill and serve immediately.

# INDONESIAN STUFFED PEPPERS

*Preparation time: 30 minutes*
*Cooking time: 1 hour*
*Recommended freezer life: 4 months*

6 large green peppers
40 g/1½ oz butter
1 Spanish onion, peeled and
  finely chopped
4 rashers streaky bacon, rind
  removed, diced
450 g/1 lb minced beef
2 teaspoons curry paste
1 tablespoon tomato purée
40 g/1½ oz salted peanuts
40 g/1½ oz sultanas
1 teaspoon soy sauce
1 tablespoon chopped fresh
  parsley
1 teaspoon dried marjoram
300 ml/½ pint beef stock
salt
freshly ground black pepper
2 tablespoons cornflour
4 tablespoons water
50 g/2 oz cooked rice
2 tablespoons double cream
TO SERVE:
300 ml/½ pint Demi-Glace
  Sauce (page 61)

1. Cut off and reserve the tops of the peppers.
2. Carefully remove the cores and seeds from the peppers, then blanch them with the tops in boiling salted water for 10 minutes. Drain and set them aside.
3. Melt the butter in a pan, add the onion and fry gently until soft and transparent.
4. Increase the heat and stir in the bacon and minced beef. Fry until the meat is browned, stirring occasionally.
5. Stir in the curry paste, and continue cooking for 2-3 minutes.
6. Add the tomato purée, peanuts, sultanas, soy sauce, chopped parsley, marjoram, stock and salt and pepper, and cook for 7-8 minutes.
7. Mix the cornflour with the water, stir into the mixture and continue cooking for 2-3 minutes.
8. Remove from the heat and stir in the cooked rice and cream.
9. Stuff the peppers with the meat mixture and place the reserved lids on top of them.

TO FREEZE: Allow to go cold, then pack together tightly in a rigid container, cover and freeze.

TO SERVE: Allow to thaw at room temperature for 6 hours. Pour the Demi-Glace Sauce into a shallow earthenware dish, and stand the peppers in the sauce. Cover with foil, and cook in a preheated oven at 180°C, 350°F, Gas Mark 4 for 35-40 minutes, basting occasionally with the sauce. Serve with a green salad and crusty French bread.

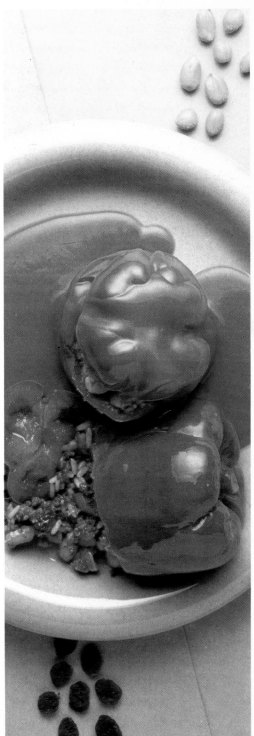

# ITALIAN MEAT SAUCE

*Preparation time: 25 minutes*
*Cooking time: 2¾ hours*
*Recommended freezer life: 4 months*

3 tablespoons oil
1 Spanish onion, peeled and
  diced
1 small green pepper, cored,
  seeded and diced
450 g/1 lb minced beef
2 garlic cloves, crushed
1×400 g/14 oz can tomatoes or
  450 g/1 lb fresh tomatoes,
  skinned and chopped
3 tablespoons tomato purée
150 ml/¼ pint red wine
150 ml/¼ pint beef stock
2 teaspoons dried oregano
1-2 teaspoons caster sugar
2 bay leaves
salt
freshly ground black pepper
100 g/4 oz button mushrooms,
  sliced

To serve with all types of pasta.

1. Heat the oil in a saucepan, add the onion and green pepper and fry gently until the onion is soft and light golden.
2. Stir in the minced beef, and continue cooking until the meat is browned.
3. Add the garlic, tomatoes, tomato purée, wine, stock, oregano, sugar, bay leaves and salt and pepper. Simmer gently, uncovered, for 2 hours, stirring occasionally.
4. Stir in the mushrooms, cover and simmer for a further 30 minutes.

TO FREEZE: Allow to go cold. Pour into a rigid container, cover and freeze.

TO SERVE: Turn the frozen sauce into a pan, and thaw over a low heat for about 20 minutes, stirring from time to time. Bring to the boil and serve.

# CIDERED PORK CHOP PARCELS

*Preparation time: 10 minutes*
*Cooking time: 35 minutes*
*Recommended freezer life: 4 months*

25 g/2 oz butter
2 tablespoons oil
4 × 225 g/8 oz pork chops, trimmed
seasoned flour
4 pineapple rings, fresh or canned
4 tablespoons cider
salt
freshly ground black pepper
4 fresh sage leaves

1. Heat the butter and the oil together in a heavy pan. Coat the chops with the seasoned flour, add them to the pan and quickly fry on both sides until brown.
2. Remove the chops from the pan, and place each one on an individual square of buttered foil.
3. Put a pineapple ring on top of each chop, and pour 1 tablespoon of cider over each. Add salt and pepper, and place a sage leaf on top of each chop. Fold the foil around to form 4 parcels and place them on a baking sheet.
4. Cook the parcels in a preheated oven at 200°C, 400°F, Gas Mark 6 for 25 minutes.

TO FREEZE: Allow to go cold, wrap in a polythene bag, seal and freeze.

TO SERVE: Allow to thaw at room temperature for 4-5 hours. Place in a preheated oven at 200°C, 400°F, Gas Mark 6 for 20 minutes, or on a barbecue. Serve with baked potatoes and a green salad.

# MEDALLIONS OF PORK WITH ORANGE & GINGER

*Preparation time: 20 minutes*
*Cooking time: 30 minutes*
*Recommended freezer life: 4 months*

2 pork tenderloin
2 oranges
50 g/2 oz butter
100 g/4 oz soft brown sugar
1 tablespoon syrup from preserved ginger
1 tablespoon cornflour
4 tablespoons wine vinegar
150 ml/¼ pint chicken stock
salt
freshly ground black pepper
25 g/1 oz preserved ginger, thinly sliced
TO SERVE:
1 orange, peeled and sliced

1. Cut the tenderloins into 2.5 cm/1 inch thick slices, and lay them between two sheets of greaseproof paper. Beat them with a rolling pin until they are about 5 mm/¼ inch thick.
2. Using a potato peeler, remove the rind from half an orange, and cut it into very thin strips. Squeeze the juice from both the oranges, and set aside.
3. Melt the butter in a frying pan, add the pork slices and fry on both sides until lightly browned. Remove the slices and arrange them in a serving dish or foil container.
4. Mix together the orange juice, brown sugar, ginger syrup, cornflour, vinegar, stock and salt and pepper, and pour into the pan.
5. Bring the mixture to the boil, then cover and simmer for 5-6 minutes. Stir in the sliced ginger and orange rind strips, and simmer for a further 2-3 minutes. Pour the sauce over the meat.

TO FREEZE: Allow to go cold, cover and freeze.

TO SERVE: Allow to thaw at room temperature for 5-6 hours, then turn into a heavy pan and heat through gently. Bring to the boil and simmer for 2-3 minutes, stirring occasionally. Serve garnished with the orange slices.

# STUFFED BLADE OF PORK

*Preparation time: 20 minutes*
*Cooking time: 1½ hours*
*Recommended freezer life: 4 months*

1 × 1½ kg/3 lb blade of pork, boned
salt
freshly ground black pepper
Apple and Raisin Stuffing (page 65)
1 tablespoon oil
½ teaspoon salt

1. Lay the pork rind side down on a wooden board, and beat it with a wetted rolling pin to flatten and tenderize the meat.
2. Sprinkle the meat with salt and pepper, then spread over the stuffing.
3. Roll the meat up, and secure with string.
4. Place the joint with the join at the bottom in a roasting tin, and rub it with the oil. Sprinkle on the salt and rub it into the slits in the rind to ensure good crackling.
5. Place in a preheated oven at 200°C, 400°F, Gas Mark 6 for 30 minutes, then reduce the heat to 180°C, 350°F, Gas Mark

4 and cook for a further 1 hour.

**TO FREEZE:** Allow to go cold, then open freeze for 4 hours. Place in a polythene bag and return to the freezer.

**TO SERVE:** To serve hot, allow to thaw at room temperature for 8 hours, then place on a baking sheet in a preheated oven at 160°C, 325°F, Gas Mark 3 for 45 minutes. Serve with a Demi-Glace Sauce (page 61). To serve cold, allow to thaw at room temperature for 8 hours. Cut the joint into slices and arrange the meat on a serving platter.

# NORMANDY PORK TENDERLOIN

*Preparation time: 20 minutes, plus soaking time*
*Cooking time: 1 hour*
*Recommended freezer life: 4 months*

1 × 25 g/1 oz can anchovy fillets, drained
14 almonds, shelled and peeled
7 prunes, soaked in water overnight and stoned
2 pork tenderloin
50 g/2 oz butter
1 tablespoon oil
1 large onion, peeled and cut into rings
1 Bramley apple, peeled, cored and sliced
2 tablespoons demerara sugar
150 ml/¼ pint dry cider
150 ml/¼ pint stock
1 teaspoon lemon juice
4 fresh sage leaves, roughly chopped
salt
freshly ground black pepper
1 tablespoon cornflour
3 tablespoons water
50 ml/2 fl oz double cream
**TO SERVE:**
sprigs of parsley

1. Wrap each anchovy fillet around two almonds and use to stuff the prunes.
2. Remove the thin transparent skin from the pork and any excess fat. Slit each pork tenderloin lengthwise, cutting to within 1 cm/½ inch of the base, and open out.
3. Place the stuffed prunes in a row down the length of one of the fillets, then cover with the second fillet. Tie together with string, tucking in the ends.
4. Melt the butter and oil in a flameproof casserole and brown the pork on all sides. Remove from the pan.
5. Add the onion rings and apple slices to the dish. Sprinkle over the sugar, then pour in the cider, stock and lemon juice. Add the sage, and salt and pepper.
6. Lay the pork joint over this mixture, cover and cook in a preheated oven at 160°C, 325°F, Gas Mark 3 for 40 minutes.
7. Using a slotted spoon, lift the apple and onion out of the dish and arrange in the bottom of a foil container or serving dish. Lay the pork joint on top and remove the string.
8. Transfer the pan juices to a saucepan and simmer for 5 minutes.
9. Mix the cornflour with the water, and stir into the sauce. Simmer for a further 2-3 minutes, then remove from the heat and stir in the cream. Pour the sauce over the pork joint.

**TO FREEZE:** Allow to go cold, cover and freeze.

**TO SERVE:** Allow to thaw in the refrigerator for at least 8 hours, or overnight. Loosen the lid and place in a preheated oven at 160°C, 325°F, Gas Mark 3 for 35 minutes. Serve garnished with parsley sprigs.

# CHICKEN GALANTINE

*Preparation time: 1 hour*
*Cooking time: 1½ hours*
*Recommended freezer life: 4 months*

1×2 kg/4½ lb chicken
**STUFFING:**
2 onions, peeled and finely
   diced
225 g/8 oz minced veal
225 g/8 oz minced pork
100 g/4 oz minced pork fat
2 tablespoons chopped fresh
   tarragon
3 tablespoons port
salt
freshly ground black pepper
1 egg, beaten
**LAYERS:**
2 thin ham slices, cut in strips
50 g/2 oz blanched almonds
**TO COOK:**
75 g/3 oz butter, softened
salt
freshly ground black pepper

1. Bone the chicken carefully, removing the leg bones, but keeping the wings intact. Take care not to pierce the skin of the chicken. Place the boned chicken on a wooden board, skin side down.
2. Mix all the stuffing ingredients together, and push some of the stuffing into the legs of the chicken.
3. Form layers of stuffing, ham strips and almonds in the main body of the bird.
4. Bring up the sides of the bird, and sew together with a trussing needle and fine string, keeping a good shape.
5. Carefully sew up the ends of the legs to keep the stuffing intact.
6. Place the chicken, breast side up on a sheet of foil in a roasting tin. Smear it with the softened butter and sprinkle over some salt and pepper. Draw up the foil to prevent the chicken breast from becoming too brown during the cooking.
7. Cook in a preheated oven at 160°C, 325°F, Gas Mark 3 for 1 hour. Fold back the foil, baste the chicken, then return it to the oven and cook for another 30 minutes, or until the breast is golden brown.
8. Remove the chicken from the oven, and allow it to go cold.

**TO FREEZE:** Wrap in clean foil, place in a freezer bag, seal and freeze.

**TO SERVE:** Allow to thaw at room temperature for 7-8 hours. Serve sliced on a bed of salad, or pack the slices in a polythene box to take on a picnic.

# MILD MALAYAN CHICKEN CURRY

*Preparation time: 20 minutes*
*Cooking time: 1 hour 10 minutes*
*Recommended freezer life: 3 months*

50 g/2 oz butter
1×1½ kg/3½ lb chicken, cut into
   8 joints
2 Spanish onions, peeled and
   sliced
1 tablespoon plain flour
1 tablespoon curry paste
450 ml/¾ pint milk
juice of 1 lemon
1 tablespoon peach chutney
75 g/3 oz unsalted peanuts
salt
freshly ground black pepper
1 tablespoon cornflour
4 tablespoons water

1. Melt the butter in a heavy pan, add the chicken joints and brown them on all sides. Remove the joints and set aside.
2. Add the onions to the pan and fry them for 6-8 minutes, until light golden.
3. Stir in the flour and the curry paste and cook for 1-2 minutes.
4. Stir the milk, lemon juice, chutney, peanuts and salt and pepper into the sauce. Bring to the boil, stirring well.
5. Return the chicken to the pan, cover and simmer for 30-40 minutes.
6. Remove the chicken and arrange in a foil container or serving dish.
7. Mix together the cornflour and water and stir into the sauce. Bring to the boil, then simmer for 2-3 minutes, stirring. Pour the sauce over the chicken.

**TO FREEZE:** Allow to go cold, cover and freeze.

**TO SERVE:** Allow to thaw for 3-4 hours at room temperature. Loosen the lid and place in a preheated oven at 160°C, 325°F, Gas Mark 3 for 35-40 minutes. Serve on a bed of boiled brown rice, with poppadoms, sliced bananas sprinkled with lemon juice, and chopped hard-boiled egg.

**Above, left to right: Chicken galantine; Parmesan baked chicken; Supremes of chicken with tarragon**
**Right: Mild Malayan chicken curry**

# PARMESAN BAKED CHICKEN

*Preparation time: 30 minutes*
*Cooking time: 45 minutes*
*Recommended freezer life: 4 months*

1 × 1½ kg/3½ lb chicken
seasoned flour
100 g/4 oz fresh white
    breadcrumbs
50 g/2 oz Parmesan cheese,
    grated
2 tablespoons chopped fresh
    parsley
1 egg, beaten
150 g/5 oz butter
1 garlic clove, crushed
**TO SERVE:**
bacon rolls
sprigs of parsley

1. Joint the chicken into 8 pieces, and coat them in the seasoned flour.
2. Mix the breadcrumbs with the Parmesan cheese and chopped parsley.
3. Dip the chicken pieces into beaten egg, then coat them thickly with the breadcrumb mixture.
4. Lay the joints in a well greased roasting tin, and cook in a preheated oven at 200°C, 400°F, Gas Mark 6 for 10-15 minutes.
5. Melt the butter in a pan, stir in the crushed garlic, then pour over the chicken, making sure that all the joints are well basted.
6. Lower the oven temperature to 180°C, 350°F, Gas Mark 4, and continue cooking the chicken for 30 minutes.

**TO FREEZE:** Allow to go cold, then pack in a foil container, cover and freeze.

**TO SERVE:** Thaw overnight in the refrigerator, then place on a buttered ovenproof serving dish for 20 minutes in a preheated oven at 180°C, 350°F, Gas Mark 4. Serve garnished with bacon rolls and parsley sprigs.

# SUPREMES OF CHICKEN WITH TARRAGON

*Preparation time: 10 minutes*
*Cooking time: 1 hour*
*Recommended freezer life: 4 months*

75 g/3 oz butter
1 tablespoon oil
6 chicken suprêmes, skinned
2 tablespoons chopped fresh
    tarragon
salt
freshly ground black pepper
600 ml/1 pint chicken stock
2 tablespoons cornflour
4 tablespoons water
250 ml/8 fl oz double cream
**TO SERVE:**
sprigs of fresh tarragon

1. Melt the butter and oil in a frying pan, add the chicken pieces and brown them on both sides.
2. Transfer the chicken and the pan juices to a casserole, and sprinkle the chopped tarragon over the top. Add salt and pepper, then pour over the stock.
3. Cover and cook in a preheated oven at 180°C, 350°F, Gas Mark 5 for 40 minutes.
4. Arrange the chicken in a serving dish or foil container. Mix the cornflour and water together, stir into the casserole and simmer the sauce for 2-3 minutes, stirring. Remove from the heat and stir in the cream, then pour the sauce over the chicken.

**TO FREEZE:** Allow to go cold, cover and freeze.

**TO SERVE:** Allow to thaw at room temperature for 5-6 hours. Loosen the lid and place in a preheated oven at 160°C, 325°F, Gas Mark 3 for 35 minutes, stirring once. Serve garnished with sprigs of fresh tarragon.

# CHICKEN GOUGÈRE

*Preparation time: 20 minutes*
*Cooking time: 35 minutes*
*Recommended freezer life: 4 months*

100 g/4 oz butter
300 ml/½ pint water
150 g/5 oz plain flour, sifted
3 eggs
50 g/2 oz Cheddar cheese,
    finely diced
salt
freshly ground black pepper
**FILLING:**
25 g/1 oz butter
1 onion, peeled and chopped
15 g/½ oz plain flour
300 ml/½ pint chicken stock
100 g/4 oz button mushrooms,
    sliced
1 tablespoon cornflour
2 tablespoons water
3 tomatoes, peeled, seeded and
    quartered
450 g/1 lb cooked chicken, cut
    into large cubes
pinch of dried tarragon
1 tablespoon finely chopped
    fresh parsley
salt
freshly ground black pepper
1 tablespoon grated Parmesan
    cheese

1. Melt the butter in the water over a low heat.
2. When the butter has melted completely, bring the mixture to the boil, and quickly add the flour all at once.
3. Beat vigorously, until the mixture thickens, and forms a smooth paste.
4. Cook the mixture for 2-3 minutes, beating continually, until it leaves the sides of the pan.
5. Allow the mixture to cool for 1-2 minutes, then beat in the eggs one at a time.
6. Fold in the diced Cheddar cheese, and add salt and pepper to taste.
7. Grease a 1.2 litre/2 pint gratin dish or shallow foil container, and spoon in the choux pastry to form a thick border around the edge. Set aside.
8. To make the filling, melt the butter in a pan, add the onion and fry gently until soft and transparent.
9. Stir in the flour and cook for 2-3 minutes. Gradually stir in the stock. Add the mushrooms and bring the sauce to the boil.
10. Mix the cornflour with the water, stir into the sauce, and simmer for 3-4 minutes, stirring.
11. Allow the sauce to cool, then fold in the tomatoes, chicken, tarragon, parsley and salt and pepper.
12. Spoon the mixture into the centre of the choux pastry ring, and sprinkle it with the Parmesan cheese.

**TO FREEZE:** Cover and freeze.

**TO SERVE:** Uncover, then place in a preheated oven 200°C, 400°F, Gas Mark 6, and cook for 45 minutes, until the pastry is risen and golden. Reduce the heat to 180°C, 350°F, Gas Mark 4 and continue cooking for 15-20 minutes to set the pastry. If not frozen, reduce the cooking times by one-third.

# CREAMY CHICKEN WITH OLIVES

*Preparation time: 20 minutes*
*Cooking time: 25 minutes*
*Recommended freezer life: 4 months*

50 g/2 oz butter
75 g/3 oz back bacon, cut into thin strips
100 g/4 oz button mushrooms, sliced
25 g/1 oz plain flour
250 ml/8 fl oz chicken stock
salt
freshly ground black pepper
750 g/1½ lb cooked chicken, cut into large dice
75 g/3 oz stuffed olives, sliced
250 ml/8 fl oz double cream
1 tablespoon cornflour
2 tablespoons water

1. Melt the butter in a large frying pan, add the bacon and fry gently for 4-5 minutes.
2. Add the mushrooms and continue cooking for a further 2-3 minutes, stirring gently.
3. Stir in the flour, and cook the mixture until it is well blended.
4. Stir in the stock, and salt and pepper, bring to the boil, then stir in the chicken, olives and cream.
5. Mix the cornflour and water together, and stir into the sauce. Continue simmering the sauce for a further 2-3 minutes, stirring.

**TO FREEZE:** Allow the mixture to go cold, then spoon it into a foil container, cover and freeze.

**TO SERVE:** Loosen the lid and place in a preheated oven at 160°C, 325°F, Gas Mark 3 for 45 minutes, stirring occasionally. Serve the chicken on a bed of boiled rice.

# CHICKEN WITH ARTICHOKE HEARTS

*Preparation time: 25 minutes*
*Cooking time: 5 minutes (for the croûtons)*
*Recommended freezer life: 4 months*

2 × 425 g/15 oz cans artichoke hearts, drained and quartered
750 g/1½ lb cooked chicken, roughly shredded
2 × 275 g/10 oz cans condensed cream of chicken soup
175 ml/6 fl oz mayonnaise
1 teaspoon curry powder
2 teaspoons lemon juice
freshly ground black pepper
100 g/4 oz Cheddar cheese, grated
50 g/2 oz butter
4 thick slices white bread, crusts removed and cubed

1. Arrange the artichoke heart pieces evenly over the base of a well buttered gratin dish or foil freezer container. Place the chicken in a layer over the artichokes.
2. Combine the soup, mayonnaise, curry powder, lemon juice and pepper in a bowl, then pour the mixture over the chicken.
3. Sprinkle the grated cheese over the top of the dish.
4. Melt the butter in a large saucepan, then remove from the heat. Do not allow it to brown. Add the cubes of bread to the melted butter and toss them gently until they are well soaked. Arrange the bread over the cheese.

**TO FREEZE:** Cover and freeze.

**TO SERVE:** Allow to thaw at room temperature for 3-4 hours, then uncover and place in a preheated oven at 190°C, 375°F, Gas Mark 5 for 45 minutes, until heated through and crisp on the top.

# CHICKEN ROULADE WITH BACON & MUSHROOMS

*Preparation time: 30 minutes*
*Cooking time: 30 minutes*
*Recommended freezer life: 4 months*

40 g/1½ oz butter
100 g/4 oz bacon, rind removed
  and chopped
100 g/4 oz button mushrooms,
  chopped
25 g/1 oz plain flour
15 g/½ oz cornflour
450 ml/¾ pint milk
225 g/8 oz cooked chicken,
  finely diced
4 eggs, separated
1 teaspoon dried tarragon
salt
freshly ground black pepper
pinch of ground nutmeg
25 g/1 oz Cheddar cheese,
  grated
TO SERVE:
sprigs of watercress

1. Line a 20 × 30 cm/8 × 12 inch Swiss roll tin with oiled greaseproof paper, securing the corners with paper clips.
2. Melt the butter in a pan, add the bacon and mushrooms and fry gently for 3-4 minutes. Remove them from the pan with a slotted spoon, and set aside.
3. Stir the flour into the butter remaining in the pan, and cook for 2-3 minutes, then remove from the heat.
4. Blend the cornflour with the milk, and gradually stir it into the pan, mixing well. Bring the sauce to the boil, and simmer it for 2-3 minutes.
5. Place the diced chicken in a large mixing bowl, and stir in 3 tablespoons of the sauce.
6. Beat the egg yolks one at a time into this mixture, adding the tarragon and salt and pepper.
7. Stiffly whisk the egg whites and fold them into the chicken mixture.
8. Spoon the chicken mixture into the prepared tin smoothing it into the corners.
9. Cook in a preheated oven at 200°C, 400°F, Gas Mark 6, for 10-15 minutes until

set and golden brown on the surface.
10. Meanwhile, stir the cooked bacon and mushrooms into the remaining white sauce, with salt, pepper and the nutmeg.
11. When the roulade is cooked, remove it from the oven, and invert it on to a wire tray covered with a piece of clean greaseproof paper.
12. Peel away the lining paper, and leave the roulade to cool slightly.
13. Spread the sauce evenly over the surface and roll up the roulade like a Swiss roll. Sprinkle the top with the grated cheese.

**TO FREEZE:** Place in a rigid plastic container, cover and freeze.

**TO SERVE:** Allow to thaw at room temperature for 2-3 hours, then place on a baking sheet in a preheated oven at 180°C, 350°F, Gas Mark 4 for 20-30 minutes. Serve garnished with watercress sprigs.

# CHICKEN & HAM PIE

*Preparation time: 20 minutes*
*Cooking time: 20 minutes*
*Recommended freezer life: 4 months*

50 g/2 oz butter
3 tablespoons plain flour
150 ml/¼ pint milk
300 ml/½ pint chicken stock
2 tablespoons cornflour
2 tablespoons water
175 g/6 oz button mushrooms,
  sliced
225 g/8 oz ham, diced
450 g/1 lb cooked chicken, cut
  in strips
1 tablespoon chopped fresh
  parsley
pinch of ground nutmeg
salt
freshly ground black pepper
1 × 375 g/13 oz packet frozen
  puff pastry, thawed
TO SERVE:
1 egg, beaten

1. Melt the butter in a large saucepan, stir in the flour and cook for 2-3 minutes. Gradually stir in the milk and stock.
2. Mix the cornflour with the water, stir into the sauce and simmer for 2 minutes.
3. Stir in the mushrooms, ham, chicken, parsley, nutmeg, salt and pepper, and simmer for a further 5 minutes.
4. Pour the mixture into an ovenproof or foil pie dish and allow to go cold.
5. Roll out the pastry thinly and use it to cover the pie, sealing the edges with water. Use the pastry trimmings to make leaves to garnish the pie.

**TO FREEZE:** Open freeze for 3-4 hours, then place in a polythene bag, seal and return to the freezer.

**TO SERVE:** Unwrap the frozen pie and brush with beaten egg. From frozen, cook in a preheated oven at 200°C, 400°F, Gas Mark 6 for 20-30 minutes, or until the pastry is well risen. Reduce the heat to 180°C, 350°F, Gas Mark 4 and cook for a further 30 minutes.

# CHICKEN & PRAWN PILAFF

*Serves 6*
*Preparation time: 35 minutes*
*Cooking time: 30 minutes*
*Recommended freezer life: 3 months*

175 g/6 oz long-grain rice
25 g/1 oz butter
3 tablespoons oil
1 Spanish onion, peeled and
  sliced
1 green pepper, cored and sliced
1 red pepper, cored and sliced
1 garlic clove, crushed
1 teaspoon turmeric
1 teaspoon dried oregano
75 g/3 oz button mushrooms,
  sliced
50 g/2 oz shelled unsalted
  peanuts
1 × 200 g/7 oz can red kidney
  beans, drained and rinsed in
  cold water
2 tablespoons chopped fresh
  parsley
225 g/8 oz shelled prawns
450 g/1 lb cooked chicken or
  turkey, cut in strips
salt
freshly ground black pepper
50 g/2 oz Parmesan cheese,
  grated

1. Cook the rice in a large pan of boiling salted water for 13 minutes, then drain and keep it warm.
2. Meanwhile, heat the butter and oil in a pan, add the onion, peppers and garlic and fry gently until lightly browned.
3. Stir in the turmeric, oregano, mushrooms, peanuts, red kidney beans and chopped parsley, and cook for 2-3 minutes.
4. Add the prawns and chicken or turkey and stir over the heat for 5-7 minutes. Add salt and pepper to taste.
5. Stir in the cooked rice, taking care not to break up the chicken or turkey pieces.

**TO FREEZE:** Spoon into a large foil container and sprinkle with the Parmesan cheese. Allow to go cold, cover and freeze.

**TO SERVE:** Allow to thaw at room temperature for at least 6 hours. Loosen the lid and place in a preheated oven at 160°C, 325°F, Gas Mark 3 for 30-40 minutes. Serve with a green salad and garlic bread.

# TURKEY BREASTS MARSALA

*Serves 6*
*Preparation time: 20 minutes*
*Cooking time: 30 minutes*
*Recommended freezer life: 4 months*

1 kg/2 lb turkey breasts, cut into
  7.5 cm/3 inch lengths
seasoned flour
50 g/2 oz butter
100 g/4 oz shallots, peeled and
  chopped
350 g/12 oz button mushrooms
100 g/4 oz unsweetened
  chestnut purée (optional)
175 ml/6 fl oz Marsala
2 bay leaves
salt
freshly ground black pepper
1 tablespoon cornflour
2 tablespoons water
TO SERVE:
boiled rice
2 tablespoons double cream
paprika

1. Toss the turkey breast strips in the seasoned flour.
2. Melt the butter in a frying pan, add the shallots and fry gently until soft and transparent. Stir in the mushrooms and fry for a further 4 minutes.
3. Remove the vegetables from the pan with a slotted spoon, and set aside.
4. Brown the turkey strips in the remaining butter, then replace the vegetables, and stir in the chestnut purée.
5. Pour in the Marsala and chicken stock, and stir well. Add the bay leaves, and salt and pepper, then simmer for 8-10 minutes.
6. Mix the cornflour with the water, stir into the pan and simmer for 2-3 minutes.

TO FREEZE: Allow to go cold, spoon into a foil container, cover and freeze.

TO SERVE: Allow to thaw at room temperature for 5-6 hours, then turn into a heavy saucepan, and gently reheat. Serve on a bed of boiled rice. Trickle the cream over the dish and garnish with paprika.

# STUFFED TURKEY BREASTS WITH PISTACHIO NUTS

*Preparation time: 35 minutes*
*Cooking time: 1 hour*
*Recommended freezer life: 3 months*

2 × 350 g/12 oz turkey breasts
STUFFING:
50 g/2 oz pistachio nuts,
  chopped
100 g/4 oz full fat soft cheese
100 g/4 oz fresh white
  breadcrumbs
2 tablespoons grated onion
1 teaspoon grated lemon rind
1 egg, beaten
salt
freshly ground black pepper

25 g/1 oz butter
2 tablespoons lemon juice
TO SERVE:
300 ml/½ pint Demi-Glace
  Sauce (page 61)
potato crisps
sprigs of watercress

1. Split each turkey breast lengthwise, not quite cutting right through, and open out.
2. Lay a sheet of greaseproof paper over each breast, and beat with a rolling pin to flatten the meat.
3. To make the stuffing, put all the ingredients in a mixing bowl and blend together.
4. Divide the stuffing between the two turkey breasts and roll each one up, securing with a skewer.
5. Melt the butter in a frying pan, add the turkey breasts one at a time, and fry them until lightly browned on both sides.
6. Remove the breasts from the pan and lay them on a sheet of buttered foil. Sprinkle with the lemon juice, and fold up the foil to form a parcel.
7. Place the parcels on a baking sheet and cook in a preheated oven at 180°C, 350°F, Gas Mark 4 for 35 minutes. Open the foil, and cook for a further 8-10 minutes to brown the tops of the turkey breasts.

TO FREEZE: Allow to go cold, wrap each one in clean foil, pack into a polythene bag, seal and freeze.

TO SERVE: Allow to thaw at room temperature for 5-6 hours. Place the breasts in an ovenproof dish, pour over the Demi-Glace Sauce and cover with foil. Place in a preheated oven at 180°C, 350°F, Gas Mark 4 for 25-30 minutes. Serve garnished with watercress sprigs and hot potato crisps.

**Above, clockwise from the top: Turkey breasts Marsala; Braised duckling with cherry sauce; Stuffed turkey breasts with pistachio nuts**

# BRAISED DUCKLING WITH CHERRY SAUCE

*Preparation time: 20 minutes*
*Cooking time: 2½ hours*
*Recommended freezer life: 4 months*

1 × 2¼ kg/5 lb duckling
oil
salt
**SAUCE:**
1 Spanish onion, peeled and
    finely chopped
150 ml/¼ pint red wine
450 ml/¾ pint chicken stock
3 tablespoons cornflour
6 tablespoons water
225 g/8 oz ripe black cherries, or
    1 × 425 g/15 oz can black
    cherries, drained (stoned, if
    preferred)
salt
freshly ground black pepper

1. Prick the skin of the duckling several times with a fork. Rub a little oil on the skin, and sprinkle with a little salt.
2. Place the duckling on a wire tray in a large roasting tin, and cook in a preheated oven at 200°C, 400°F, Gas Mark 6 for 45 minutes.
3. Turn the bird over on to the breast side and cook it for a further 45 minutes.
4. Cover the skin of the bird with foil to prevent it from becoming too brown. Return the bird to the original position, and cook it for about 30 minutes until the juices run clear and the meat is tender.
5. Remove the duckling from the oven and allow it to cool slightly.
6. Divide the duckling into 4 joints with poultry shears or kitchen scissors. Arrange the joints on a serving platter or in a large foil container.
7. To make the sauce, place 2 tablespoons of the duckling fat from the bottom of the roasting tin into a pan. Add the chopped onion and fry gently until soft and golden.

8. Pour in the wine and the stock. Bring to the boil, then boil rapidly, uncovered until reduced to approximately 450 ml/ ¾ pint.
9. Mix the cornflour with the water and stir into the sauce. Simmer for 2-3 minutes, stirring, then add the cherries, and salt and pepper.
10. Simmer gently until the cherries are heated through, then pour the sauce over the duckling joints.

**TO FREEZE:** Allow to go cold, cover and freeze.

**TO SERVE:** Allow to thaw at room temperature for 4-5 hours, then loosen the lid and place in a preheated oven at 160°C, 325°F, Gas Mark 3 for 35-40 minutes, basting the duckling joints with the sauce from time to time.

# CHICKEN LIVER & KIDNEY KEBABS

*Preparation time: 15 minutes,*
 *plus marinating*
*Cooking time: 25 minutes*
*Recommended freezer life: 4 months*

100 g/4 oz chicken livers, halved
4 lamb's kidneys, skinned,
 halved lengthwise and cored
8 bacon rashers, rind removed
 and rolled
4 chipolata sausages, twisted
 and halved
**MARINADE:**
2 tablespoons grated onion
2 teaspoons peanut butter
1 tablespoon tomato purée
1 tablespoon Worcestershire
 sauce
1 tablespoon wine vinegar
1 tablespoon oil
2 teaspoons clear honey
1 teaspoon dried thyme
1 tablespoon syrup from
 preserved ginger
salt
freshly ground black pepper

2 tablespoons oil
**SAUCE:**
300 ml/½ pint chicken stock
1 tablespoon cornflour
2 tablespoons water

1. Place all the meats in a large shallow dish.
2. Combine the marinade ingredients and pour over the meats. Leave for 30 minutes.
3. Heat the oil in a pan. Remove the meat from the marinade, and fry in the hot oil until evenly browned. Remove from the pan and set aside.
4. Stir any remaining marinade into the pan then pour in the stock and bring the mixture to the boil. Mix the cornflour with the water and stir into the sauce. Simmer for 2-3 minutes, stirring.
5. Divide the meats between 4 kebab skewers.

**TO FREEZE:** Wrap each kebab skewer in foil, then place all 4 in a polythene bag, seal and freeze. Pour the sauce into a rigid container, cover and freeze separately.

**TO SERVE:** Allow both the meat and sauce to thaw at room temperature for 3-4 hours. The kebabs may be placed in a preheated oven at 200°C, 400°F, Gas Mark 6 for 20 minutes, or cooked on a barbecue. Turn the sauce into a pan and bring slowly to boiling point before pouring over the kebabs. Serve with boiled rice or baked potatoes.

# KIDNEYS TURBIGO

*Preparation time: 15 minutes*
*Cooking time: 45 minutes*
*Recommended freezer life: 4 months*

25 g/1 oz butter
1 tablespoon oil
225 g/½ lb chipolata sausages,
 halved
12 lamb's kidneys, skinned,
 halved and cored
25 pickling onions, peeled
100 g/½ lb button mushrooms,
 sliced
300 ml/½ pint Demi-Glace
 Sauce (page 61)
1 tablespoon cornflour
3 tablespoons water
1 tablespoon chopped fresh
 parsley
**TO SERVE:**
croûtons
sprigs of parsley

1. Melt the butter and oil in a heavy frying pan, add the sausages and kidneys and fry until lightly browned, then remove from the pan and set aside.
2. Add the onions to the pan and fry gently for 2-3 minutes, then add the button mushrooms and continue cooking for a further 2 minutes.
3. Return the sausages and kidneys to the pan and pour over the Demi-Glace Sauce. Cover and simmer for 25 minutes, stirring occasionally.
4. Mix the cornflour with the water, stir into the pan and simmer for 2-3 minutes, stirring.
5. Stir in the chopped parsley, then taste and adjust the seasoning.

**TO FREEZE:** Pour into a rigid container and allow to go cold. Cover and freeze.

**TO SERVE:** Allow to thaw at room temperature for 3-4 hours. Turn into a heavy frying pan and heat through gently. Bring to the boil and simmer for 2-3 minutes, stirring occasionally. Serve garnished with croûtons and parsley sprigs.

# LIVER & BACON WITH TOMATO SAUCE

*Preparation time: 15 minutes*
*Cooking time: 1 hour*
*Recommended freezer life: 4 months*

25 g/1 oz butter
1 tablespoon oil
6 rashers shortback bacon
750 g/1½ lb lamb's liver, thinly sliced
1 Spanish onion, peeled and sliced
2 garlic cloves, crushed
1 tablespoon tomato purée
450 g/1 lb tomatoes, peeled, seeded and chopped
1 teaspoon granulated sugar
salt
freshly ground black pepper
1 tablespoon cornflour
2 tablespoons water
**TO SERVE:**
sprigs of parsley

1. Melt the butter and oil in a frying pan, add the bacon rashers and fry quickly on both sides, then remove from the pan.
2. Add the liver and brown lightly all over. Set the bacon and liver aside.
3. Add the onion to the pan and fry until light golden.
4. Stir in the crushed garlic, tomato purée, tomatoes, sugar, and salt and pepper. Simmer for 5 minutes.
5. Mix the cornflour with the water and stir into the sauce, then simmer for 2-3 minutes, stirring.
6. Layer the liver, bacon and sauce in a foil dish or casserole, finishing with a layer of sauce. Cover tightly with a sheet of foil or a lid.
7. Place in a preheated oven at 160°C, 325°F, Gas Mark 3 for 40 minutes.

**TO FREEZE:** Allow to go cold, then freeze.

**TO SERVE:** Allow to thaw for 4-5 hours at room temperature, then loosen the lid, and place in a preheated oven at 160°C, 325°F, Gas Mark 3 for 40 minutes. Serve garnished with parsley sprigs.

# LAMB'S SWEETBREADS IN SHERRY SAUCE

*Preparation time: 10 minutes*
*Cooking time: 40 minutes*
*Recommended freezer life: 4 months*

450 g/1 lb lamb's sweetbreads
50 g/2 oz butter
1 onion, peeled and finely chopped
175 g/6 oz button mushrooms, sliced
2 tablespoons plain flour
150 ml/¼ pint chicken stock
150 ml/¼ pint sherry
pinch of ground mace
salt
freshly ground black pepper
1 teaspoon cornflour
2 tablespoons water
50 ml/2 fl oz single cream
2 tablespoons chopped fresh parsley

1. Remove the skin-like tissue from the sweetbreads. Cook in boiling water for 3 minutes, then drain and pat dry.
2. Melt the butter in a frying pan, add the sweetbreads and fry gently until lightly browned on all sides. Remove from the pan and set aside.
3. Add the onion and mushrooms to the pan and fry gently for 6 minutes.
4. Stir in the flour, then add the stock, sherry, mace and salt and pepper. Bring the sauce to the boil.
5. Return the sweetbreads to the pan, cover and simmer for 15-20 minutes.
6. Mix the cornflour with the water and stir into the sauce. Simmer for 2-3 minutes, stirring.
7. Remove the pan from the heat and stir in the cream and parsley.

**TO FREEZE:** Pour into a rigid container and allow to go cold. Cover and freeze.

**TO SERVE:** Allow to thaw at room temperature for 2-3 hours. Loosen the lid and place in a preheated oven at 180°C, 350°F, Gas Mark 4 for 35-40 minutes, stirring occasionally. Serve with rice.

# VEGETABLES

## BROAD BEANS WITH WALNUTS

*Preparation time: 10 minutes*
*Cooking time: 35 minutes*
*Recommended freezer life: 4 months*

450 g/1 lb broad beans, shelled
25 g/1 oz butter
15 g/½ oz plain flour
300 ml/½ pint milk
1 teaspoon grated lemon rind
salt
freshly ground black pepper
50 g/2 oz ham, cut into thin
  strips
50 g/2 oz walnut halves
1 tablespoon cornflour
2 tablespoons water
2 tablespoons double cream

1. Cook the beans in boiling salted water until just tender. Drain and set aside.
2. Melt the butter in a saucepan and stir in the flour. Cook for 2-3 minutes, then gradually stir in the milk over a low heat. Bring gently to the boil. Add the lemon rind, salt and pepper.
3. Stir the beans, ham and walnuts into the sauce and cover and simmer for 4-5 minutes. Blend the cornflour with the water, add to the sauce and simmer for 2-3 minutes, to allow the sauce to thicken. Stir in the cream.

**TO FREEZE:** Pour into a foil container and allow to go cold. Cover and freeze.

**TO SERVE:** Allow to thaw at room temperature for 3-4 hours then gently reheat in a pan stirring occasionally.

## PETITS POIS A LA FRANCAISE

*Preparation time: 15 minutes*
*Cooking time: 35 minutes*
*Recommended freezer life: 4 months*

40 g/1½ oz butter
8 pickling onions, peeled
2 rashers back bacon, rind
  removed and chopped
450 g/1 lb fresh peas, shelled
salt
freshly ground black pepper
1 teaspoon caster sugar
pinch of ground nutmeg
250 ml/8 fl oz water
1 tablespoon cornflour
2 tablespoons water
4 lettuce leaves, shredded
2 tablespoons double cream
TO SERVE:
chopped fresh parsley

1. Melt the butter in a saucepan and stir in the onions and bacon. Cook over a gentle heat, tossing occasionally, for 6-8 minutes. Add the peas, a little salt and pepper, sugar, nutmeg and 250 ml/8 fl oz water to the mixture and bring to the boil. Cover and gently simmer the peas until just tender.
2. Blend the cornflour with 2 tablespoons water and add to the pan. Bring back to the boil. Stir in the lettuce and cream, and simmer gently for a further 2-3 minutes, stirring.

**TO FREEZE:** Pour into a foil container and allow to go cold. Cover and freeze.

**TO SERVE:** Allow to thaw at room temperature for 2-3 hours, loosen the lid and place in a preheated oven 160°C, 325°F, Gas Mark 3 for 20-30 minutes, stirring once during the reheating period. Serve the peas sprinkled with chopped fresh parsley.

# COURGETTE, TOMATO & BACON CASSEROLE

*Preparation time: 10 minutes*
*Cooking time: 10 minutes*
*Recommended freezer life: 4 months*

750 g/1½ lb courgettes, sliced
25 g/1 oz butter
8 rashers streaky bacon, rind
  removed, chopped
175 g/6 oz Mozzarella cheese,
  grated
6 tomatoes, skinned, quartered
  and seeded
freshly ground black pepper

1. Blanch the courgettes in boiling salted water for 3 minutes, drain and pat dry with kitchen paper. Melt the butter in a pan and gently fry the bacon until browned.
2. Grease a foil container and line the base with some of the courgettes. Cover the courgettes with a layer of the grated cheese, bacon and then tomato, adding a little pepper between layers. Repeat layers until all the ingredients have been used, finishing with a layer of cheese.

**TO FREEZE:** Allow to go cold, cover and freeze.

**TO SERVE:** Allow to thaw at room temperature for 3-4 hours. Bake in a preheated oven 160°C, 325°F, Gas Mark 3 for 35-40 minutes.

# CHINESE VEGETABLES

*Serves 6*
*Preparation time: 30 minutes*
*Cooking time: 10 minutes*
*Recommended freezer life: 4 months*

2 tablespoons vegetable oil
1 Spanish onion, peeled and
  roughly chopped
1 teaspoon peeled and finely
  slithered fresh ginger or 1
  teaspoon ground ginger
1 garlic clove, peeled and very
  finely chopped
bunch of spring onions,
  trimmed and cut into 5 cm/
  2 inch pieces, including a
  little of the green part
1 medium green pepper, cored,
  seeded and roughly chopped
1 medium red pepper, cored,
  seeded and roughly chopped
a selection of the following
  vegetables to a total of
  350 g/12 oz:
100 g/4 oz mange tout peas,
  trimmed
100 g/4 oz French beans,
  trimmed and cut into 5 cm/
  2 inch pieces
100 g/4 oz celery, cut diagonally
  into 5 cm/2 inch pieces
100 g/4 oz fresh bean-sprouts
100 g/4 oz small cauliflower
  florets
freshly ground black pepper
1 teaspoon caster sugar
**TO SERVE:**
450 g/1 lb Chinese cabbage or
  any green cabbage, roughly
  chopped
2 tablespoons soy sauce
salt

This dish is best prepared in a Chinese wok, but can successfully be prepared in a heavy deep frying pan.

1. Heat the oil in the wok or frying pan, and cook the Spanish onion, fresh or powdered ginger and garlic quickly for 2-3 minutes, stirring constantly. Add the spring onions, green and red pepper and all the selected vegetables and cook, stirring, for a further 3-4 minutes. Do not allow the vegetables to brown. Season the mixture with pepper and add the sugar.

**TO FREEZE:** Turn into a rigid container and allow to go cold. Cover and freeze.

**TO SERVE:** Allow to thaw at room temperature for 2-3 hours. Turn into a wok or large heavy frying pan. Add the cabbage, soy sauce and salt to taste, and cook the mixture quickly, stirring, over a medium heat until the cabbage is just cooked, but still crisp. Turn the vegetables into a dish and serve immediately.

# RATATOUILLE

*Serves 6*
*Preparation time: 25 minutes*
*Cooking time: 1 hour*
*Recommended freezer life: 4 months*

4 tablespoons oil
2 Spanish onions, peeled and
    sliced
2 cloves garlic, crushed
2 medium aubergines, roughly
    chopped
1 green pepper, cored, seeded
    and sliced
1 red pepper, cored, seeded and
    sliced
350 g/12 oz courgettes, sliced
750 g/1½ lb tomatoes, peeled,
    seeded and chopped
3 tablespoons tomato purée
salt
freshly ground black pepper
1 bay leaf
sprig of thyme
TO SERVE:
2 tablespoons chopped fresh
    parsley

1. Heat the oil in a large heavy pan and gently fry the onions until soft and light golden. Add the garlic and the chopped aubergines and cook for 3-4 minutes, stirring. Add the peppers and courgettes to the pan and cook the mixture for a further 4-5 minutes.
2. Stir in all the remaining ingredients, cover and stew the vegetables over a gentle heat for 35-40 minutes, tossing the pan occasionally to ensure even cooking. When cooked the vegetables should be tender, but with their shape retained.

TO FREEZE:  Turn into a rigid container and allow to go cold. Cover and freeze.

TO SERVE:  Allow to thaw at room temperature for 3-4 hours. Gently heat in a pan. Stir in the chopped parsley and serve hot.

# CASSEROLE OF CUCUMBER, SPRING ONION & TOMATO

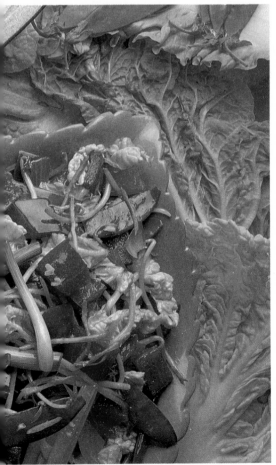

*Preparation time: 15 minutes*
*Cooking time: 25 minutes*
*Recommended freezer life: 4 months*

40 g/1½ oz butter
1 small onion, peeled and
    chopped
bunch of spring onions,
    trimmed and cut into
2.5 cm/1 inch pieces
1 cucumber, peeled and cut into
    1 cm/½ inch lengths
150 ml/¼ pint chicken stock
pinch of sugar
1 teaspoon tomato purée
4 sprigs mint
salt
freshly ground black pepper
2 teaspoons cornflour
2 tablespoons water
4 tomatoes, skinned, quartered
    and seeded

1. Melt the butter in a large saucepan and gently cook the onion and spring onions for 5 minutes. Add the cucumber and continue cooking gently for a further 5 minutes.
2. Pour in the chicken stock and add the sugar, tomato purée, sprigs of mint, and salt and pepper. Cover and simmer for 10 minutes.
3. Blend the cornflour with the water and stir into the mixture. Bring back to the boil, add the tomatoes and simmer for 2-3 minutes, stirring occasionally but taking care not to break up the vegetables.

TO FREEZE:  Spoon into a foil container and allow to go cold. Cover and freeze.

TO SERVE:  Allow to thaw at room temperature for 3-4 hours. Turn into a pan and reheat over a low flame, stirring gently.

**From left to right: Casserole of cucumber, spring onion and tomato; Courgette, tomato and bacon casserole; Chinese vegetables**

# STUFFED AUBERGINES

*Preparation time: 45 minutes*
*Cooking time: 30 minutes*
*Recommended freezer life: 4 months*

2 medium aubergines, stalks
    removed
salt
3 tablespoons oil
40 g/1½ oz butter
2 onions, peeled and finely
    chopped
40 g/1½ oz plain flour
250 ml/8 fl oz milk
freshly ground black pepper
1 teaspoon cornflour
1 tablespoon water
75 g/3 oz Gruyère cheese,
    grated
1 egg yolk
TO SERVE:
chopped fresh chives

1. Cut the aubergines in half lengthwise. Slash the flesh, sprinkle with salt and place the aubergine halves flesh side down on a wire tray. Leave for 20-30 minutes.
2. Rinse and dry the flesh with kitchen paper.
3. Heat the oil in a frying pan and fry the aubergines on both sides until the flesh is tender. Scoop out the flesh and chop roughly. Arrange the shells in an ovenproof dish or foil container.
4. To make the filling, melt the butter in a saucepan and gently fry the onions until transparent. Stir in the flour and cook for 2-3 minutes. Gradually stir in the milk, bring to the boil and add salt and pepper. Blend the cornflour with the water, add to the sauce and simmer for a further 2-3 minutes.

5. Remove from the heat and stir in 50 g/2 oz of the cheese and the egg yolk. Add the chopped aubergine flesh. Fill the aubergine shells with the mixture and sprinkle with the remaining cheese.

**TO FREEZE:** Allow to go cold, cover and freeze.

**TO SERVE:** Allow to thaw at room temperature for 3-4 hours. Place in a preheated oven 160°C, 325°F, Gas Mark 3 for 35 minutes. If not frozen, cook for only 20 minutes. Put briefly under a hot grill to brown the topping and serve garnished with chopped chives.

# CHEESY STUFFED PEPPERS

*Preparation time: 10 minutes*
*Cooking time: 15 minutes*
*Recommended freezer life: 4 months*

4 small green peppers, cut in
    half lengthwise, cored and
    seeded
25 g/1 oz butter
25 g/1 oz plain flour
250 ml/8 fl oz milk
1 teaspoon cornflour
1 tablespoon water
2 eggs, separated
225 g/8 oz cottage cheese
175 g/6 oz canned red kidney
    beans, drained
75 g/3 oz Cheddar cheese,
    grated
salt
freshly ground black pepper
pinch of ground nutmeg
40 g/1½ oz flaked almonds

Use leftover kidney beans from the can to add to salads.

1. Blanch the pepper halves in boiling salted water for 7 minutes, drain and dry with kitchen paper.
2. To make the filling, melt the butter in a saucepan, stir in the flour and cook for 2-3 minutes. Gradually stir in the milk over a low heat. Blend the cornflour with the water and add to the sauce. Bring to the boil and simmer for 2-3 minutes, stirring.
3. Remove from the heat, beat in the egg yolks and stir in the cottage cheese, kidney beans, grated cheese, salt, pepper and nutmeg. Whip the egg whites stiffly, and fold into the mixture.
4. Arrange the peppers in a greased ovenproof dish or foil container and fill with the cheese mixture. Sprinkle with the almonds.

**TO FREEZE:** Allow to go cold, cover and freeze.

**TO SERVE:** Allow to thaw at room temperature for 2-3 hours. Uncover and place in a preheated oven 190°C, 375°F, Gas Mark 5 for 25-30 minutes, until the peppers have risen slightly and are golden brown on top.

**Clockwise from the top: Stuffed aubergines; Spinach ring; Cheesy stuffed peppers**

# SPINACH RING

*Serves 6*
*Preparation time: 20 minutes*
*Cooking time: 55 minutes*
*Recommended freezer life: 4 months*

1¾ kg/4 lb fresh spinach,
   stalks removed
50 g/2 oz butter
50 g/2 oz plain flour
600 ml/1 pint milk
salt
freshly ground black pepper
pinch of ground nutmeg
3 eggs, beaten
65 g/2½ oz butter, melted
**TO SERVE:**
150 ml/¼ pint single cream,
   warmed and seasoned

1. Grease a 25 cm/10 inch ring mould.
2. Wash the spinach thoroughly and cook in the minimum amount of boiling salted water for 8 minutes. Drain well, pressing with the back of a spoon to remove excess moisture. Roughly chop.
3. To make a white sauce, melt the butter in a saucepan, add the flour and cook for 2-3 minutes. Gradually stir in the milk over a low heat. Add salt, pepper and the nutmeg. Remove from the heat and beat in the eggs.
4. Mix together the spinach and the white sauce and fold in the melted butter.
5. Pour the mixture into the ring mould and cook in a preheated oven 180°C, 350°F, Gas Mark 4 for 40 minutes.

**TO FREEZE:** Allow to go cold, place in a polythene bag, seal and freeze.

**TO SERVE:** Allow to thaw at room temperature for 5-6 hours. Cover with buttered greaseproof paper, and place the ring in a roasting tin half filled with water. Gently heat through in a preheated oven 180°C, 350°F, Gas Mark 4 for 30 minutes. Turn the ring out on to a serving dish and pour over the warm, seasoned cream.

# POMMES BOULANGÈRE

*Serves 6*
*Preparation time: 30 minutes*
*Cooking time: 35-40 minutes*
*Recommended freezer life: 4 months*

3 onions, peeled and thinly
    sliced
1 kg/2 lb potatoes, peeled and
    thinly sliced
75 g/3 oz Cheddar cheese,
    grated
pinch of ground nutmeg
salt
freshly ground black pepper
300 ml/½ pint chicken stock
3 tablespoons fresh white
    breadcrumbs
50 g/2 oz butter, melted

1. Butter a large shallow ovenproof dish or foil container and arrange a layer of onion and potato, overlapping, in the bottom. Sprinkle with a little of the grated cheese and the nutmeg, and add salt and pepper. Repeat these layers using the remaining onion, potato and cheese.
2. Pour the stock over the vegetables and sprinkle with the breadcrumbs. Dribble the melted butter evenly over the breadcrumbs and cover the dish with a piece of buttered greaseproof paper.
3. Cook the potatoes in a preheated oven 190°C, 375°F, Gas Mark 5 for 35-40 minutes.

**TO FREEZE:** Remove the piece of greaseproof paper and allow to go cold. Cover and freeze.

**TO SERVE:** Allow to thaw at room temperature for 2-3 hours, uncover and place in a preheated oven 190°C, 375°F, Gas Mark 5 for 30 minutes, until the potatoes are tender and the breadcrumb topping is browned.

# SAVOY POTATOES

*Serves 6*
*Preparation time: 20 minutes*
*Cooking time: 35 minutes*
*Recommended freezer life: 4 months*

75 g/3 oz butter
1¼ kg/2½ lb potatoes, peeled
    and diced
3 onions, peeled and sliced
salt
freshly ground black pepper
about 200 ml/⅓ pint chicken
    stock
100 g/4 oz Gruyère cheese,
    cut into wafer thin slices

1. Melt the butter in a heavy pan, add the potatoes, onions, and salt and pepper. Cover the vegetables with a sheet of buttered greaseproof paper and a lid. Cook over a low heat until tender, occasionally shaking the pan gently to prevent the vegetables from sticking.
2. Put the vegetables into a buttered ovenproof dish or foil container and pour over enough chicken stock to cover partially the vegetables.
3. Place the slices of cheese over the top.

**TO FREEZE:** Allow to go cold, cover and freeze.

**TO SERVE:** Allow to thaw at room temperature for 2-3 hours. Uncover and bake the vegetables in a preheated oven 200°C, 400°F, Gas Mark 6 for 25-30 minutes and serve.

**Top left: Pommes boulangère**
**Below left: Savoy potatoes**
**Right: Stuffed baked potatoes – from the top,**
**Ham and cheese; Bacon and asparagus;**
**Curried tomato; Liver pâté and horseradish**

# STUFFED BAKED POTATOES

*Preparation time: 20 minutes*
*Cooking time: 1½ hours*
*Recommended freezer life: 4 months*

4 large potatoes
50 g/2 oz butter
2 tablespoons double cream
1 egg yolk
salt
freshly ground black pepper

*Ham and Cheese*
100 g/4 oz ham, diced
2 teaspoons wholegrain mustard
50 g/2 oz Cheddar cheese, grated

*Bacon and Asparagus*
4 rashers streaky bacon, rind
removed, grilled until crisp,
then crumbled
1 × 400 g/14 oz can asparagus
    tips, drained
squeeze of lemon juice

*Curried Tomato*
6 tomatoes, skinned, seeded
and chopped
2 teaspoons curry paste
pinch of caster sugar
2 teaspoons tomato purée

*Liver Pâté and Horseradish*
100 g/4 oz liver pâté
1 tablespoon horseradish sauce
2 teaspoons chopped chives

1. Scrub, dry and prick the potatoes with a fork. Bake in a preheated oven 190°C, 375°F, Gas Mark 5 for 1-1½ hours or until they feel soft.
2. Slice each potato in half lengthwise, scoop out the flesh into a bowl and mash with a fork.
3. Beat in the butter, cream and egg yolk. Add salt and pepper and return the mixture to the potato shells.

**VARIATIONS:**
There are many different stuffings which can be added to the basic potato mixture. Simply beat the extra ingredients together with the basic mixture and heap it all into the potato shells.

**TO FREEZE:** Open freeze for 2 hours, pack in separate bags, seal and return to the freezer.

**TO SERVE:** From frozen, place on a baking sheet in a preheated oven 190°C, 375°F, Gas Mark 5 for 35-40 minutes, or until heated through. If not frozen, reheat after stuffing for only 15-20 minutes.

# PARSNIP PURÉE

*Serves 6*
*Preparation time: 15 minutes*
*Cooking time: 30 minutes*
*Recommended freezer life: 4 months*

1 kg/2 lb parsnips, peeled and
   cut into even-sized chunks
50 g/2 oz butter
salt
freshly ground black pepper
pinch of ground nutmeg
6 tablespoons double cream
**TO SERVE:**
paprika

This dish is equally good when prepared with turnips, carrots or swedes.

1. Boil the parsnips in salted water for about 20 minutes until tender, drain and allow them to stand in a colander for a few minutes to dry off. Mash with a fork or purée in a food processor and beat in the butter, salt, pepper, nutmeg and cream.

**TO FREEZE:** Spoon into a rigid container and allow to go cold. Cover and freeze.

**TO SERVE:** Allow to thaw at room temperature for 3-4 hours. Gently heat through in a pan and serve sprinkled with paprika.

# LEEKS & HAM IN MORNAY SAUCE

*Serves 6*
*Preparation time: 20 minutes*
*Cooking time: 10 minutes*
*Recommended freezer life: 4 months*

6 large leeks, trimmed, left
   whole and washed well in
   salted water
6 wafer thin slices Gruyère
   cheese
6 slices ham
300 ml/½ pint Special Mornay
   Sauce (page 60)
50 g/2 oz stale white
   breadcrumbs
50 g/2 oz Cheddar cheese,
   grated

1. Boil the leeks in salted water for about 15 minutes until just tender, drain and dry on kitchen paper. Wrap each leek in a slice of Gruyère cheese and then in ham.
2. Arrange the wrapped leeks in a serving dish or foil container, and pour over the mornay sauce. Mix together the breadcrumbs and grated Cheddar cheese and sprinkle over the sauce.

**TO FREEZE:** Allow to go cold, cover and freeze.

**TO SERVE:** Allow to thaw at room temperature for 3-4 hours. Uncover and place in a preheated oven 190°C, 375°F, Gas Mark 5 until the leeks are heated through and browned on top.

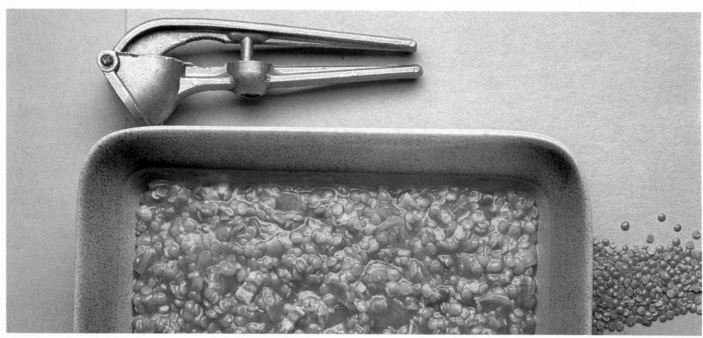

# LENTILS LORRAINE

*Preparation time: 10 minutes, plus
 soaking time*
*Cooking time: 45 minutes*
*Recommended freezer life: 4 months*

225 g/8 oz red lentils, soaked in
 water overnight
50 g/2 oz butter
2 onions, peeled and chopped
6 rashers streaky bacon, rind
 removed and cut into strips
2 tablespoons cornflour
4 tablespoons water
1 clove garlic, crushed
1 tablespoon tomato purée
1 teaspoon lemon juice
pinch of caster sugar
salt
freshly ground black pepper

1.  Cook the lentils in boiling salted water
for about 30 minutes until tender. Drain
and reserve about 450 ml/¾ pint of the
cooking liquid.
2.  Melt the butter in a large pan and
gently fry the onions and bacon until
cooked and the onions are pale golden.
Add the cooked lentils to the pan and
enough of the reserved cooking liquid to
make a thin sauce. Cook the mixture for 5
minutes, stirring occasionally.
3.  Blend the cornflour with the water and
add to the lentils with the crushed garlic,
tomato purée, lemon juice and sugar.
Season with salt and pepper and simmer
for a further 2-3 minutes to thicken the
sauce.

**TO FREEZE:**  Pour into a rigid container
and allow to go cold. Cover and freeze.

**TO SERVE:**  Allow to thaw at room
temperature for 3-4 hours. Gently reheat
in a heavy pan, stirring occasionally.

**Above: Parsnip purée; Leeks and ham in
mornay sauce
Left: Lentils lorraine**

# GARLIC FRENCH BEANS

*Serves 6*
*Preparation time: 2 minutes*
*Cooking time: 10 minutes*

450 g/1 lb frozen whole French
  beans
25 g/1 oz butter
2 tablespoons oil
2 garlic cloves, crushed
freshly ground black pepper

This dish may be eaten hot, or cold as a salad.

1. Cook the beans in boiling salted water until just tender. Drain and set aside.
2. Melt the butter and oil together in a saucepan and add the crushed garlic. Toss the beans in the garlic butter and season them with pepper.

# FRENCH BEANS WITH BACON & TOMATO

*Serves 6*
*Preparation time: 10 minutes*
*Cooking time: 20 minutes*

750 g/1½ lb frozen French beans
100 g/4 oz streaky bacon, rind
  removed and cut into strips
225 g/8 oz tomatoes, skinned,
  seeded and cut into strips
1 teaspoon caster sugar
salt
freshly ground black pepper
chopped fresh chervil or
  parsley, to garnish

1. Cook the beans in boiling salted water until just tender. Drain and cut into 5 cm/3 inch lengths.
2. Cook the bacon strips gently in their own fat for 3-4 minutes, then stir in the tomatoes, sugar, salt and pepper. Add the beans to the tomato mixture and cook for 6-8 minutes, stirring occasionally.
3. Turn the beans into a serving dish and garnish with chopped chervil or parsley.

# CRUNCHY TOPPED CAULIFLOWER

*Serves 6*
*Preparation time: 10 minutes*
*Cooking time: 10 minutes*

450 g/1 lb frozen cauliflower
  florets
4 rashers streaky bacon, rind
  removed
50 g/2 oz fresh white
  breadcrumbs
1 hard-boiled egg
freshly ground black pepper

1. Cook the cauliflower florets in boiling salted water until just tender. Drain and arrange the florets in a serving dish. Keep hot while preparing the topping.
2. Fry the bacon in its own fat until crispy. Drain on kitchen paper then crumble the bacon in a bowl. Fry the breadcrumbs in the bacon fat until crisp, drain and add to the bacon.
3. Halve the egg, scoop out the yolk and sieve into the breadcrumb mixture. Finely chop and add the egg white and mix all the ingredients thoroughly with pepper.
4. Sprinkle the topping over the cauliflower florets, flash the dish under the grill and serve hot.

# BELGIAN CARROTS

*Serves 6*
*Preparation time: 5 minutes*
*Cooking time: 15 minutes*

750 g/1½ lb frozen whole baby
   carrots
25 g/1 oz butter
1 onion, peeled and finely
   chopped
15 g/½ oz plain flour
120 ml/4 fl oz dry white wine
120 ml/4 fl oz chicken stock
1 teaspoon dried sage
1 tablespoon chopped fresh
   parsley
1 teaspoon caster sugar
salt
freshly ground black pepper

1. Cook the carrots in boiling salted water until just tender, drain and set aside.
2. Melt the butter and gently fry the onion until soft and light golden. Stir in the flour and cook for 2-3 minutes. Gradually stir in the wine and stock, then bring the sauce to the boil, add the sage, parsley, sugar and salt and pepper.
3. Add the carrots to the sauce, heat through for 2-3 minutes and turn into a serving dish.

# CARROTS VICHY

*Serves 6*
*Preparation time: 5 minutes*
*Cooking time: 15 minutes*

40 g/1½ oz butter
750 g/1½ lb frozen baby carrots
75 g/3 oz caster sugar
2 tablespoons chopped fresh
   parsley
salt
freshly ground black pepper

1. Melt the butter in a heavy saucepan and add the carrots. Cover and cook the carrots over a gentle heat, stirring occasionally, until the carrots have defrosted.
2. Add the sugar, parsley, salt and pepper, raise the heat and cook the carrots, tossing from time to time, until the juice evaporates and the melted sugar coats the carrots with a light glaze.
3. Turn the carrots into a serving dish and serve hot.

# BRUSSELS SPROUTS WITH CHESTNUTS & BACON

*Serves 6*
*Preparation time: 5 minutes*
*Cooking time: 10 minutes*

750 g/1½ lb frozen Brussels
   sprouts
50 g/2 oz butter
4 rashers back bacon, rind
   removed and cut into strips
1 × 275 g/10 oz can whole
   chestnuts, drained
salt
freshly ground black pepper

This dish is delicious when served as an accompaniment to poultry or game.

1. Cook the sprouts in boiling salted water until just tender. Meanwhile melt the butter in a pan and gently cook the bacon strips for 5 minutes. Add the chestnuts and toss with the bacon until heated through.
2. Drain the sprouts and add to the bacon and chestnuts with salt and pepper. Turn the mixture into a serving dish.

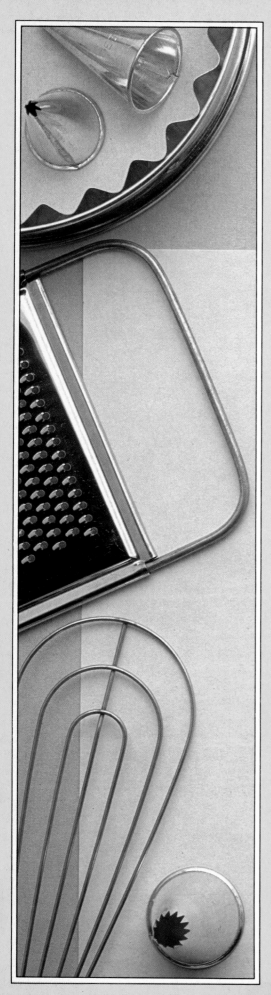

# ICE-CREAMS & DESSERTS

## LEMON MINT SORBET

*Serves 6*
*Preparation time: about 20 minutes*
*Cooking time: 15 minutes*
*Recommended freezer life: 4 months*

300 ml/½ pint water
225 g/8 oz caster sugar
250 ml/8 fl oz fresh lemon juice
rind of 1 lemon
rind of 2 oranges
1 tablespoon Crème de Menthe
2 egg whites, whipped
**TO SERVE:**
Sponge Finger Biscuits (page 141)

1. Bring the water and sugar slowly to the boil in a pan, stirring occasionally. Simmer for 10 minutes, until the colourless syrup forms a firm ball when a small amount is dropped into a cup of cold water, then cool.
2. Stir in the lemon juice, and add the lemon and orange rind. Pour the sorbet into ice cream trays and place in the freezer. Stir from time to time until the mixture becomes mushy. Remove from the freezer, and stir in the Crème de Menthe and egg whites and mix thoroughly. Return the sorbet to the freezer for at least 2-3 hours.

**TO SERVE:** Scoop into individual glass dishes and serve with Sponge Finger Biscuits.

## WATERMELON SORBET

*Serves 6*
*Preparation time: about 20 minutes*
*Cooking time: 15 minutes*
*Recommended freezer life: 4 months*

1½ kg/3 lb (about ½) watermelon, peeled and pips removed
300 ml/½ pint water
225 g/8 oz caster sugar
juice of ½ lemon
2 egg whites, whipped
1 teaspoon chopped fresh mint
**TO SERVE:**
Almond Tiles (page 140)

1. Sieve or liquidize the melon flesh and set aside. Bring the water, sugar and lemon juice slowly to the boil, stirring occasionally. Simmer for 10 minutes, until the colourless syrup forms a firm ball when a small amount is dropped into a cup of cold water, then cool.
2. Pour the syrup into the watermelon purée and stir thoroughly. Place in the freezer, and stir from time to time, until the mixture becomes mushy.
3. Remove from the freezer and fold in the egg whites and mint. Pour into ice trays and return to the freezer for at least 2-3 hours.

**TO SERVE:** Scoop into individual glasses and serve with Almond Tiles.

# VANILLA ICE CREAM

*Makes 1 pint*
*Preparation time: about 20 minutes*
*Cooking time: about 30 minutes*
*Recommended freezer life: 3 months*

3 egg yolks
100 g/4 oz caster sugar
300 ml/½ pint milk
1 teaspoon vanilla essence
150 ml/¼ pint double cream

**Ice creams, clockwise from the top: Praline; Orange and lemon; Brown breadcrumb; Vanilla; Chocolate**

1. Place the egg yolks and the sugar in a mixing bowl and beat with a wooden spoon until the mixture becomes pale and creamy. Warm the milk, add the vanilla essence and pour on to the eggs and sugar, stirring well.
2. Strain the mixture into a bowl placed over a pan of simmering water, and cook over a gentle heat for about 30 minutes, stirring continually, until the custard is thick enough to coat the back of the spoon. Do not allow to boil or it will curdle.
3. Allow the custard to cool, then stir in the cream and pour into a shallow ice tray or ice cream maker, and place in the freezer for at least 2-3 hours. If using the ice tray method the ice cream will need to be stirred several times during the freezing process to prevent crystals from forming. If using an ice cream maker, it is best to follow the maker's instructions.

**VARIATIONS:**

*Orange & Lemon Ice Cream*
Follow the basic vanilla ice cream recipe. Omit the vanilla and infuse the grated rind of 1 orange and 1 lemon with the milk.

*Praline Ice Cream*
Make up the praline (see recipe for Praline Profiteroles page 123). Follow the basic vanilla ice cream recipe, stirring in 50 g/2 oz ground praline with the cream.

*Brown Breadcrumb Ice Cream*
Crisp 50 g/2 oz fresh brown breadcrumbs in the oven and allow to go cold. Follow the basic vanilla ice cream recipe, stirring in the breadcrumbs with the cream.

*Chocolate Ice Cream*
Follow the basic vanilla ice cream recipe, but delete the vanilla essence and stir 100 g/4 oz melted plain chocolate into the custard as it cools.

# LYCHEE ICE CREAM

*Preparation time: about 45 minutes*
*Cooking time: 15 minutes*
*Recommended freezer life: 3 months*

1 × 225 g/8 oz can lychees
75 g/3 oz caster sugar
1 tablespoon lemon juice
300 ml/½ pint plain
    unsweetened yogurt
150 ml/¼ pint double cream,
    lightly whipped

1. Strain the lychees and put the syrup in a pan with the sugar and lemon juice. Simmer over a low heat until the syrup forms a firm ball when a small amount is dropped into a cup of cold water. Allow to go cold, then stir in the yogurt.
2. Pour the mixture into a shallow rigid container and freeze, stirring occasionally, until a mushy consistency, then remove from the freezer.
3. Chop the lychees and fold into the yogurt base, then fold in the lightly whipped cream. Pour the ice cream into a rigid container, cover and freeze for at least 2-3 hours.

**VARIATIONS:**

*Pineapple Ice Cream*
Use the same recipe as for the lychee ice cream, using 1 × 225 g/8 oz can pineapple in place of the lychees.

*Mandarin Ice Cream*
Use the same recipe as for the lychee ice cream, using 1 × 225 g/8 oz can mandarin oranges in place of the lychees.

*Apricot Ice Cream*
Use the same recipe as for the lychee ice cream, using 1 × 225 g/8 oz can apricot halves in place of the lychees.

*Pear Ice Cream*
Use the same recipe as for the lychee ice cream, using 1 × 225 g/8 oz can pear halves in place of the lychees.

**Ice creams, clockwise from the top: Mandarin; Lychee; Pineapple**

# STRAWBERRY ICE CREAM

*Serves 6*
*Preparation time: about 30 minutes*
*Recommended freezer life: 3 months*

450 g/1 lb fresh strawberries,
    hulled or frozen strawberries,
    thawed
225 g/8 oz icing sugar, sifted
300 ml/½ pint double cream,
    lightly whipped

This is a very quick method of making ice cream, and needs no stirring during the freezing period.

1. Strain or purée the strawberries in a liquidizer or food processor. (Straining through a sieve removes the pips.) Gradually stir in the icing sugar, then fold in the whipped cream. Pour the ice cream into ice trays and freeze for at least 2-3 hours.

**TO SERVE:** Spoon into individual dishes and serve with Sponge Finger Biscuits (page 141).

**VARIATION:**
This ice cream may also be made with raspberries or blackberries.

# SWEET PASTRY AND MERINGUE RING

*Serves 8*
*Preparation time: 40 minutes*
*Cooking time: 1½ hours*
*Recommended freezer life: 4 months*

150 g/5 oz plain flour
75 g/3 oz butter, cut into chunks
50 g/2 oz caster sugar
2 egg yolks
*Meringue:*
4 (120 ml/4 fl oz) egg whites
225 g/8 oz caster sugar
**TO SERVE:**
450 g/1 lb fresh strawberries or
    frozen strawberries, thawed
300 ml/½ pint double cream,
    whipped

1. To make the pastry, sift the flour on to a board and make a well in the centre. Place the butter, sugar and egg yolks in the well and work all the ingredients thoroughly together with the fingertips. Knead lightly, then chill in the refrigerator for 30 minutes.
2. Roll out to form a 23 cm/9 inch circle and place on a baking sheet. Crimp the edges and prick with a fork. Mark the pastry into 8 wedges with the back of a knife.
3. Bake in a preheated oven at 160°C, 325°F, Gas Mark 3 for 15 minutes, until lightly browned, then allow to cool.
4. To make the meringue, whip the egg whites until stiff, then whisk in 2 tablespoons of the caster sugar. Fold in the remaining caster sugar and place the mixture into a large piping bag fitted with a star nozzle.
5. Pipe whirls of meringue round the edge of the pastry base, allowing one whirl per marked wedge. Place the ring in a preheated oven at 150°C, 300°F, Gas Mark 2 for approximately 1 hour, or until the meringue is set. Allow to cool.

**TO FREEZE:** Place in a rigid container, cover and freeze. (Meringue remains brittle when frozen, so pack it carefully.)

**TO SERVE:** Allow to thaw at room temperature for 2-3 hours. Select 6 strawberries for the decoration, then chop up the remaining strawberries and fold into the whipped cream. Pile this mixture into the centre of the ring and decorate with the whole strawberries.

**VARIATION:**
Other fruits, such as raspberries, apricots, ripe cherries, chopped pineapple, black and white grapes, or blackberries, may be used in place of the strawberries.

# GOOSEBERRY & GINGER FOOL

*Preparation time: 30 minutes*
*Cooking time: 10 minutes*
*Recommended freezer life: 4 months*

450 g/1 lb fresh or frozen
  gooseberries, topped and
  tailed
3 tablespoons water
3 tablespoons caster sugar
pinch of ground ginger
2 tablespoons ginger syrup from
  preserved ginger
2 tablespoons preserved ginger,
  chopped
300 ml/½ pint double cream,
  whipped
**TO SERVE:**
Cigarettes Russes (page 141)

1. Place the gooseberries, water, sugar and ground ginger in a saucepan, bring to the boil, cover and simmer gently for 8-10 minutes, until the fruit is tender. Allow to cool.
2. Pass the mixture through a sieve to remove any traces of pips. Stir in the ginger syrup and chopped ginger, then fold in the whipped cream.

**TO FREEZE:** Pour into a rigid container, cover and freeze.

**TO SERVE:** Allow to thaw at room temperature for 5-6 hours. Spoon into individual glass dishes and serve with Cigarettes Russes.

**VARIATION:**
This sweet can also be prepared with fresh or frozen apricots.

# CRÈME BRÛLÉE WITH GRAPES

*Serves 6*
*Preparation time: 20 minutes*
*Cooking time: about 1 hour*
*Recommended freezer life: 4 months*

175 g/6 oz white grapes, halved
  and pips removed
6 egg yolks
2 tablespoons caster sugar
600 ml/1 pint double cream
1 vanilla pod
**TO SERVE:**
4 tablespoons demerara sugar

1. Arrange the grapes in the base of a 900 ml/1½ pint shallow ovenproof dish. Cream together the egg yolks and the caster sugar until pale.
2. Gently heat the double cream with the vanilla pod until the cream is tepid, remove the vanilla pod and pour the cream on to the egg yolks. Blend well and strain over the grapes.
3. Place the dish in a roasting tin half filled with boiling water and cook the brûlée in a preheated oven at 120°C, 250°F, Gas Mark ½ for 1 hour, or until the custard is set.

**TO FREEZE:** Allow to go cold, then place in a polythene bag, seal and freeze.

**TO SERVE:** Remove from the polythene bag and sprinkle the demerara sugar evenly over the top. Place under a hot grill until the sugar melts, then leave to stand at room temperature for 2 hours before serving.

**VARIATION:**
Other fresh fruits, such as strawberries, raspberries, chopped apricots or ripe cherries, can be used in place of the grapes.

# CHOCOLATE CARAQUE GÂTEAU

*Preparation time: 30 minutes*
*Cooking time: 1 hour*
*Recommended freezer life: 4 months*

4 eggs
100 g/4 oz caster sugar
100 g/4 oz plain flour, sifted
40 g/1½ oz butter, melted and
  cooled

**FRENCH BUTTER CREAM:**
65 g/2½ oz caster sugar
150 ml/¼ pint water
2 egg yolks, beaten
150 g/5 oz unsalted butter,
  softened
100 g/4 oz plain chocolate,
  melted and cooled

**CARAQUE DECORATION:**
50 g/2 oz plain chocolate

**TO FINISH:**
25 g/1 oz plain chocolate, grated
icing sugar for dusting

1. Grease an 18 cm/7 inch deep cake tin.
2. To make the cake base, put the eggs and the sugar into a bowl, and place over a pan of gently simmering water. Whisk the mixture well until it is light, creamy and stiff enough to hold the impression of the whisk. Remove the bowl from the pan and continue whisking until cool.
3. Fold in the sifted flour and the melted butter. Pour into the prepared tin and bake in a preheated oven at 180°C. 350°F, Gas Mark 4 for 35-40 minutes, or until the cake is firm to the touch and begins to shrink from the sides of the tin.
4. Turn out of the tin and allow to cool on a wire tray.
5. To make the French butter cream, boil the sugar and the water in a small pan until the colourless syrup forms a firm ball when a small amount is dropped into a cup of cold water. Pour slowly on to the beaten egg yolks, whisking constantly. When cool, thick and fluffy, beat in the butter, little by little. Stir in the melted chocolate and chill in the refrigerator.

6. Meanwhile, make the caraque decoration. Melt the 50 g/2 oz of plain chocolate in a bowl over hot water, taking care that it does not become too warm, or the gloss will be spoilt. Pour the melted chocolate on to a lightly greased baking sheet, and spread thinly with a palette knife. When completely cold, scrape the chocolate off the baking sheet with a sharp knife to form thin cigarette rolls.
7. Now assemble the gâteau.
Cut the cake in half and sandwich together with half of the butter cream. Spread the rest of the butter cream on the top and sides of the cake and sprinkle with the grated chocolate. Decorate the top with the caraque rolls, and dust with a little icing sugar.

**TO FREEZE:** Open freeze for 2-3 hours, then place in a rigid container, cover and freeze.

**TO SERVE:** Allow to thaw at room temperature for 3-4 hours before serving.

# CHOCOLATE WHISKY MALAKOFF

*Serves 6-8*
*Preparation time: 1 hour*
*Cooking time: 5 minutes*
*Recommended freezer life: 4 months*

18 Sponge Finger Biscuits
  (page 141)
100 g/4 oz butter
100 g/4 oz caster sugar
3 eggs, separated
100 g/4 oz plain chocolate
2 tablespoons water
2 tablespoons whisky
dash of angostura bitters
2 tablespoons powdered
  gelatine
6 tablespoons water

**TO SERVE:**
300 ml/½ pint double cream,
  whipped
grated plain chocolate

1. Lightly oil a 15 cm/6 inch charlotte mould. Draw round the base and top of the mould and cut out two circles of greaseproof paper to fit. Cover the base of the mould with the relevant round of greaseproof paper, oiled. Line the sides of the tin with sponge finger biscuits and set aside.
2. Cream the butter with the sugar. Beat in the egg yolks, one at a time, continue beating until the sugar has dissolved and the mixture is pale and thick.
3. Gently melt the chocolate with the 2 tablespoons water and stir into the egg mixture. Add the whisky and bitters.
4. Dissolve the gelatine in the 6 table-spoons water and add to the mixture. Allow to cool till on the point of setting.
5. Whisk the egg whites until they form stiff white peaks, then fold into the mixture. Pour into the lined tin and cover with the second round of greaseproof paper, oiled. Allow to set in the refrigerator.

**TO FREEZE:** Place in a polythene bag, seal and freeze.

**TO SERVE:** Allow to thaw in the refrigerator for 8 hours, then turn out on to a serving plate. Decorate with florets of whipped cream, and sprinkle with the grated chocolate.

# PRALINE PROFITEROLES WITH CHOCOLATE SAUCE

*Makes 20 profiteroles*
*Preparation time: 30 minutes*
*Cooking time: 50 minutes*
*Recommended freezer life: 4 months*

100 g/4 oz butter
300 ml/½ pint water
150 g/5 oz plain flour, sifted
3 eggs
PRALINE FILLING:
50 g/2 oz whole almonds,
   unpeeled
50 g/2 oz caster sugar

250 ml/8 fl oz double cream
TO SERVE:
225 g/8 oz plain chocolate
100 g/4 oz caster sugar
120 ml/4 fl oz water

**From left to right: Chocolate
whisky malakoff; Chocolate
caraque gâteau; Praline
profiteroles with chocolate
sauce**

For convenience make double the
quantity of praline given here and the
extra amount can be stored for about 3
months in a screw-topped jar. Use to
decorate gâteaux, and flavour ice cream
and soufflés.

1. Melt the butter in the 300 ml/½ pint
water over a low heat.
2. Bring the mixture to the boil, and
quickly add the flour.
3. Beat vigorously, until the mixture
thickens, and forms a smooth paste.
4. Cook the mixture beating continually
for 2-3 minutes, until it leaves the sides of
the pan.
5. Allow to cool for 3-4 minutes, then
beat in the eggs one at a time.
6. Grease a baking sheet and spoon the
pastry out in rough ball shapes to form 20
buns. Bake in a preheated oven at 220°C,
425°F, Gas Mark 7 for 20 minutes until
well risen and light golden. Pierce each
bun with a skewer to allow the air to
escape, then return to the oven for 2-3
minutes to dry out.

7. Allow the profiteroles to cool on a wire
tray while preparing the filling.
8. Put the almonds and sugar in a small
saucepan and heat gently until the sugar
dissolves. Boil the mixture until the sugar
becomes nut brown in colour, then pour
out into a well oiled tin and allow to set.
9. Grind the praline to a powder in a
coffee grinder or liquidizer.
10. Whip the cream stiffly and fold in the
praline. Split the profiteroles and fill with
the cream mixture.

**TO FREEZE:** Pack the profiteroles into a
rigid container, cover and freeze.

**TO SERVE:** Allow to thaw at room
temperature for 3-4 hours, then arrange
on a serving dish in a pyramid shape.

To make the sauce, melt the chocolate,
sugar and water over a gentle heat,
stirring gently. When thoroughly blended
raise the heat and allow to boil, without
stirring, until the sauce thickens. (This
should take approximately 10 minutes.)

Cool slightly, then pour over the
profiteroles and serve immediately.

# CHESTNUT CREAM

*Preparation time: 15 minutes*
*Cooking time: 5 minutes*
*Recommended freezer life: 4 months*

1 × 225 g/8 oz can sweetened
  chestnut purée
2 tablespoons milk
100 g/4 oz plain chocolate,
  melted and slightly cooled
50 g/2 oz walnuts, chopped
150 ml/¼ pint double cream,
  stiffly whipped
TO SERVE:
75 ml/3 fl oz double cream,
  whipped
4 walnut halves

1. Place the chestnut purée in a mixing bowl and gradually stir in the milk. Stir in the melted chocolate and chopped walnuts, then fold in the cream. Spoon the mixture into 4 individual pots and allow to set in the refrigerator for about 20 minutes.

TO FREEZE: Cover with cling film and freeze.

TO SERVE: Allow to thaw in the refrigerator for 5-6 hours. Decorate with whirls of whipped cream and walnut halves.

# LITTLE CHOCOLATE POTS

*Preparation time: 30 minutes*
*Cooking time: 5 minutes*
*Recommended freezer life: 4 months*

2 eggs, separated
50 g/2 oz caster sugar
100 g/4 oz plain chocolate,
  melted and cooled
75 ml/3 fl oz single cream
TO SERVE:
75 ml/3 fl oz double cream,
  whipped
coarsely grated chocolate

1. Put the egg yolks and sugar in a bowl placed over a pan of gently simmering water. Whisk until the mixture is fluffy.
2. Remove the bowl from the heat and continue whisking until the mixture is cool. Mix together the melted chocolate and the cream and fold into the egg yolk mixture until thoroughly blended.
3. Whip the egg whites until stiff and fold into the chocolate mixture. Divide the mixture between 4 individual pots, and allow to set in the refrigerator.

TO FREEZE: Cover with cling film and freeze.

TO SERVE: Allow to thaw in the lower part of the refrigerator for 4-5 hours. Decorate with cream and chocolate.

# ALMOND & APRICOT MERINGUE CAKE

*Serves 6*
*Preparation time: 30 minutes,*
  *plus soaking time*
*Cooking time: 40 minutes*
*Recommended freezer life: 4 months*

225 g/8 oz caster sugar
100 g/4 oz flaked almonds
4 (120 ml/4 fl oz) egg whites
FILLING:
100 g/4 oz dried apricots,
  soaked overnight in water or
  1 × 200 g/7 oz can apricots,
  drained, finely chopped
1 tablespoon dark rum
300 ml/½ pint double cream,
  stiffly whipped
50 g/2 oz flaked almonds, toasted
TO DECORATE:
icing sugar for dusting
grated plain chocolate

1. Sift the caster sugar into a bowl and stir in the flaked almonds. Whisk the egg whites to form stiff peaks and beat in 1 tablespoon of the sugar and almond mixture. Fold in the remaining sugar and almonds.
2. Oil a large baking sheet, cover with greaseproof paper and oil the surface of the paper. Spread out the meringue mixture to make 2 circles, each 18 cm/ 7 inches in size.
3. Cook in a preheated oven at 160°C, 325°F, Gas Mark 3 for 40 minutes. Cool on a wire tray while preparing the filling.
4. Put the apricots into a small bowl and add the rum. Fold in the whipped cream and toasted almonds.
5. Sandwich the two circles of meringue together with the cream mixture, and dust the top of the cake with icing sugar

and sprinkle with grated chocolate.

TO FREEZE: Open freeze for 3-4 hours, then, because meringue remains fragile, pack into a rigid plastic container, cover and return to the freezer.

TO SERVE: Allow to thaw for at least 5 hours at room temperature.

**Right: Almond and apricot meringue cake**

# EMPRESS RICE MOULD

*Serves 6*
*Preparation time: 10 minutes*
*Cooking time: 1 hour*
*Recommended freezer life: 4 months*

90 g/3½ oz Carolina rice
450 ml/¾ pint milk

CUSTARD:
150 ml/¼ pint milk
4 egg yolks
90 g/3½ oz caster sugar
1½ tablespoons powdered
    gelatine
4 tablespoons water

150 ml/¼ pint double cream
90 g/3½ oz crystallized fruits,
    chopped

TO SERVE:
4 tablespoons redcurrant jelly
1 tablespoon Kirsch

1. Blanch the rice in boiling water for 3 minutes, drain and place the rice in a saucepan. Pour over the 450 ml/¾ pint milk and bring gently to simmering point. Cover and gently cook the rice until tender, then set aside to cool.
2. Heat the 150 ml/¼ pint milk in a small saucepan. Beat the egg yolks with the sugar in a bowl, and stir in the hot milk.
3. Strain the custard into a bowl placed over a pan of simmering water and cook gently, stirring with a wooden spoon, until it thickens.
4. Blend the gelatine with the water and add to the custard, stirring until the gelatine has dissolved. Stir the custard into the cooked rice and milk mixture, and leave to go cold, stirring occasionally, until the mixture is on the point of setting.
5. Whip the cream and fold into the mixture with the fruits. Pour into a lightly oiled 1.2 litre/2 pint ring mould, and allow to set in the refrigerator.

TO FREEZE:  Place in a polythene bag, seal and freeze.

TO SERVE:  Allow to thaw at room temperature for 5-6 hours, then turn out on to a serving dish. Melt the redcurrant jelly and stir in the Kirsch. Cool the sauce, then pour over the rice mould just before serving.

# CINNAMON RASPBERRY TART

*Serves 6*
*Preparation time: 40 minutes*
*Cooking time: 50 minutes*
*Recommended freezer life: 4 months*

150 g/5 oz plain flour
1 tablespoon ground cinnamon
65 g/2½ oz ground almonds
1 teaspoon grated lemon rind
50 g/2 oz butter, cut into pieces
1 egg
**FILLING:**
225 g/8 oz fresh or frozen
  raspberries, or 350 g/12 oz
  raspberry jam
225 g/8 oz caster sugar

4 tablespoons redcurrant jelly

1.  Sift the flour on to a board. Sprinkle the cinnamon, ground almonds and lemon rind on to the flour, then make a well in the centre. Place the butter and the egg in the well and work together with the fingertips, until the mixture forms a stiff dough. Chill in the refrigerator for 20 minutes.
2.  If using fresh or frozen raspberries, place them in a pan with the sugar and cook over a gentle heat for 15-20 minutes. Allow the raspberry mixture to go cold.
3.  Roll out the pastry and use it to line an 18 cm/7 inch flan dish. Fill the flan with the cooked raspberries, or the raspberry jam. Re-roll the pastry trimmings and cut into long strips, to make a lattice pattern over the top of the tart.

4.  Bake in a preheated oven at 190°C, 375°F, Gas Mark 5 for 25-30 minutes. Allow to cool slightly, then melt the redcurrant jelly and brush over the top of the tart to form a glaze.

**TO FREEZE:** Allow to go cold, then place in a polythene bag, seal and freeze.

**TO SERVE:** Allow to thaw at room temperature for 5-6 hours. Serve cold or gently warm the tart through, and serve with lightly whipped cream.

# DUTCH APPLE & MINCEMEAT TART

*Serves 6*
*Preparation time: 35 minutes*
*Cooking time: 45 minutes*
*Recommended freezer life: 4 months*

150 g/5 oz plain flour
75 g/3 oz butter, cut into pieces
50 g/2 oz caster sugar
2 egg yolks
FILLING:
450 g/1 lb cooking apples,
    peeled, cored and quartered
1 teaspoon grated lemon rind
pinch of ground cinnamon
pinch of ground nutmeg
2 cloves
2 tablespoons water
150 g/5 oz mincemeat
40 g/1½ oz demerara sugar

1. To make the pastry, sift the flour on to a board and make a well in the centre. Place the butter, sugar and egg yolks in the well and work all the ingredients thoroughly together with the fingertips. Knead lightly, then chill in the refrigerator for 30 minutes.
2. Roll out the pastry and use to line an 18 cm/7 inch fluted flan tin with a loose bottom. Set the flan aside while making the filling.
3. Place two-thirds of the apples with the lemon rind, cinnamon, nutmeg, cloves and water in a saucepan, cover and stew for 15 minutes, then allow to cool.
4. Spread the base of the tart with the mincemeat and then cover with the stewed apples. Slice the remaining apples very thinly and arrange, overlapping, on top. Sprinkle with the demerara sugar and bake in a preheated moderately hot oven at 190°C, 375°F, Gas Mark 5 for 30 minutes.

TO FREEZE:  Allow to go cold, then place in a polythene bag, seal and freeze.

TO SERVE:  Allow to thaw for 5 hours at room temperature. This dish may be served cold with lightly whipped cream, or warmed through gently and served with whipped cream.

# APPLE & ORANGE PIE

*Serves 6*
*Preparation time: 30 minutes*
*Cooking time: 1 hour 10 minutes*
*Recommended freezer life: 4 months*

350 g/12 oz frozen shortcrust
    pastry, thawed
3 tablespoons orange juice
1 teaspoon lemon juice
grated rind of 1 orange
½ teaspoon ground cinnamon
pinch of ground nutmeg
6 cloves (optional)
50 g/2 oz sultanas
1 kg/2 lb cooking apples,
    peeled, cored and sliced
4 tablespoons demerara sugar
1 egg, beaten
1 tablespoon caster sugar

1. Roll out half of the shortcrust pastry and use to line the base of a 25 cm/10 inch pie plate. Prick the pastry with a fork and bake blind in a preheated oven at 180°C, 350°F, Gas Mark 4 for 10 minutes. Lift off the greaseproof paper and dried beans and allow the pastry to cool.
2. Mix together the orange juice, lemon juice, orange rind, cinnamon, nutmeg and cloves.
3. Sprinkle half of the sultanas over the pastry base and place a layer of half the apples on top. Sprinkle with half the demerara sugar and pour over half of the juice mixture.
4. Repeat these layers, then roll out the remaining pastry and use to cover the pie, sealing the edges with a little beaten egg. Decorate the top with leaves made from pastry trimmings. Brush the pie with beaten egg, and sprinkle with caster sugar.
5. Cook in a preheated oven at 190°C, 375°F, Gas mark 5 for 30 minutes. Cover with foil, reduce the oven temperature to moderate 160°C, 325°F, Gas Mark 3 and cook for a further 30 minutes.

TO FREEZE:  Allow to go cold, then place in a polythene bag, seal and freeze.

TO SERVE:  Allow to thaw at room temperature for 6-8 hours, cover with foil and reheat in a preheated oven at 160°C, 325°F, Gas Mark 3 for 25-30 minutes. Serve with cream or warm custard.

**Top: Dutch apple and mincemeat tart**
**Below: Apple and orange pie**

# TIPSY ALMOND TRIFLE

*Serves 6*
*Preparation time: 25 minutes*
*Cooking time: 10 minutes (for custard)*
*Recommended freezer life: 4 months*

1 × 100 g/4 oz packet trifle sponges
4 tablespoons raspberry jam
150 ml/¼ pint sherry
75 g/3 oz ground almonds
50 g/2 oz ratafia biscuits, crumbled
3 tablespoons double cream
600 ml/1 pint hot custard
**TO SERVE:**
150 ml/¼ pint double cream, whipped
glacé cherries
angelica leaves
ratafia biscuits

1. If making the trifle for the freezer, line a straight sided china or pyrex serving dish with foil, allowing a border of it to come up above the rim of the bowl.
2. Halve the trifle sponges and sandwich them together with the raspberry jam. Cut each sponge into 4 and arrange in the bottom of the dish. Pour over the sherry and sprinkle the ground almonds and crumbled ratafia biscuits on top.
3. Stir the cream into the hot custard and pour the mixture over the trifle. Cover the dish with cling film to prevent a skin from forming while the custard is cooling.

**TO FREEZE:** Allow to go cold, then open freeze for 5-6 hours. When frozen, lift out of the dish by the foil border, place in a polythene bag, seal and return to freezer.

**TO SERVE:** Peel the foil away from the frozen trifle and return to the original dish. Allow to thaw at room temperature for at least 6 hours. Decorate the top with whirls of whipped cream, glacé cherries, angelica leaves and ratafia biscuits.

# GÂTEAU PITHIVIERS

*Serves 6*
*Preparation time: 25 minutes*
*Cooking time: 30 minutes*
*Recommended freezer life: 4 months*

50 g/2 oz butter
50 g/2 oz caster sugar
1 egg yolk
50 g/2 oz ground almonds
1 × 375 g/13 oz packet puff pastry, thawed
1 egg, beaten
**TO SERVE:**
icing sugar for dredging

1. Cream the butter with the sugar. Add the egg yolk and mix well, then stir in the ground almonds.
2. Roll out the pastry to a thin rectangle and cut out 2 circles, each 18 cm/7 inches in size. Place one of the pastry circles on a wetted baking sheet and spoon the almond mixture in a mound on to the middle, leaving a 2.5 cm/1 inch edge.
3. Roll out the pastry trimmings and cut a thin strip 5 mm/¼ inch wide. Brush the border of the almond filled pastry circle with beaten egg and place the pastry strip around the edge. Brush the strip with beaten egg and place the second pastry circle over the top of the almond filling.
**VARIATIONS:**
4. Crimp the edge of the gâteau to seal and with the back of a knife, scallop the edge. Using the point of a knife, make a small hole in the centre to allow the steam to escape. Prick the surface with a fork and brush lightly with beaten egg.
5. Bake in a preheated oven at 220°C, 425°F, Gas Mark 7 for 30 minutes, or until the pastry is risen and golden brown.

**TO FREEZE:** Allow to go cold, then place in a polythene bag, seal and freeze.

**TO SERVE:** Allow to thaw at room temperature for 6-8 hours. Dredge with icing sugar and serve with double cream.

# APPLE & BLACKBERRY PLAIT

*Serves 6-8*
*Preparation time: 25 minutes*
*Cooking time: 40 minutes*
*Recommended freezer life: 4 months*

1 × 375 g/13 oz packet puff
   pastry, thawed
225 g/8 oz blackberries
1 large cooking apple, peeled,
   cored and diced
1 tablespoon caster sugar
50 g/2 oz flaked almonds
1 egg, beaten
1 tablespoon demerara sugar

1. Roll out the pastry to form a rectangle 20 × 30 cm/9 × 12 inches in size. With the pastry rectangle upright, make diagonal slashes at 2 cm/¾ inch intervals down both lengths, leaving a 10 cm/4 inch panel down the centre.
2. Mix together the blackberries, apple, caster sugar and almonds, and spread evenly down the centre panel. Turn the 2 ends of the pastry in, then plait the pastry strips over the filling, securing the last two strips under the plait with a little beaten egg.
3. Place on a baking sheet, brush with beaten egg and sprinkle the top with demerara sugar. Bake the plait in a preheated oven at 200°C, 400°F, Gas Mark 6 for 15-20 minutes, until well risen, then reduce the heat to 180°C, 350°F, Gas Mark 4, and continue cooking for 20 minutes.

**TO FREEZE:** Allow to go cold, place in a polythene bag, seal and freeze.

**TO SERVE:** Allow to thaw at room temperature for 3-4 hours. Place on a baking sheet and heat through in a preheated oven at 160°C, 325°F, Gas Mark 3 for 15 minutes.

Serve the plait with double cream.

## VARIATIONS:

*Apple & Mincemeat Plait*
Use the same recipe as for apple and blackberry plait, omitting the sugar and replacing the blackberries with mincemeat.

*Apple & Raspberry Plait*
Use the same recipe as for apple and blackberry plait, replacing the blackberries with fresh raspberries.

*Apple & Apricot Plait*
Use the same recipe as for apple and blackberry plait, replacing the blackberries with 275 g/10 oz fresh apricots, halved and stoned.

**Left: Gâteau pithiviers**
**Right: Apple and blackberry plait**

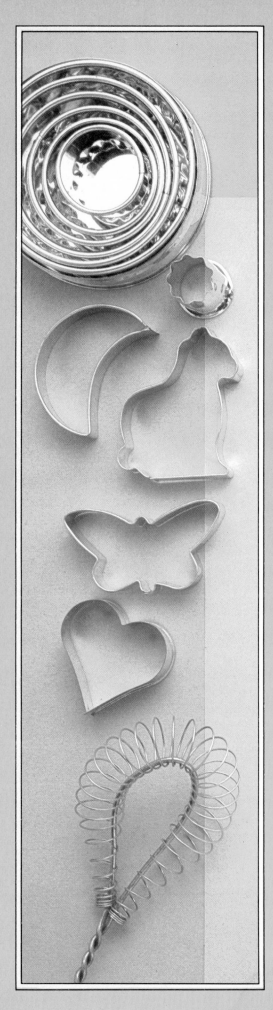

# BAKING

## FRUIT & NUT TEA LOAF

*Makes 1 × 1 kg/2 lb loaf*
*Preparation time: 25 minutes*
*Cooking time: 1¼-1½ hours*
*Recommended freezer life: 6 months*

350 g/12 oz self-raising flour
½ teaspoon salt
pinch of ground cinnamon
pinch of ground cloves
75 g/3 oz caster sugar
40 g/1½ oz currants
40 g/1½ oz sultanas
75 g/3 oz shelled walnuts,
  roughly chopped
300 ml/10 fl oz milk
2 eggs
50 g/2 oz butter, melted

1. Sift the flour, salt, cinnamon and cloves together into a large mixing bowl.
2. Add the sugar, currants, sultanas and walnuts and mix well together.
3. Beat together the milk and eggs, and pour them in. Add the melted butter, beat well for 2-3 minutes.
4. Line a 1 kg/2 lb loaf tin with greased greaseproof paper and spoon in the mixture.
5. Cook in a preheated oven at 180°C, 350°F, Gas Mark 4 for 1½ hours.
6. Allow the bread to cool in the tin for 15 minutes, then turn it on to a wire tray, peel off the paper and leave to cool.

**TO FREEZE:** When cold, place in a polythene bag, seal and freeze.

**TO SERVE:** Allow to thaw at room temperature for 2-3 hours. Serve sliced and buttered.

## TREACLE SODA BREAD

*Makes 1 loaf*
*Preparation time: 25 minutes*
*Cooking time: 35-40 minutes*
*Recommended freezer life: 6 months*

225 g/8 oz plain flour
225 g/8 oz wholemeal flour
2 tablespoons baking powder
1 teaspoon salt
50 g/2 oz butter
75 g/3 oz sultanas
300 ml/½ pint milk
1 teaspoon vinegar
2 tablespoons black treacle

1. Blend the flours together in a large mixing bowl, and mix in the baking powder and salt.
2. Rub in the butter until the mixture resembles fine breadcrumbs, then stir in the sultanas.
3. Place the milk, vinegar and treacle in a saucepan, and heat them gently, stirring.
4. Allow the liquid to cool a little, then stir it into the flour to form a dough.
5. Turn the dough on to a floured board, and knead it gently for 2 minutes.
6. Shape the dough into a ball, and place it on a lightly greased baking sheet. Cut a deep cross in the loaf.
7. Cook in a preheated oven at 200°C, 400°F, Gas Mark 6 for 35-40 minutes, until well risen and golden brown.
8. Test the loaf with a skewer, which will come out clean when the bread is cooked.
9. Cool the loaf on a wire tray.

**TO FREEZE:** When cold, place in a polythene bag, seal and freeze.

**TO SERVE:** Allow to thaw at room temperature for 1½-2 hours. Serve with butter and strawberry jam.

# WHOLEMEAL BREAD

*Makes 2 × 450 g /1 lb loaves
or 1 × 1 kg /2 lb loaf*
*Preparation time: 2 hours*
*Cooking time: 35-45 minutes
(depending on size)*
*Recommended freezer life: 6 months*

750 g/1½ lb wholemeal flour
1 teaspoon salt
15 g/½ oz butter
20 g/¾ oz fresh yeast or 3
teaspoons dried yeast with 1
teaspoon sugar
500 ml/18 fl oz tepid water
25 g/1 oz cracked wheat

1. Place the flour and salt in a large warm mixing bowl and rub in the butter.
2. Blend the yeast with a little of the tepid water. If using dried yeast add the sugar at the same time and leave until frothy. Add the yeast mixture to the remaining water.
3. Add the yeast mixture to the flour. Beat the flour and liquid together, using your hands or a wooden spoon, until they form a dough.
4. Alternatively, knead the dough for 5-6 minutes using the dough hook attachment of an electric mixer.
5. Turn the dough on to a floured board, and knead it thoroughly for about 5 minutes.
6. Place the kneaded dough in the mixing bowl and cover it with an oiled polythene bag. Leave in a warm place until it has doubled in size.
7. Turn the risen dough on to a floured board and knead it gently.
8. Shape the dough and place it in greased tin(s).
9. Place the tin(s) in large oiled polythene bags and tie the bags loosely. Allow the dough to prove in a warm place until double in size.
10. Uncover and sprinkle the tops of the loaves with the cracked wheat, then cook in a preheated oven at 220°C, 425°F, Gas Mark 7 for 20 minutes.
11. Reduce the heat to 200°C, 400°F, Gas Mark 6 for a further 15 minutes for the 450 g/1 lb tins and 25 minutes for the 1 kg/2 lb tin.
12. When cooked the bread will sound hollow if tapped on the bottom.
13. Cool the bread on a wire tray.

**TO FREEZE:** When cold, place in polythene bags, seal and freeze.

**TO SERVE:** Allow to thaw at room temperature for 2-3 hours, then if you wish to serve it warm, place in a preheated oven at 200°C, 400°F, Gas Mark 6 for 10 minutes.

# COB LOAF

*Makes 2 loaves*
*Preparation time: 2 hours*
*Cooking time: 30 minutes*
*Recommended freezer life: 6 months*

1 quantity Wholemeal Bread
dough
50 g/2 oz cracked wheat

1. Make the dough following the recipe for Wholemeal Bread up to step 8.
2. Divide the dough into 2 even sized pieces and shape each piece into a round.
3. Place the rounds on a lightly floured baking sheet.
4. Leave in a warm place until the loaves have doubled in size.
5. Brush the tops with water, then sprinkle the loaves with the cracked wheat and cook in a preheated oven at 230°C, 450°F, Gas Mark 8 for 30 minutes.

6. When cooked the bread will sound hollow if tapped on the bottom.
7. Cool the bread on a wire tray.

**TO FREEZE:** When cold, place in polythene bags, seal and freeze.

**TO SERVE:** Allow to thaw at room temperature for 2-3 hours, then if you wish to serve it warm, place in a preheated oven at 200°C, 400°F, Gas Mark 6 for 10 minutes.

# WHITE BREAD

*Makes 1 × 1 kg /2 lb loaf or*
*2 × 450 g /1 lb loaves*
*Preparation time: 2 hours*
*Cooking time: 30-45 minutes*
*(depending on size)*
*Recommended freezer life: 6 months*

450 g /1 lb strong white flour
2 teaspoons salt
15 g /½ oz fresh yeast, or 2
  teaspoons dried yeast with 1
  teaspoon sugar
about 300 ml /½ pint tepid water
beaten egg, milk or salted water

Some flours require more than the measured liquid, and some less, so a little extra flour or water may be necessary to correct the consistency of the dough when mixing.

1. Sift the flour and the salt into a warm mixing bowl.
2. Blend the yeast with a little of the tepid water. If using dried yeast add the sugar at the same time and leave until frothy. Stir into the remaining water.
3. Add the yeast mixture to the flour. Beat the flour and the liquid together, using your hands or a wooden spoon, until they form a dough.
4. Alternatively, knead the dough for about 5 minutes using the dough hook attachment of an electric mixer.
5. Turn the dough on to a floured board, and knead it thoroughly for 10 minutes until it is smooth and elastic.
6. Place the kneaded dough in the mixing bowl and cover it with an oiled polythene bag. Leave in a warm place until it has doubled in size.

7. Turn the risen dough on to a floured board and knead it gently.
8. Shape the dough and place it in greased tin(s).
9. Place the tin(s) in large oiled polythene bags and tie the bags loosely. Allow the dough to prove in a warm place until double in size. Uncover.
10. For a golden, shiny crust, brush the dough with beaten egg or milk, or salted water for a plain loaf.
11. Cook in a preheated oven at 230°C, 450°F, Gas Mark 8 for 30-45 minutes until well risen and golden brown.
12. When cooked, the bread will sound hollow if tapped on the bottom.
13. Cool the bread on a wire tray.

**TO FREEZE:** When cold, pack in polythene bags, seal and freeze.

**TO SERVE:** Allow to thaw at room temperature for 2-3 hours, then if you wish to serve it warm, place in a preheated oven at 200°C, 400°F, Gas Mark 6 for 10 minutes.

# HERB & ONION ROLLS

*Makes 12 rolls*
*Preparation time: 2 hours*
*Cooking time: 15-20 minutes*
*Recommended freezer life: 6 months*

1 quantity White Bread dough
  (page 133), using half and
  half milk and water for the
  liquid
25 g /1 oz butter, melted
2 tablespoons mixed dried herbs
3 tablespoons finely chopped
  onion

1. Make the dough following the recipe for White Bread up to step 8 (shaping).
2. Divide the dough into 12 even sized pieces and form each one into a round.
3. Place the rolls on a greased baking sheet, and make a light indentation in the top of each one with the backs of two fingers.
4. Brush each roll with the melted butter, and divide the herbs and chopped onion between the tops of the rolls.
5. Leave the rolls to prove in a warm

place until they have doubled in size.
6. Cook the rolls in a preheated oven at 220°C, 425°F, Gas Mark 7 for 15-20 minutes. Cool on a wire tray.

**TO FREEZE:** When cold, pack in a polythene bag, seal and freeze.

**TO SERVE:** Allow to thaw at room temperature for 1-2 hours, then warm through in a preheated oven at 200°C, 400°F, Gas Mark 6 for 5 minutes.

# MILK BREAD

*Preparation time: 2 hours*

450 g/1 lb strong white flour
1 teaspoon salt
40 g/1½ oz butter
300 ml/10 fl oz tepid milk
15 g/½ oz fresh yeast
2 teaspoons caster sugar
1 egg, beaten

1. Sift the flour and salt into a warm mixing bowl.
2. Melt the butter in a small pan, then pour on the milk.
3. Place the yeast and the sugar in a small bowl, and pour over a little of the milk mixture.
4. Cream the yeast until it has dissolved, then pour it back into the remaining milk. Add the beaten egg, stirring well.
5. Make a well in the centre of the flour, and pour in the liquid. Beat the flour and the liquid together, using your hands, until they form a dough.

6. Turn out the dough on to a lightly floured board, and knead it for 8-10 minutes.
7. Return the dough to the bowl, then place the bowl in a large lightly oiled polythene bag. Leave in a warm place, until the dough has doubled in size.
8. Turn the risen dough on to a floured board and knead it gently for 1-2 minutes.
9. The dough is now ready for shaping, either for a batch of rolls or a poppy seed plait (below), or as a base for a pizza (page 52).

# POPPY SEED PLAIT

*Makes 1 loaf*
*Preparation time: 2 hours 10 minutes*
*Cooking time: 35-40 minutes*
*Recommended freezer life: 6 months*

1 quantity Milk Bread dough (above)
1 egg, beaten with 1 tablespoon milk
1 teaspoon poppy seeds

1. Make the dough following the recipe for Milk Bread up to step 9 (shaping).
2. Divide the dough into 3 equal portions, and form each portion into a sausage shape, thicker in the middle than at the ends.
3. Join the 3 pieces together at one end, then plait them together, turning the ends under.
4. Place the plaits on a greased baking sheet, and leave to prove in a warm place for 30 minutes.
5. Brush the loaf lightly with the egg and milk and sprinkle over the poppy seeds.
6. Cook in a preheated oven at 200°C,

400°F, Gas Mark 6 for 35-40 minutes until well risen and golden brown.
7. When cooked, the bread will sound hollow if tapped on the bottom.
8. Cool the bread on a wire tray.

**TO FREEZE:** When cold, place in a polythene bag, seal and freeze.

**TO SERVE:** Allow to thaw at room temperature for 2-2½ hours, then if you wish to serve it warm, place in a preheated oven at 200°C, 400°F, Gas Mark 6 for 10 minutes.

# WHITE ROLLS

*Makes 12 rolls*
*Preparation time: 2½ hours*
*Cooking time: 20-25 minutes*
*Recommended freezer life: 6 months*

1 quantity Milk Bread dough (page 134)
1 egg, beaten with 1 tablespoon milk
poppy seeds
sesame seeds

1. Make the dough following the recipe for Milk Bread up to step 9 (shaping).
2. Divide the dough into 12 portions and make them into any of the following shapes. Allow the shapes to prove for 20 minutes in a warm place. Brush them with the egg and milk mixture, and sprinkle with poppy seeds or sesame seeds, or leave them plain. Then cook them in a preheated oven at 200°C, 400°F, Gas Mark 6 for 20-25 minutes until they are well risen and golden brown. Cool on a wire tray.

### TREFOILS
Divide one of the portions of dough into 3 balls, and place them close together on a greased baking sheet in a clover shape. Depending on how many trefoil rolls you require, continue shaping the portions of dough.

### SMALL PLAITS
Divide one of the portions of dough into 3, and form the 3 pieces into sausage shapes, thicker in the middle than at the

ends. Join the 3 pieces at one end, then plait them together, turning in the ends. Place the plait on a greased baking sheet, and continue shaping the portions depending on how many small plaits you require.

### COTTAGE LOAF ROLLS
Divide one of the portions of dough into 1 large and 1 small ball. Place the small ball on top of the large ball, and press the handle of a wooden spoon or a finger down through the middle of the roll to make a dimple. Place the roll on a greased baking sheet, and continue shaping the portions of dough depending on how many cottage loaf rolls you require.

**TO FREEZE:** When cold, pack in a polythene bag, seal and freeze.

**TO SERVE:** From frozen, place in a preheated oven at 200°C, 400°F, Gas Mark 6 for 5-10 minutes.

# CHEESE BREAD

*Makes 2 × 450 g /1 lb loaves*
*Preparation time: 2 hours*
*Cooking time: 45 minutes*
*Recommended freezer life: 6 months*

450 g/1 lb strong white flour
2 teaspoons salt
freshly ground black pepper
2 teaspoons dry mustard
175 g/6 oz Cheddar cheese,
   grated
15 g/½ oz fresh yeast, or 2
   teaspoons dried yeast with 1
   teaspoon water
300 ml/½ pint tepid water
25 g/1 oz Cheddar cheese,
   grated, to finish

1. Sift the flour, salt, pepper and mustard into a large warm mixing bowl, and stir in the grated cheese.
2. Continue as for White Bread (page 133) up to step 8 (shaping).
3. Divide the dough between 2 greased 450 g/1 lb loaf tins, cover with oiled polythene bags, and prove them in a warm place until doubled in size.
4. Uncover and cook in a preheated oven at 220°C, 424°F, Gas Mark 7 for 10 minutes, then reduce the heat to 190°C, 375°F, Gas Mark 5 for a further 35 minutes.
5. Sprinkle the grated cheese over the loaves, and return them to the oven for a further 5 minutes.
6. When cooked, the bread will sound hollow if tapped on the bottom.
7. Cool on a wire tray.

**TO FREEZE:** When cold, place in polythene bags, seal and freeze.

**TO SERVE:** Allow to thaw at room temperature for 2-3 hours, then if you wish to serve it warm, place in a preheated oven at 200°C, 400°F, Gas Mark 6 for 10 minutes.

**Top: White bread; Poppy seed plait**
**Below: Cottage loaf roll; Trefoils; Small plait; Cheese bread**

# SAVOURY PICNIC SCONES

*Makes 8 scones*
*Preparation time: 30 minutes*
*Cooking time: 20 minutes*
*Recommended freezer life: 6 months*

350 g/12 oz wholemeal flour
½ teaspoon salt
4 teaspoons baking powder
50 g/2 oz butter
1 onion, peeled and finely
   chopped
75 g/3 oz ham, finely diced
50 g/2 oz salami, finely diced
½ red pepper, cored, seeded
   and finely chopped
3 tablespoons chopped fresh
   parsley
pinch of paprika
freshly ground black pepper
150 ml/¼ pint milk

1. Place the flour in a large mixing bowl, and stir in the salt and baking powder.
2. Rub the butter into the flour until the mixture resembles fine breadcrumbs.
3. Stir in the onion, ham, salami, red pepper, chopped parsley, paprika and pepper.
4. Slowly add the milk, stirring it gently with a round bladed knife, until the mixture forms a dough.
5. Turn the dough on to a floured board and knead it gently, then roll it out to form a 23 cm/9 inch circle.
6. Cut the dough into 8 wedges, and place them on a baking tray.
7. Cook in a preheated oven at 220°C, 425°F, Gas Mark 7 for 20 minutes, until well risen and golden brown.
8. Cool the scones on a wire tray.

**TO FREEZE:** When cold, pack into a polythene bag, seal and freeze.

**TO SERVE:** Allow to thaw in the bag for 2-3 hours at room temperature.

# FRUITY TEA SCONES

*Makes 12-14 scones*
*Preparation time: 25 minutes*
*Cooking time: 10-12 minutes*
*Recommended freezer life: 6 months*

225 g/8 oz plain flour
pinch of salt
1 teaspoon mixed spice
½ teaspoon cream of tartar
½ teaspoon bicarbonate of soda
40 g/1½ oz chilled butter,
   chopped
25 g/1 oz caster sugar
25 g/1 oz sultanas
15 g/½ oz currants
15 g/½ oz chopped mixed peel
about 150 ml/¼ pint milk
a little milk, to glaze

1. Sift the flour into a mixing bowl with the salt, mixed spice, cream of tartar and bicarbonate of soda.
2. Add the butter, and rub it in until the mixture resembles fine breadcrumbs.
3. Stir in the sugar and the sultanas, currants and mixed peel.
4. Stir in enough milk to make a soft manageable dough.
5. Knead the mixture on a floured board for 1 minute, then roll it out to 1 cm/½ inch thick, and cut it into 12-14 rounds each 5 cm/2 inches across.
6. Place the scones on a floured baking sheet, and brush the tops with a little milk.
7. Cook in a preheated oven at 230°C, 450°F, Gas Mark 8 for 10-12 minutes, until well risen and golden brown.
8. Cool the scones on a wire tray.

**TO FREEZE:** When cold, place in a polythene bag, seal and freeze.

**TO SERVE:** From frozen, place in a preheated oven at 180°C, 350°F, Gas Mark 4 for approximately 10 minutes. Serve split and buttered.

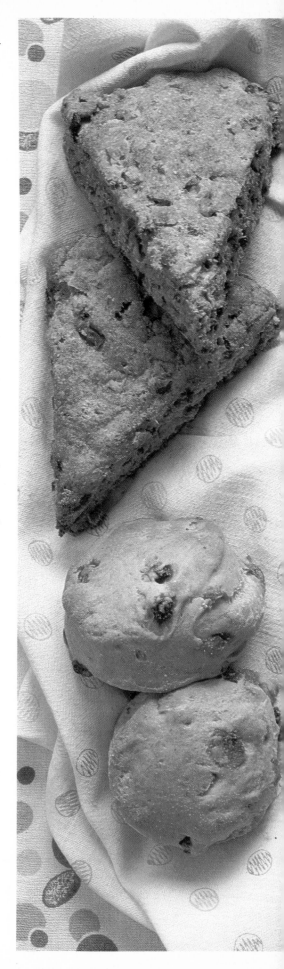

**Top: Savoury picnic scones**
**Below left: Fruity tea scones**
**Below right: Nutty shortbread fingers**

# ALICE'S ROCK CAKES

*Makes 12 rock cakes*
*Preparation time: 20 minutes*
*Cooking time: 10-15 minutes*
*Recommended freezer life: 6 months*

225 g/8 oz self-raising flour
100 g/4 oz butter, cut into pieces
75 g/3 oz demerara sugar
75 g/3 oz sultanas
1 egg, beaten
about 1 tablespoon milk
    (optional)

1. Sift the flour into a bowl, and rub in the butter until the mixture resembles fine breadcrumbs.
2. Stir in the sugar and sultanas, then bind the mixture with the beaten egg, stirring gently with a fork. If the mixture is too dry, add a little milk.
3. Put dessertspoonfuls of the mixture on to a greased baking sheet in rocky lumps.
4. Cook in a preheated oven at 200°C, 400°F, Gas Mark 6 for 10-15 minutes.
5. Cool the rock cakes on a wire tray.

**TO FREEZE:** When cold, place in a polythene bag, seal and freeze.

**TO SERVE:** Allow to thaw at room temperature for 1½-2 hours.

# NUTTY SHORTBREAD FINGERS

*Makes 16 biscuits*
*Preparation time: 20 minutes*
*Cooking time: 20-25 minutes*
*Recommended freezer life: 6 months*

100 g/4 oz plain flour
50 g/2 oz rice flour
50 g/2 oz caster sugar
100 g/4 oz butter, cut into pieces
50 g/2 oz blanched almonds,
    chopped

1. Place the plain flour, rice flour and sugar together in a mixing bowl.
2. Rub in the butter until the mixture comes together to form a light dough, working in the nuts towards the end. Do not overwork the dough, or the shortbread will be heavy when cooked.
3. Roll out the mixture on a lightly floured board to about 1 cm/½ inch thick, and cut it into finger shapes 2 × 5 cm/ ¾ × 2 inches.
4. Arrange the fingers on a lightly greased baking sheet and cook in a preheated oven at 180°C, 350°F, Gas Mark 4 for 20-25 minutes, until pale golden and firm.
5. Cool the biscuits on a wire tray.

**TO FREEZE:** Pack into a rigid container, cover and freeze.

**TO SERVE:** Allow to thaw at room temperature for 2-3 hours.

# OLD FASHIONED CHOCOLATE CAKE

*Makes 1 × 18 cm/7 inch cake*
*Preparation time: 35 minutes*
*Cooking time: 25-30 minutes*
*Recommended freezer life: 6 months*

175 g/6 oz butter
175 g/6 oz caster sugar
3 eggs, beaten
4 tablespoons cocoa powder, mixed to a thick paste with a little hot water
175 g/6 oz self-raising flour, sifted
3 drops vanilla essence
**BUTTER CREAM:**
175 g/6 oz icing sugar
2 tablespoons cocoa powder
100 g/4 oz unsalted butter

1. Grease 2 × 18 cm/7 inch sandwich tins with a little butter and set them aside.
2. Cream the butter and sugar together in a large mixing bowl until light and fluffy.
3. Add the eggs, a little at a time, beating well between each addition. A little of the measured flour may be added if there is any sign of the mixture curdling.
4. Beat the cocoa paste into the mixture, fold in the sifted flour, and add the vanilla essence.
5. Divide the mixture evenly between the 2 cake tins and smooth it over.
6. Cook in a preheated oven at 180°C, 350°F, Gas Mark 4 for 25-30 minutes.
7. Test the cake with a skewer which will come out clean when the cake is ready.
8. Turn the cakes on to a wire tray to cool.

9. To make the butter icing, sift the icing sugar and the cocoa powder together. Cream the butter in a mixing bowl, then gradually beat in the icing sugar and cocoa.
9. Beat the icing well until it is smooth.
10. Sandwich the cooled cakes together with half the butter icing. Spread the remaining icing over the top of the cake, and make a pattern by swirling the icing with the prongs of a fork.

**TO FREEZE:** Open freeze for 2-3 hours, then place in a polythene bag, seal and freeze.

**TO SERVE:** Allow to thaw at room temperature for 2-3 hours before serving.

# BELGIAN BISCUIT CAKE

*Makes 8 wedges*
*Preparation time: 30 minutes*
*Cooking time: 5 minutes*
*Recommended freezer life: 6 months*

50 g/2 oz butter
50 g/2 oz caster sugar
1 tablespoon double cream
100 g/4 oz plain chocolate, melted
175 g/6 oz rich tea biscuits, broken into small pieces
50 g/2 oz glacé cherries, chopped
50 g/2 oz blanched almonds, chopped
1 egg yolk

1. Melt the butter with the sugar over a low heat until the sugar has completely dissolved, then bring to the boil, stirring occasionally.
2. Stir the cream into the melted chocolate and pour them into the butter mixture.
3. Mix all the ingredients well together, then remove from the heat and add the broken biscuits.
4. Set aside 1 tablespoon of the cherries and almonds for decoration, and stir the rest into the mixture with the egg yolk, combining well.
5. Spoon the mixture into a well oiled 18 cm/7 inch shallow cake tin, pressing it down firmly around the edges.

6. Smooth over the surface of the cake, sprinkle it with the reserved cherries and almonds and press them slightly into the biscuit mixture.
7. Put the cake in the refrigerator to set for about 1 hour.

**TO FREEZE:** Place the cake in its tin in a polythene bag, seal and freeze.

**TO SERVE:** Allow to thaw at room temperature for 5-6 hours. Cut into 8 wedges, and serve.

# CHOCOLATE CHUNK CAKE

*Makes 1 × 20 cm/8 inch cake*
*Preparation time: 25 minutes*
*Cooking time: 45-50 minutes*
*Recommended freezer life: 6 months*

175 g/6 oz butter
175 g/6 oz caster sugar
3 eggs, beaten
175 g/6 oz self-raising flour, sifted
100 g/4 oz plain chocolate, chopped
**TO SERVE:**
icing sugar

1. Butter a 20 cm/8 inch loose bottomed cake tin, and dust it with flour.
2. Cream the butter and sugar together in a large mixing bowl until light and fluffy.
3. Add the eggs, a little at a time, beating well between each addition. A little of the measured flour may be added if there is any sign of the mixture curdling.
4. Fold the remaining flour and the chopped chocolate into the mixture, then spoon it into the prepared tin and smooth the top.
5. Cook in a preheated oven at 160°C, 325°F, Gas Mark 3 for 45-50 minutes.
6. Test the cake with a skewer which will come out clean when the cake is ready.
7. Turn out the cake on to a wire tray and leave to cool.

**TO FREEZE:** When cold, place in a polythene bag, seal and freeze.

**TO SERVE:** Allow to thaw in the polythene bag for 6 hours at room temperature, then place on a wire tray. Cut 12 × 1 cm/½ inch wide strips of thin card, and lay them in a lattice pattern over the top of the cake. Dust the cake with icing sugar, then carefully remove the strips of card, leaving a diamond pattern on the top of the cake.

# LIGHT SPONGE CAKE

*Makes 1 × 20 cm/8 inch cake*
*Preparation time: 20 minutes*
*Cooking time: about 40 minutes*
*Recommended freezer life: 6 months*

4 eggs
120 g/4½ oz caster sugar
100 g/4 oz plain flour, sifted
225 g/8 oz jam
**TO SERVE:**
icing sugar

1. Lightly grease a 20 cm/8 inch round cake tin with butter, then use about 1 teaspoon flour to thinly coat the surfaces.
2. Place the eggs and sugar in a large mixing bowl over a pan of gently simmering water, and whisk them together until thick and creamy.
3. Remove the bowl from the heat and continue whisking the mixture until it is cool.
4. Lightly fold the flour into the mixture in 3 batches then pour the mixture into the prepared tin.
5. Cook in a preheated oven at 180°C, 350°F, Gas Mark 4 for about 40 minutes. When the cake is cooked it will begin to shrink from the sides of the tin.
6. Turn the cake on to a wire tray to cool, right side up.

7. When the cake is cold, split it in half, then sandwich the 2 halves together with the jam of your choice.

**TO FREEZE:** Pack in a rigid container, cover and freeze.

**TO SERVE:** Allow to thaw at room temperature for 2-3 hours. Place a paper doyley over the cake, and sift a little icing sugar over the top. Remove the doyley carefully to leave a lace pattern on the top of the cake.

**Clockwise from the top: Old-fashioned chocolate cake; Light sponge cake; Chocolate chunk cake; Belgian biscuit cake**

# MACAROONS

*Makes 12 macaroons*
*Preparation time: 25 minutes*
*Cooking time: 15 minutes*
*Recommended freezer life: 6 months*

100 g/4 oz ground almonds
225 g/8 oz caster sugar
2 egg whites
15 g/½ oz rice flour
2 sheets rice paper
1 egg white, lightly beaten
15 g/1 oz blanched almonds,
   split

1.  Place the ground almonds in a mixing bowl with the caster sugar and the 2 egg whites, and mix them together.
2.  Add the rice flour to the mixture, and beat with a wooden spoon for 7-8 minutes.
3.  Place the rice paper on to 2 baking sheets. Spoon the macaroon mixture into a piping bag fitted with a 1 cm/½ inch plain nozzle and pipe it on to the rice paper in rounds of about 4 cm/1½ inches in diameter.
4.  Carefully brush the macaroons with the beaten egg white, and place a split almond in the centre of each one.

5.  Cook in a preheated oven at 190°C, 375°F, Gas Mark 5 for 15 minutes.
6.  Turn the macaroons on to a wire tray to cool. When cold, gently tear off any surplus rice paper.

**TO FREEZE:** Pack into a rigid container, cover and freeze.

**TO SERVE:** Allow to thaw at room temperature for 2-3 hours.

# ALMOND TILES

*Makes 12-14 tiles*
*Preparation time: 10 minutes*
*Cooking time: about 20 minutes*
*Recommended freezer life: 6 months*

50 g/2 oz butter
2 egg whites
65 g/2½ oz caster sugar
50 g/2 oz plain flour
50 g/2 oz blanched almonds,
   chopped

For best results it is advisable to cook only 3 biscuits at a time, as speed is required in moving them from the baking sheet to the rolling pin before they harden.

1.  Melt the butter over a gentle heat and set it aside to cool.
2.  Whisk the egg whites to a stiff froth, then add the sugar and whisk again for 3-4 minutes.
3.  Sift the flour on to the whites, and fold it in with the melted butter and the almonds.
4.  Lightly grease 3 baking sheets and a rolling pin. Drop teaspoonfuls of the mixture on to the greased sheets.
5.  Spread each one into a very thin circle approximately 6 cm/2½ inches in diameter.
6.  Cook in a preheated oven at 200°C,

400°F, Gas Mark 6 for approximately 5 minutes, or until pale golden but still soft.
7.  Loosen the biscuits from the baking sheet with a palette knife, and lay them over the lightly greased rolling pin, pressing them gently with your hand to make them curve into a tile shape.
8.  Allow the tiles to cool until they are hard, then carefully transfer them to a wire tray.

**TO FREEZE:** When cold, pack carefully into a rigid container, cover and freeze.

**TO SERVE:** Allow to thaw at room temperature for 1 hour. The tiles may be crisped in a preheated oven at 180°C, 350°F, Gas Mark 4 for about 3 minutes, then allowed to cool before serving. Serve with ice cream.

# SPONGE FINGER BISCUITS

*Makes 16 biscuits*
*Preparation time: 20 minutes*
*Cooking time: 10-12 minutes*
*Recommended freezer life: 6 months*

3 eggs, separated
75 g/3 oz caster sugar
90 g/3½ oz plain flour, sifted
icing sugar, sifted

1. Cut some strips of greaseproof paper approximately 15 cm/6 inches wide, and the length of the baking sheets to be used.
2. Cream the egg yolks and the sugar together until thick and light in colour.
3. Whisk the egg whites until stiff, then fold them gently into the yolk mixture together with the flour.
4. Place the mixture in a piping bag fitted with a plain 1 cm/½ inch nozzle.
5. Pipe finger lengths of the mixture on to the greaseproof paper strips. Dust the biscuits lightly with sifted icing sugar.
6. Cook in a preheated oven at 180°C, 350°F, Gas Mark 4 for 10-12 minutes until light golden brown. Remove the papers carefully from the biscuits, and cool them on a wire tray.

**TO FREEZE:** When cold, pack into a rigid container, cover and freeze.

**TO SERVE:** Allow to thaw at room temperature for 1-2 hours. These biscuits may be served with ice cream, or used to line tins when making charlottes.

**VARIATION:**
The ends of the cooked, cooled biscuits may be dipped in melted chocolate.

# CIGARETTES RUSSES

*Makes 10-12 cigarettes*
*Preparation time: 10 minutes*
*Cooking time: 20 minutes*
*Recommended freezer life: 6 months*

50 g/2 oz butter
2 egg whites
65 g/2½ oz caster sugar
50 g/2 oz plain flour

It is best to cook these biscuits 3 at a time, as speed is required to roll them around the spoon handles before they harden.

1. Melt the butter over a gentle heat, then set it aside to cool.
2. Whisk the egg whites until frothy, then add the sugar and whisk again for 2-3 minutes.
3. Sift the flour on to the egg whites, and fold it in together with the melted butter.
4. Lightly grease 3 baking sheets, and drop the mixture in teaspoonfuls on to the sheets. Spread each one out to form a 7.5 cm/3 inch circle.
5. Cook in a preheated oven at 200°C, 400°F, Gas Mark 6 for about 5 minutes or until pale golden, but still pliable.
6. Remove the biscuits from the oven, and loosen them from the baking sheet with a palette knife.
7. Quickly roll each one around the handle of a wooden spoon, then set the spoons down on a flat surface to prevent the cigarettes from unrolling as they cool.
8. When the cigarettes are set firm, remove them from the spoon handles and allow to finish cooling on a wire tray.

**TO FREEZE:** When cold, pack carefully in a rigid container, cover and freeze.

**TO SERVE:** Allow to thaw at room temperature for 1 hour. The cigarettes may be crisped in a preheated oven at 180°C, 350°F, Gas Mark 4 for about 3 minutes, if you desire.

# INDEX

## A

Alice's rock cakes 137
Almond:
    Almond and apricot meringue cake 124
    Almond tiles 140
    Apricot and almond stuffing 65
    Tipsy almond trifle 128
Aluminium foil 14
Aluminium foil containers 14
Anchovy and mozzarella pizza 52
Apple:
    To freeze apples 23
    Apple and apricot plait 129
    Apple and blackberry plait 129
    Apple and mincemeat plait 129
    Apple and orange pie 127
    Apple and raisin stuffing 65
    Apple and raspberry plait 129
    Apple sauce 62
    Dutch apple and mincemeat tart 127
Apricot:
    To freeze apricots 23
    Almond and apricot meringue cake 124
    Apple and apricot plait 129
    Apricot and almond stuffing 65
Artichoke:
    To freeze globe or Jerusalem artichokes and artichoke hearts 30
    Artichoke soup 43
    Chicken with artichoke hearts 97
Asparagus, to freeze 31
Asparagus peas, to freeze 34
Aubergine:
    To freeze aubergines 31
    Stuffed aubergines 108
Avocado pear:
    To freeze avocados 23
    Avocado ice cream 45

## B

Baby foods, puréed 17
Bacon:
    Brussels sprouts with chestnuts and bacon 115
    Chicken roulade with bacon and mushrooms 98
    Courgette, tomato and bacon casserole 106
    French beans with bacon and tomato 114
    Liver and bacon with tomato sauce 103
    Mushroom and bacon stuffing 65
    Storage time in freezer 21
Bananas, to freeze 24
Batch cooking 16

Bean:
    To freeze broad, French or runner beans 31
    Broad beans with walnuts 104
    French beans with bacon and tomato 114
    Garlic French beans 114
Béarnaise sauce 64
Beef:
    Cottage pie 88
    Hungarian goulash 86
    Indonesian stuffed peppers 91
    Italian meat sauce 91
    Lasagne 90
    Mild beef curry 87
    Picnic pasties 89
    Spanish beef 87
    Steak, kidney and mushroom pie 88
    Storage time in freezer 21
    Summer beef casserole 86
Beetroot, to freeze 31
Belgian biscuit cake 138
Belgian carrots 115
Bilberry, to freeze 24
Biscuits see Cakes and biscuits
Blackcurrant:
    To freeze blackcurrants 25
    Blackcurrant sauce 63
Blanching vegetables 30
Blue cheese dip 56
Blueberry, to freeze 24
Boil-in bags 14
Bombay dip 57
Bouquet garni 18
Bread:
    To thaw bread 20
    Cheese bread 135
    Cob loaf 132
    Fruit and nut tea loaf 130
    Herb and onion rolls 133
    Milk bread 134
    Poppy seed plait 134
    Storage time in freezer 21
    Treacle soda bread 130
    White bread 133
    White rolls 134
    Wholemeal bread 132
Breadcrumbs, fresh 17
Broad bean see Bean
Broccoli, to freeze 31
Brown breadcrumb ice cream 118
Brussels sprout:
    To freeze Brussels sprouts 32
    Brussels sprouts with chestnuts and bacon 115
Bulk-buying meat 16
Butter:
    To freeze and thaw butter 18
    Flavoured butters 17
    Storage time in freezer 21

## C

Cabbage:
    To freeze white or red cabbage 32
Cakes and biscuits:
    To freeze cakes and biscuits 18
    To thaw cakes and biscuits 20
    Alice's rock cakes 137
    Almond tiles 140
    Belgian biscuit cake 138
    Chocolate chunk cake 138
    Cigarrettes russes 141
    Fruity tea scones 136
    Light sponge cake 139

Macaroons 140
    Nutty shortbread fingers 137
    Old-fashioned chocolate cake 138
    Savoury picnic scones 136
    Sponge finger biscuits 141
    Storage time in freezer 21
Calabrese, to freeze 31
Camembert crescents 44
Canapés 54–5
Capons, storage time in freezer 21
Carrot:
    To freeze carrots 32
    Belgian carrots 115
    Carrots Vichy 115
Cauliflower:
    To freeze cauliflower 32
    Crunchy topped cauliflower 114
Celeriac, to freeze 32
Celery, to freeze 33
Ceramic containers 15
Cheese:
    To freeze and thaw cheese 18
    Blue cheese dip 56
    Camembert crescents 44
    Cheese bread 135
    Cheesy stuffed peppers 108
    Cocktail beignets 54
    Cream cheese and tomato dip 56
    Nutty cheese triangles 54
    Potted cheese with port 47
    Ricotta cannelloni with tomato sauce 49
    Special Mornay sauce 60
    Storage time in freezer 21
    Twisty cheese straws 55
Cherry sauce, braised duckling with 101
Chest freezer 11
Chestnut:
    Brussels sprouts with chestnuts and bacon 115
    Chestnut cream 124
Chicken:
    Chicken with artichoke hearts 97
    Chicken galantine 94
    Chicken gougère 96
    Chicken and ham pie 98
    Chicken liver and kidney kebabs 102
    Chicken and liver terrine 46
    Chicken and prawn pilaff 99
    Chicken roulade with bacon and mushrooms 98
    Creamy chicken with olives 97
    French chicken liver pâté 47
    Mild Malayan chicken curry 94
    Parmesan baked chicken 95
    Storage time in freezer 21
    Supremes of chicken with tarragon 95
Chicory, to freeze 33
Chilli:
    To freeze chillis 33
    Chilli sauce 57
Chinese seafood rolls 71
Chinese vegetables 106
Chocolate:
    Belgian biscuit cake 138
    Chocolate caraque gâteau 122
    Chocolate chunk cake 138
    Chocolate ice cream 118
    Chocolate sauce 123
    Chocolate whisky Malakoff 122
    Little chocolate pots 124
    Old-fashioned chocolate cake 138

Cidered pork chop parcels 92
Cigarettes russes 141
Cinnamon raspberry tart 126
Cob loaf 132
Cocktail beignets 54
Coconut, to freeze 24
Cod:
    Cod steaks with parsley and lemon sauce 76
    Special cod pie 74
Coffee cubes, concentrated 17
Conservators 11
Containers for freezing 14–15
Corn, to freeze 33
Cottage loaf rolls 134
Cottage pie 88
Courgette:
    To freeze courgettes 33
    Courgette, tomato and bacon casserole 106
Cranberries, to freeze 25
Cream, to freeze and thaw 18; storage time in freezer 21
Cream cheese and tomato dip 56
Creamy chicken with olives 97
Creamy onion sauce 60
Creamy prawn curry 70
Crème brûlée with grapes 121
Croûtons 17
Crunchy topped cauliflower 114
Cucumber:
    To freeze cucumber 34
    Casserole of cucumber, spring onion and tomato 107
Currants, black, red and white, to freeze 25. See also Blackcurrants, etc.
Curried dishes:
    Bombay dip 57
    Creamy prawn curry 70
    Iced curried soup 40
    Mild beef curry 87
    Mild Malayan chicken curry 94

## D

Dairy products, to freeze 17–18; to thaw 20. See Butter, Cream, etc.
Damsons, to freeze 25
Date plums, to freeze 28
Dates, to freeze 25
Defrosting 12–13
Delicatessen meats, storage time in freezer 21
Demi-glace sauce 61
Desserts. See also Ice creams
    Almond and apricot meringue cake 124
    Apple and apricot plait 129
    Apple and blackberry plait 129
    Apple and mincemeat plait 129
    Apple and orange pie 127
    Apple and raspberry plait 129
    Chestnut cream 124
    Chocolate caraque gâteau 122
    Chocolate whisky Malakoff 122
    Cinnamon raspberry tart 126
    Crème brûlée with grapes 121
    Dutch apple and mincemeat tart 127
    Empress rice mould 125
    Gâteau Pithiviers 128

Gooseberry and ginger fool 121
Little chocolate pots 124
Praline profiteroles with chocolate sauce 123
Sweet pastry meringue ring 120
Tipsy almond trifle 128
Dips:
    Blue cheese dip 56
    Bombay dip 57
    Cream cheese and tomato dip 56
Dover sole in orange sauce 69
Duchesse potatoes 53
Duck, duckling:
    Braised duckling with cherry sauce 101
    Storage time in freezer 21
Dutch apple and mincemeat tart 127

**E**

Egg:
    To freeze and thaw eggs 18
    Omelette fillings 17
    Storage time in freezer 21
Empress rice mould 125

**F**

Fast freezing 10
Fennel, to freeze 34
Figs, to freeze 25
Fish. *See also* Cod, Haddock, etc.
    To thaw and cook fish 20
    Storage time in freezer 21
Florence fennel, to freeze 34
Freezer foil 14
Freezer tape 15
Freezers:
    Buying a second-hand freezer 12
    Cleaning and defrosting 12–13
    Choosing a freezer 11–12
    Coping with power failures 13
    Moving house with a freezer 13
    Packaging for the freezer 13–15
    Record of frozen food 15
    Running costs 12
    Stocking a freezer 16
    Types of freezer 11–12
French bean *see* Bean
French chicken liver pâté 47
French onion tart 52
French roast lamb 80
Fruit. *See also* Apple, Apricot, etc.
    To freeze fruit 22–9
    To thaw and cook fruit 20
    To use frozen fruit for jam and jelly making 23
    Fruit juices 22
    Fruit and nut tea loaf 130
    Fruity tea scones 136
    Storage time in freezer 21

**G**

Game:
    To thaw and cook game 20
Storage time in freezer 21
Garlic French beans 114
Gâteau Pithiviers 128
Gelatine, to freeze dishes containing 19
Glass jars and bottles 15
Glazed leg of lamb with port and honey 80
Globe artichoke *see* Artichoke
Goose, storage time in freezer 21
Gooseberry:
    To freeze gooseberries 25
    Gooseberry and ginger fool 121
Grape:
    To freeze grapes 26
    Crème brûlée with grapes 121
Grapefruit; to freeze 26
Greengage, to freeze 26

**H**

Haddock:
    Haddock maison 75
    Seafood crumble 77
    Smoked haddock soup 42
    Smoked haddock and tomato shells 53
Ham:
    Chicken and ham pie 98
    Leeks and ham in mornay sauce 112
Herbs:
    To freeze herbs 18
    Herb and onion rolls 133
    Storage time in freezer 21
Herring:
    Soft herring roe pâté 48
Hollandaise sauce 64
Honeydew soup 40
Hungarian goulash 86

**I**

Ice cream maker 17
Ice creams and sorbets:
    Avocado ice cream 45
    Brown breadcrumb ice cream 118
    Chocolate ice cream 118
    Lemon mint sorbet 116
    Lychee ice cream 119
    Mandarin ice cream 119
    Orange and lemon ice cream 118
    Pineapple ice cream 119
    Praline ice cream 118
    Storage time in freezer 21
    Strawberry ice cream 120
    Vanilla ice cream 118
    Watermelon sorbet 116
Ice cubes 17
Iced curried soup 40
Indonesian stuffed peppers 91
Irish stew 83
Italian meat sauce 91

**J**

Jellies 19
Jerusalem artichoke *see* Artichoke

**K**

Kidney:
    Chicken liver and kidney kebabs 102
    Kidneys turbigo 102
    Steak, kidney and mushroom pie 88
Kohlrabi, to freeze 34

**L**

Labelling 15
Lamb:
    French roast lamb 80
    Glazed leg of lamb with port and honey 80
    Irish stew 83
    Lamb chops with orange 85
    Lamb cutlets Wellington 84
    Lamb with yogurt and dill 83
    Spicy lamb chops 85
    Spinach stuffed breast of lamb 78
    Storage time in freezer 21
    Stuffed shoulder of lamb en croûte 82
    Winter braised lamb 81
Lamb's sweetbreads in sherry sauce 103
Lasagne 90
Leek:
    To freeze leeks 34
    Leek and potato soup 43
    Leeks and ham in mornay sauce 112
Lemon:
    To freeze lemons 26
    Lemon mint sorbet 116
Lemon sole véronique 68
Lentils lorraine 113
Limes, to freeze 26
Liver:
    Chicken liver and kidney kebabs 102
    Chicken and liver terrine 46
    French chicken liver pâté 47
    Liver and bacon with tomato sauce 103
Loganberries, to freeze 29
Lychee:
    To freeze lychees 26
    Lychee ice cream 119

**M**

Macaroons 140
Main courses, complete frozen 16
Mandarin ice cream 119
Mange tout (Sugar peas), to freeze 34
Mangoes, to freeze 26
Marrow, to freeze 34
Meat. *See also* Beef, Lamb, etc.
    To bulk-buy 16
    To thaw and cook meat 20
    Storage time in freezer 21
Melba sauce 63
Melon:
    Honeydew soup 40
Watermelon sorbet 116
Microwave cooker 17
Microwave oven containers 15
Milk:
    To freeze and thaw milk 18
    Milk bread 134
    Storage time in freezer 21
Mornay sauce, special 60
Mousse:
    Smoked trout mousse 51
    Tuna fish mousse 51
Mushroom:
    To freeze mushrooms 35
    Chicken roulade with bacon and mushrooms 98
    Mushroom and bacon stuffing 65
    Mushroom sauce 58
    Spinach parcels with mushroom sauce 74
    Steak, kidney and mushroom pie 88

**N**

Nectarines, to freeze 27
Normandy pork tenderloin 93
Nuts, to freeze 19
Nutty cheese triangles 54
Nutty shortbread fingers 137

**O**

Offal, storage time in freezer 21
Okra (Ladies' fingers), to freeze 35
Old-fashioned chocolate cake 138
Omelette fillings 17
Onion:
    To freeze onions 35
    Creamy onion sauce 60
    French onion tart 52
    Herb and onion rolls 133
Open freezing 17
Orange:
    To freeze oranges 27
    Apple and orange pie 127
    Dover sole in orange sauce 69
    Lamb chops with orange 85
    Medallions of pork with orange and ginger 92
    Orange and lemon ice cream 118
    Tomato and orange soup 42

**P**

Packaging for freezing 13–15
Parmesan baked chicken 95
Parsley and lemon sauce 76
Parsnip:
    To freeze parsnips 35
    Parsnip purée 112
Passion fruit, to freeze 27
Pasta, to freeze 19; storage time in freezer 21
Pastry, storage time in freezer 21
Pastry dishes, to freeze 18

Pâté:
French chicken liver pâté 47
Sardine and pimento pâté 48
Smoked salmon and cream cheese pâté 45
Soft herring roe pâté 48
Taramasalata 48
Pawpaw or papaya, to freeze 27
Pea:
To freeze peas and petits pois 35
Petits pois à la française 104
Peaches, to freeze 27
Pears, to freeze 28
Pepper:
To freeze sweet, red or green peppers 36
Cheesy stuffed peppers 108
Indonesian stuffed peppers 91
Sardine and pimento pâté 48
Persimmon, to freeze 28
Petits pois à la française 104
Picnic pasties 89
Picnic scones, savoury 136
Pies. See also Tarts
Apple and orange pie 127
Chicken and ham pie 98
Cottage pie 88
Special cod pie 74
Steak, kidney and mushroom pie 88
Pineapple:
To freeze pineapple 28
Pineapple ice cream 119
Pistachio nuts, stuffed turkey with 100
Pizza, anchovy and mozzarella 52
Plaice:
Fillets of plaice duglere 70
Stuffed fillets of plaice in prawn sauce 68
Plastic cling film 14
Plastic containers 14
Plums, to freeze 28
Polythene bags, containers 14
Pomegranate, to freeze 28
Pommes boulangère 110
Poppy seed plait 134
Pork:
Cidered pork chop parcels 92
Medallions of pork with orange and ginger 92
Normandy pork tenderloin 93
Storage time in freezer 21
Stuffed blade of pork 93
Potato:
To freeze potatoes 36
Baked potatoes provençale 76
Leek and potato soup 43
Pommes boulangère 110
Savoy potatoes 110
Stuffed baked potatoes 111
Potted cheese with port 47
Poultry. See also Chicken, etc.
To thaw and cook poultry 20
Power failures, to cope with 13
Praline ice cream 118
Praline profiteroles with chocolate sauce 123
Prawn:
Baked potatoes provençale 76
Chicken and prawn pilaff 99
Creamy prawn curry 70
Seafood crumble 77
Stuffed fillets of plaice in prawn sauce 68
Puddings see Desserts, Ices
Pumpkin, to freeze 36

R

Raspberry:
To freeze raspberries 29
Apple and raspberry plait 129
Cinnamon raspberry tart 126
Melba sauce 63
Ratatouille 107
Redcurrants, to freeze 25

S

Salmon fishcakes 72
Salmon surprise 66
Salsify, Oyster plant, to freeze 36
Sandwiches, to freeze 19; to thaw 20; storage time in freezer 21
Sardine crescents 55
Sardine and pimento pâté 48
Sauces:
To thaw and heat sauces 20
Apple sauce 62
Béarnaise sauce 64
Blackcurrant sauce 63
Chilli sauce 57
Chocolate sauce 123
Cornflour stabilizer 64
Creamy onion sauce 60
Demi-glace sauce 61
Fresh tomato sauce 58
Hollandaise sauce 64
Italian meat sauce 91
Melba sauce 63
Mushroom sauce 58
Special mornay sauce 60
Storage time in freezer 21
Sweet and sour sauce 62
Sausages, storage time in freezer 21
Savoury picnic scones 136
Savoy potatoes 110
Scallop:
Scallop nests 50
Scallops à la bretonne 73
Scones 136; to thaw and heat 20
Scorzonera, to freeze 36
Seafood crumble 77
Seafood rolls, Chinese 71
Shellfish, storage time for 21
Shortbread fingers, nutty 137
Smoked haddock soup 42
Smoked haddock and tomato shells 53
Smoked salmon and cream cheese pâté 45
Smoked trout mousse 51
Soda bread, treacle 130
Sole:
Dover sole in orange sauce 69
Lemon sole Véronique 68
Sorbets 116
Soup:
To thaw and cook soup 19
Artichoke soup 43
Honeydew soup 40
Iced curried soup 40
Leek and potato soup 43
Smoked haddock soup 42
Storage time in freezer 21
Tomato and orange soup 42
Spanish beef 87
Spicy lamb chops 85
Spinach:
To freeze spinach 37
Spinach parcels 74

Spinach ring 109
Spinach stuffed lamb 78
Sponge cake, light 139
Sponge finger biscuits 141
Starters. See also Pâté, Soup
Anchovy and mozzarella pizza 52
Avocado ice cream 45
Camembert crescents 44
Canapés 54–5
Chicken and liver terrine 46
Dips 56–7
French onion tart 52
Potted cheese with port 47
Ricotta cannelloni with tomato sauce 49
Scallop nests 50
Smoked haddock and tomato shells 53
Smoked salmon and cream cheese pâté 45
Smoked trout mousse 51
Tuna fish mousse 51
Steak, kidney and mushroom pie 88
Stock:
To thaw and cook stock 19
Concentrated stock cubes 17
Storage time in freezer 21
Stocking a freezer 16
Storage of frozen food 11; -times in freezer 21
Strawberry:
To freeze strawberries 29
Strawberry ice cream 120
Stuffed aubergines 108
Stuffed baked potatoes 111
Stuffed blade of pork 93
Stuffed fillets of plaice in prawn sauce 68
Stuffed shoulder of lamb en croûte 82
Stuffed trout parcels 73
Stuffed turkey with pistachio nuts 100
Stuffing:
Apple and raisin stuffing 65
Apricot and almond stuffing 65
Mushroom and bacon stuffing 65
Summer beef casserole 86
Supremes of chicken with tarragon 95
Swede, to freeze 37
Sweet pastry meringue ring 120
Sweet potatoes, to freeze 37
Sweet and sour sauce 62
Sweetbread:
Lamb's sweetbreads in sherry sauce 103

T

Taramasalata 48
Tarragon, supremes of chicken with 95
Tarts:
Cinnamon raspberry tart 126
Dutch apple and mincemeat tart 127
French onion tart 52
Tea cubes, concentrated 17
Thawing and cooking frozen food 19–20
Time saving ideas and equipment 17
Tipsy almond trifle 128

Toast toppings 17
Tomato:
To freeze tomatoes 37
Courgette, tomato and bacon casserole 106
French beans with bacon and tomato 114
French tomato sauce 58
Smoked haddock and tomato shells 53
Tomato and orange soup 42
Toughened glass containers 15
Treacle soda bread 130
Trefoild 134
Trout:
Smoked trout mousse 51
Stuffed trout parcels 73
Tuna fish mousse 51
Turkey:
Storage time in freezer 21
Stuffed turkey with pistachio nuts 100
Turkey breasts Marsala 100
Turnips, to freeze 37

U

Ugli fruit, to freeze 29
Upright freezer 11

V

Vanilla ice cream 118
Veal, storage time in freezer 21
Vegetables. See also Artichoke, etc.
To blanch vegetables 30
To freeze vegetables 30–7
To thaw and cook vegetables 20
Chinese vegetables 106
Mixed vegetables and vegetable stew packs, to freeze 37
Ratatouille 107
Storage time in freezer 21

W

Walnuts, broad beans with 104
Watermelon sorbet 116
Waxed containers 14
White bread 133
White rolls 134
Whitecurrants, to freeze 25
Whiting:
Spinach parcels with mushroom sauce 74
Wholemeal bread 132
Whortleberries to freeze 29
Winter braised lamb 81

Y

Yams, to freeze 37
Yeast and yeast mixtures, to freeze 19; storage time in freezer 21